The Elements of Confederate Defeat

The Elements
of Confederate Defeat

Nationalism, War Aims, and Religion

Richard E. Beringer, Herman Hattaway, Archer Jones,
and William N. Still, Jr.

The University of Georgia Press

Athens and London

© 1988 by the University of Georgia Press
Athens, Georgia 30602
This book is an abridged edition
of *Why the South Lost the Civil
War* (Georgia, 1986).

Designed by Nighthawk Design
Set in 10.5/13 Linotron 202 Ehrhardt
Typeset by The Composing Room of Michigan, Inc.
Printed and bound by Thomson-Shore

The paper in this book meets the guidelines for
permanence and durability of the Committee on
Production Guidelines for Book Longevity of the
Council on Library Resources.

Printed in the United States of America

92 91 90 89 88   5 4 3 2 1

Library of Congress Cataloging in Publication Data
The Elements of Confederate defeat: nationalism, war
aims, and religion/Richard E. Beringer . . . [et al.].
p.   cm.
Abridged ed. of: Why the South lost the Civil War, 1986.
Bibliography: p.
Includes index.
ISBN 0-8203-1076-X (alk. paper)
ISBN 0-8203-1077-8 (pbk.: alk. paper)
1. Confederate States of America—Historiography.
2. United States—History—Civil War, 1861–1865—
Historiography. I. Beringer, Richard E. 1933–
II. Why the South lost the Civil War.
E487.W482   1988
973.7'13—dc19   88-17311
CIP

British Library Cataloging in Publication Data available

The map on pages 48–49 is from *How the North Won:
A Military History of the Civil War* by Herman
Hattaway and Archer Jones (University of Illinois
Press, 1983). Copyright 1983 by the Board of Trustees
of the University of Illinois.

To Our Parents:

Martha Miriam Wupper Beringer, 1895–1970
William Beringer, 1887–1975

Mary Amelia Cook Hattaway, 1915–1986
Samuel Morell Hattaway, 1913–1979

Helen Johnston Skinner
M. Osborne Jones, 1896–1979

Helen Morris Still
William N. Still, 1908–1963

Contents

Introduction

FIVE EMINENT HISTORIANS gathered in November 1958 for a conference at Gettysburg College, at which each of them probed one of the familiar interpretations of why the North won the Civil War. David Donald edited the papers, published in 1960 as *Why the North Won the Civil War*. David M. Potter chose the performance of Jefferson Davis and the impact of political factors; he believed that Jefferson Davis exhibited deficiencies in his relations with other people, his concept of the presidency, and his role as commander in chief. Potter even suggested that if Davis and Abraham Lincoln had been in each other's position, the Confederacy might have won the war. Norman A. Graebner assessed superior northern diplomacy and European neutrality, concluding that Secretary of State William H. Seward had made it clear that Europe would pay a high price if it chose to recognize the Confederacy. Richard N. Current reiterated that God had been on the side He usually chose, the one with the strongest battalions; he suggested that the real puzzle was how the Confederacy managed to stay afloat, for the economic supremacy of the Union made victory inevitable. T. Harry Williams examined the military question and cogently argued that northern victory resulted from superior northern and inferior southern military leadership because the South was undone by adherence to the place-oriented strategy of Antoine Henri Jomini. David Donald charged that the Confederacy lost the conflict because it refused to surrender its democratic ideals. Each of the five men admitted that he focused exclusively upon only one single theme for the sake of argument but that in many respects their total views overlapped. All of their essays had proved thought-provoking, but the ideas therein were hardly new or revolutionary.

The historiography of Civil War victory stretches as far back as the end of the war itself, when many northerners were convinced they had won the war because of the moral superiority of their cause, and many southerners thought they were defeated by their adversary's overwhelming resources. In the following generations interpretations became more subtle and less simplistic, as historians discussed military strategy, military superiority, leadership, political factors, diplomacy, and the tension between localism and centralism. Most historians still largely ascribe Confederate defeat to these issues, and Donald himself, in the introduction to the published version of the Gettysburg lectures, implies that all of the factors discussed on that occasion contributed to the result. Many historians have agreed with Donald's rejection of monocausation. Donald has written elsewhere that economic difficulties—including lack of resources, inflation, and the blockade; desertion; malnutrition; physical devastation; inferior manpower; and the lack of a system of political parties that would enable Jefferson Davis to mobilize political support—were all partly responsible for Confederate defeat.

Over twenty years after this important conference new research and writing warranted another book on the same theme. Since the four historians who undertook it shared the same view of the causes of the war's outcome, they felt no need to follow the model of the earlier work, a collection of essentially independent contributions, stressing different factors. Instead, they wrote a unified, interpretive volume whose title, *Why the South Lost the Civil War,* reflected the work's emphasis on the Confederacy. Further, by adopting a chronological approach and integrating political, intellectual, economic, and military factors, they could present a dynamic rather than a static approach to the causes of Confederate defeat.

This book, published by the University of Georgia Press in 1986, forms the basis of *The Elements of Confederate Defeat: Nationalism, War Aims, and Religion* by these same authors. Since it gives the source of almost every quotation used in this volume, readers can consult it and, for the most part fairly readily, find their source. *Why the South Lost,* in turn, depended for its military treatment on Herman Hattaway and Archer Jones, *How the North Won: A Military History of the Civil War,* which adopted a revisionist approach to Lincoln, H. W. Halleck, and the generals as well as to U. S. Grant and R. E. Lee. Readers curious about or questioning any interpretation or wishing amplification should go directly to *How the North Won,* except those seeking the source of quotations from Clausewitz and Jomini or a more extensive application of their ideas to the Civil War. Both books have large bibliographies and ample notes.

This book, like its parent, depends largely on the work of many others. We address the major interpretations advanced by contemporaries and subsequent scholars, including issues of the blockade, states' rights, battlefield success, economic development, resources, and the like, and attempt to show that these are not sufficient to explain the outcome of the war. Indeed, some of these factors are better able to explain why the South lasted as long as it did than to reveal why it lost; other explanations seem, upon reflection, almost irrelevant. We hope that our analysis demonstrates the relationship between military success, morale, and will and the weakness of Confederate nàtionalism when undermined by battlefield defeat. We hope to suggest not only factors that led to the ultimate result, but also to explain the dynamics of their interaction to produce an effect that was greater than the sum of the contributing parts.

We have tried to synthesize the best and most appropriate conclusions of our predecessors in this field and to present the best and most provocative of that earlier work. Our goal is not to settle the controversy over Confederate defeat, once and for all, for we recognize that that is impossible. Rather, we hope to stimulate fresh thought and to move future discussion onto more complex ground. Of course, we accept full responsibility for our interpretations of the works of other historians.

We are thankful for permission to quote from the following repositories and persons: the Samuel Latham Mitchill Barlow Papers, the Robert Alonzo Brock Papers, and the James William Eldridge Papers at the Huntington Library, San Marino, California; the Memoirs of W. S. Oldham at the Barker Texas History Center, University of Texas, Austin; the Thomas Bragg Diary, the John W. Brown Diaries, and the James G. Ramsay Papers, in the Southern Historical Collection, Library of the University of North Carolina at Chapel Hill; the Robert Charles Winthrop Papers in the Massachusetts Historical Society; the Reminiscences of J. A. Orr, Mississippi State Department of Archives and History; and Professors Dan T. Carter and William J. McNeill, for papers presented at annual meetings of the Southern Historical Association.

Chapter One

Military Conditions, Performance, and Possibilities

A COMPARATIVE LACK OF industrial development hindered the South's military performance less than the progress of the industrial revolution would cause one to expect, in part because the Civil War happened at a time when equipping armies could hardly have been simpler or less expensive. Since a man needed clothes whether soldier or civilian, the possession of a firearm defined the essential material difference between a combatant and a noncombatant. In earlier times soldiers often had required metal body armor, swords of good-quality steel, and bows or crossbows with suitable arrows. In contrast to the slow and expensive production of these handmade weapons, machines manufactured rifles relatively cheaply and quickly. The machine making of bullets and powder equally contrasted with the hand manufacture of arrows. The characteristic infrequency of battle meant that ammunition would constitute neither a problem nor a major cost. Further, since a smoothbore or rifle was far easier to learn to use than a sword or bow, both sides could quickly train effective forces. The main task was to learn how to march, drill, and deploy. Even drill had become much simplified by the new system adopted seventy years earlier during the French Revolution.

In addition to rifles, an army required artillery, one to four cannon per thousand men. Both the North and the South possessed plenty of coast-defense guns, and each had some serviceable muzzle-loading, smoothbore field guns—as well as facilities to make more. But the horses and mules that were required to move wagons and artillery and to equip the cavalry were costly. Even though the proportion of cavalry used by armies had declined steadily for a century and a half, an army was still a horse-

intensive organization. Civil life in both the North and South also depended heavily on horses, and the diversion of existing horses from civilian to military purposes soon provided an adequate supply.

Thus the American Civil War occurred at a time when the task of
preparing for war proved simpler than it had been for a long time and
than it would become by the twentieth century. The Civil War also took
place at a time when the power of the defense was approaching its ap-
ogee. Cavalry, the traditional offensive arm, already had lost much of its
effectiveness when all infantry came to be armed with smoothbores and
bayonets. The combination of volleys and a bristling wall of bayonets
presented by infantry in three lines rendered almost any frontal cavalry
charge ineffective. The pre–Civil War introduction of the accurate, long-
range rifle completed the devaluation: a cavalry charge became so nearly
impossible that bayonets lost their most basic purpose.

During the Civil War a fluke in technological development made artillery almost exclusively a defensive weapon. The Napoleonic era saw development of new, more mobile artillery that could concentrate rapidly
and fire upon infantry, which was vulnerable because the men had to
stand to fire and reload as well as to resist cavalry charges. Artillery had
the ability to come within three or four hundred yards, close enough to
use grape or canister shot but still beyond the effective range of smoothbore muskets. Grape and canister shot, loads of small balls fired from a
muzzle-loading smoothbore cannon, wreaked a devastating effect on infantry standing erect. But in the Civil War the infantryman's new rifle
outranged the artilleryman's grape or canister. Since the infantrymen
could shoot the gunners, the artillery had to stay out of the range of rifle
as well as grape and canister fire and could no longer support the attack
as in Napoleon's day. Because rifle-augmented firepower disposed of the
danger of a cavalry charge, infantry on the defensive no longer needed to
stand erect in serried ranks, vulnerable to grape, canister, and musket
balls. Instead, infantrymen usually sought, or quickly devised, some
cover against rifle bullets.

Smoothbore artillery, when firing cannon balls, had relatively little effect on infantry in defensive deployment. The available rifled artillery
had little more effect, and ordnance designers had yet to develop a means
of accurately exploding shrapnel shells in the air over the head of distant
infantry. But the smoothbore, muzzle-loading cannon were just as deadly
in the defense as ever, infantrymen fearing these more than rifled pieces.

The grape and canister could inflict serious casualties upon attacking troops even though the attacking infantry no longer used lines three ranks deep. Infantry still had to advance erect, and the artillery, often as well protected from fire as the defending infantry, still provided a formidable asset to the defense just at the time it had lost most of its offensive value.

The Civil War introduced to the North American continent the very large armies long characteristic of European warfare. But European supply conditions did not prevail in the United States. Compared to Europe, where soldiers usually could find abundant food and fodder with ease, the American South was a sparsely populated area, which, in many cotton and tobacco regions, hardly grew any food crops at all, sometimes not even enough for local consumption. This difference in population density and agricultural productivity made it especially difficult to supply large forces if they remained long in one place. Civil War armies therefore had to depend far more on large-capacity lines of communications; horses and wagons over bad American roads would not suffice for very long. Water communications fully met this criterion, as did the new railroads, though with less efficiency. This exceptional logistic constraint also limited the mobility of American armies when compared with contemporary European armies because the Americans had to depend so much more on their communications. Thus, stationary or in motion, armies in the American theater of war, especially in the South, would face unusual logistic difficulties which further strengthened the defense.

The performance of the contending armies has received a constant stream of conflicting critiques, beginning with the first battles and campaigns, continuing until the present day, and apparently destined to persist indefinitely. Of this multitude of commentaries, in recent years three interpretations of southern performance have attracted the most scholarly attention. The first of these, that of T. Harry Williams, which had antecedents in his work and that of others, reached its complete form in his contribution to David Donald's *Why the North Won the Civil War.* He explained the behavior of Union and Confederate generals as stemming from the influence of Antoine Henri Jomini, a Swiss veteran of service in the French army and prominent military historian and theorist. At the time of the Civil War Jomini had become the Western world's most influential interpreter of Napoleon and Frederick the Great. Williams depicted Jomini as an exponent of an obsolete, ineffective strategy that handicapped many Union generals and, at least hypothetically, could have given victory to the Confederates had not Lincoln and Grant, ignorant of Jomini, displayed an intuitive grasp of the proper strategy and ultimately given a firm, modern direction to the Union war effort.

According to Williams, Jomini advocated warfare divorced from political considerations and aimed only at limited and essentially territorial military objectives. These ideas stultified Union commanders by making them see "cities and territory as their objectives rather than the armies of the enemy" and seek to conquer these "by maneuvering rather than by fighting." Like Jomini, Union generals wished to circumscribe the destructiveness of war. Jomini's prescription for the offensive, which involved, Williams said, "one big effort at a time in one theatre," inhibited Union offensives because generals never did "possess enough strength to undertake the movements recommended by Jomini."

Lincoln always disagreed with these ideas, according to Williams, and, when he secured in Grant a commander not shackled by Jomini's precepts, the Union marched to victory in 1864 and 1865. Grant's strategy included the innovative and anti-Jominian elements of simultaneous advances on all fronts, aiming at the enemy's army, and the economic and psychological effect of William T. Sherman's marches.

But Williams saw Jomini's ideas as having a different effect on Confederate generals. They stressed the important offensive element in Jomini's thought, particularly as interpreted by West Point professor Dennis Hart Mahan, as an emphasis on "celerity and the headlong attack." "More Jominian than the Federals," the Confederates, the "most brilliant practitioners of Jomini," successfully applied "the principles that Jomini emphasized—the objective, the offensive, mass, economy of force, interior lines, and unity of command."

Confederates not only could not go beyond the restricted ideas of Jomini but, further, fought a strategically "conservative war" that was "designed to guard the whole circumference of the country." Because of this concern for territory, the "localistic South" could not "attempt on a grand strategic scale the movements its generals were so good at on specific battlefields—the concentrated mass offensive" prescribed by Jomini. Limited by their parochial outlook, Confederates could not concentrate in one theater and did not attempt such an offensive, which would have provided "probably the South's best chance to win its independence by a military decision."

Criticisms of this interpretation soon followed, many found or referred to in T. L. Connelly and Archer Jones's 1973 *Politics of Command: Factions and Ideas in Confederate Strategy* and Herman Hattaway and Archer Jones's *How the North Won: A Military History of the Civil War.* Although it is now clear that West Point taught very little of the strategy of Jomini or of anyone else and that Professor Dennis Hart Mahan had more influence as a teacher of the power of entrenchments than of the headlong attack, generals on both sides did read about the art of war, and many could have learned much more of Jomini than available through the brief exposure at West Point. It is also evident that Jomini was a far more faithful exponent of Napoleon than Williams believed and that an influence he had or might have had would have differed little from that resulting from an independent study of the strategy of Napoleon's campaigns.

Meanwhile, in a paper summarized in his and Jones's *Politics of Command,* T. L. Connelly argued that R. E. Lee, the South's premier general, had such a propensity for the offensive that he cost the Confederacy more casualties than the South could afford and thus exaggerated the necessary price of his long and successful defense of Virginia. This, together with his ignorance of the needs of the West, had a baneful effect on the Confederate war effort, making Lee so significant a liability as very seriously to mar Confederate military performance. Yet a decade later Hattaway and Jones, in their *How the North Won,* on examining Lee's motives in his Virginia operations, found them defensive and saw his strategy emerging as an effort to avoid battle and to exploit the turning movement as a defensive strategy. Further, in a quantitative appendix, they showed that Lee had attacked less often than the average of other Confederate army commanders and, on the average, lost no more men than other generals. Nevertheless, though the present book follows this interpretation of Lee, the issue is not settled. In 1986 Russell F. Weigley, one of the leading authorities on American warfare, reassessed Lee in his contribution to Peter Paret, ed., *Makers of Modern Strategy from Machiavelli to the Nuclear Age.* In this essay he still essentially adhered to his earlier interpretation of Lee as a too costly general who sought battles in a vain effort to destroy the opposing Union armies.

The third interpretation that has attracted attention was introduced by Grady McWhiney in the 1970s and fully stated in his and Perry D. Jamieson's 1982 book, *Attack and Die: Civil War Tactics and the Southern Heritage.* Unlike Williams, McWhiney and Jamieson stress tactics as well as strategy and see a dominant influence not in military thought but in an ethnic factor, the Celticness of the South. Like Hattaway and Jones, they emphasize the influence of the Mexican War. But their major thesis for the cause of southern defeat is that "by attacking instead of defending, the Confederates murdered themselves," suffering defeat in the war by piling up unsustainable casualties in futile frontal attacks.

In testing the implication of southern tactical ineptitude suggested by this interpretation, Hattaway and Jones found that the Confederate armies may actually have significantly surpassed Union troops in tactical skill. In *Why the South Lost* the authors used a broader data base and found that the Confederates did, in fact, attack less frequently than the Union and did not sustain more casualties than warranted by fighting a numerically superior foe armed with rifles rather than smoothbores. This examination also showed that, in spite of these heavy casualties, the nominal strength of Confederate armies remained virtually unchanged; the armies decreased in size because of the constant increase in the number of soldiers absent from their units, which steadily eroded real Confederate military strength. These absences reflect a loss in morale and in confidence in victory, an attitude on the part of both soldiers and civilians to which the war's heavy losses certainly contributed substantially. Thus it seems likely that the main effect of combat losses was not so much directly on military strength as indirectly, on civil and military morale when southerners implicitly compared the past and prospective costs of the war with the value they placed on victory.

Despite the obvious difficulties in assessing the military performance of the contestants in this war, any evaluation of the role of military factors in the conflict demands an effort to compare the competence of the Union and Confederate armies and navies as well as to determine the possibilities open to military force in making its contribution to victory. To evaluate the military performance of the contestants in the American Civil War and to determine whether the Union could have won by military efforts alone, the acknowledged experts on nineteenth-century warfare will provide the prime guide. The best-known among them in the 1800s, Antoine Henri Jomini, had studied the campaigns of Frederick the Great and Napoleon and had written detailed analytical histories of their campaigns to illustrate what he believed were certain immutable principles of warfare. In the 1830s he presented these principles in his *Summary of the Art of War,* a succinct book containing his recommendations concerning all aspects of war.

We use Jomini as an authority not because of any assumption that soldiers consciously followed him but because of the thoroughness and authority with which he had treated warfare similar to that of the Civil War. We have also depended on Jomini's contemporary Karl von Clausewitz, who also relied on military history and drew his inspiration from the campaigns of Frederick and Napoleon. Clausewitz, who explained his conclusions in his major work, *On War,* published in 1832, has a far greater reputation and impact today than does Jomini, and very properly so. Not only does Clausewitz assume a knowledge of Jomini and go beyond him, but he treats much more exhaustively the lessons of Napoleonic warfare and many of the issues raised by the question whether the Confederacy could have won militarily. He also deals with the relationship between military and political factors more extensively and with more sophistication than Jomini.

Just as with Jomini, we do not use Clausewitz because we suppose that any Civil War soldier depended on him. Rather, we rely on him as an acknowledged expert on warfare similar to that fought thirty years after his death. Unlike Jomini's, Clausewitz's principal work continues as a vital part of current military thought, having had a new, fine English translation in 1976 and a thorough application to the Vietnam War by Harry Summers in 1981. Moreover, the United States Army War College recently had an international conference on him. Just as Clausewitz accepted much of Jomini, so have many of their concepts become part of our military culture. For example, the United States Army's *Field Manual 100-5, Operations,* of August 20, 1982, employs the concepts of envelopment, the turning movement, and interior lines, ideas central to the thinking of Clausewitz and Jomini. The 1986 revision has additional references to Clausewitz. In explaining military operations we make a few references to this manual to illustrate, in the Civil War context, some of the consonance between nineteenth-century and present-day thought.

Although we rely more on Clausewitz than on Jomini, the use of both as authorities has the valuable by-product of implicitly comparing their military ideas. In showing how much they had in common and how rarely they disagreed significantly, we demonstrate—albeit indirectly—the inappropriateness of those understandings of Jomini that sharply differentiate him from Clausewitz and the Napoleonic tradition. Thus we can indirectly examine T. Harry Williams's understanding of Jomini and his application of him to the Civil War.

In appealing to these two soldier-historians whose ideas are widely accepted today and who participated in warfare under conditions similar to those of the American Civil War, we hope to have made a better and less controversial assessment of military performance and possibilities. Since they wrote, the railroad and the electric telegraph had affected logistics and strategy but only to broaden the application of one of Jomini's concepts of strategic maneuver; the ultimately universal replacement of the smoothbore by the rifle only reinforced Clausewitz's insight of the dominance of the defensive.

Because the Union began the war with a regular army too small to constitute a framework for the immense forces which both combatants rapidly created, the North did not enjoy much initial advantage over the South. On both sides the states raised these forces, which usually entered national service as regiments complete with officers from colonel down, all appointed by the state governments. Because of the small size of the regular army, Lincoln as well as Davis and their secretaries of war faced the critical task of appointing enough new general officers to command the brigades, into which the regiments must be formed, and the divisions, corps, and armies required for the management of the soon-to-be-mustered hundreds of thousands of men. Both contestants not only lacked enough experienced regular officers to supply all of the needed generals, but politicians, with and without military backgrounds, exploited the country's citizen-soldier tradition to serve as generals and, for many, to acquire military fame as a route to greater political opportunity.

The process of Union and Confederate appointments to general officer rank proceeded in much the same way. Each president divided the openings about equally between politicians and present or former regular army officers. Lincoln made some significant appointments of Democrats in an effort to rally more of the population behind the war effort. One of these, John A. Logan, a Stephen A. Douglas Democrat from Illinois, who had served as a lieutenant during the Mexican War, earned fame for his ability. Another Democratic appointee, Benjamin F. Butler of Massachusetts, became notorious largely for his military incompetence. The Confederacy enjoyed greater success with its political generals because Davis, more than Lincoln, held them to the same standard of achievement as generals without political prominence.

Thus both combatants improvised armies made up of civilians with guidance largely supplied by officers educated at West Point and, often, schooled and seasoned in the Mexican War. Abraham Lincoln began with the brilliant but elderly Winfield Scott as general in chief. Scott had led the army that captured Mexico City in the Mexican War and, in the process, had significantly contributed to the training of many West Point graduates who later became generals on both sides in the Civil War. Jefferson Davis was a West Point graduate, who had served as a colonel in the Mexican War and as a U.S. secretary of war. So similar influences, together with a reading of military history by some, had given many Civil War soldiers a grasp of two fundamentals, the primacy of the turning movement, agreed upon by Jomini and Clausewitz, and the tactical supremacy of the defense, especially when aided by entrenchments, a basic condition grasped only by Clausewitz.

Since the study of combat effectiveness has established the tactical competence of the Confederate army, our treatment of military operations will examine the quality of the strategic direction of the Union as well as the Confederate armies, using some of the points made in *On War* and *Summary of the Art of War.* By presenting this account in narrative rather than topical form, we provide the background of military developments that had such a crucial effect on the morale of Confederate soldiers and civilians and ultimately caused changes in military policy and even in war aims.

In seeking to answer the questions of whether the Confederacy conducted its military operations properly and skillfully and if it could have won in spite of northern superiority in manpower and material resources, Clausewitz and Jomini aid us by the essential similarity of their interpretations of the causes of success and failure in the military operations of Napoleon's day.

Perhaps they disagreed most over the relative power of the offensive and defensive. Clausewitz regarded this as so fundamental a question that he essentially organized his treatment around the difference between the two. Over and over Clausewitz repeated that *"the defensive form of warfare is intrinsically stronger than the offensive,"* and in his book he devoted three times as much space to defense as to attack. Jomini, on the other hand, regarded the offensive as strategically stronger and at least tactically equal to the defensive. But both disparaged a passive defense, agreeing that a defender who remained "passive and receiving all the attacks of his adversary will finally yield."

Among their many areas of essential concord, perhaps the most significant for the Civil War was Clausewitz's and Jomini's advocacy of an attack on the enemy's flank or rear. Although Civil War soldiers tended to call all such attacks "turning movements," Clausewitz and Jomini distinguished two kinds, tactical and strategic. In a tactical turning movement, two armies stand face to face and one seeks to move at least some of its force around the opposing army to attack its flank or rear. In a strategic turning movement, the attacking army marches around to the far rear and places itself astride the communications of the defending army. This move often compels the defending army to fight to recover its communications and route of retreat. Then, if a battle ensues, the army that successfully had carried out a strategic turning movement would be on the more desirable tactical defensive. Clausewitz, in particular, saw that these maneuvers had become "a general law of the nature of engagements."

Jomini preferred the strategic turning movement, the "system of modern strategy" in the "new era" created by Napoleon. He saw the opportunity for reaching the enemy's rear, where he "would have no other chance of escape than in forcing his way through your line." If Jomini had believed in the superiority of the tactical defense, he would have seen even more virtue in the strategic turning movement, for it compelled the enemy to assume the offensive to avoid being cut off from supplies and reinforcements. He disparaged the tactical turning movement, saying a general would "do better to employ strategic than tactical combinations" to seize the "enemy's communications while at the same time holding his own." He preferred the strategic because the tactical maneuver would only "dislodge" the enemy whereas the strategic would "ruin his army completely." Clearly, Jomini placed less stress on the capture and occupation of territory than T. Harry Williams believed.

Clausewitz also stressed the turning movement, aware that the use of this "most effective form" of attack was the "aim of every engagement." He also distinguished between the tactical and the strategic but, unlike Jomini, gave more emphasis to the tactical, in which the attacker in battle attempted to turn the defender and the defender sought to prevent this by choosing a good position and having a reserve to turn or assail the flank of the attacker's turning force. Not sharing Jomini's admiration for the strategic movement to the enemy's rear, Clausewitz disparaged it as "not an invention of genius" and said that these "prize exhibits of the theorists" were "seldom found in actual war" because both sides "normally take precautions against them." But he did recognize the value of

the strategic turning movement for the defense when the attacker's communication lines were long and vulnerable; he further acknowledged its
hypothetical merit when he emphasized that a decisive battle demanded
"an enveloping attack or a battle with reversed fronts." The Civil War
would prove both Clausewitz and Jomini correct about the ubiquity of the
turning movement and substantiate Clausewitz's belief in the supremacy
of the defense.

In this war, as in any other, military success, Clausewitz stressed, would
be measured by *"the political object of the war."* The Union had as its objective the complete suppression of the rebellion, the extinction of the Confederate States of America. Such a goal demanded a total victory and elic-
ited the maximum possible resistance from the South. If the North were
fighting, for example, over the fate of the border states of Missouri and
Kentucky, the Union could have defined victory as the attainment of this
limited goal. Southern resistance would have amounted to less for, as
Clausewitz pointed out, "the smaller the penalty you demand from your
opponent, the less you can expect him to try to deny it to you." And, of
course, if the South attached more significance to its defeat than the North
did to its victory, the Confederacy would make a greater proportional effort
than the Union.

Clausewitz noted that, depending on the political objective, the military means could range from "the destruction of the enemy's forces" to
"passively awaiting the enemy's attacks." But for such a total political
objective as that of the Union, Clausewitz recommended a campaign to
destroy the enemy's armed forces, that is, to put them "in such a condition that they can no longer carry on the fight." The occupation of the
enemy country and the destruction of its will to resist would follow.

But neither Clausewitz nor Jomini, who had more faith in the power of
the offensive, had any recipe for success in waging a war that aimed at the
total defeat of the enemy. Although both envisioned such a war, Jomini
calling it an "invasion," they realized that such a decisive conflict would
be rare, not only because political objectives seldom warranted so great
an effort, but also because they knew the difficulty of attaining total victory. In fact, few historical models existed because, as Clausewitz pointed
out, so many wars were limited or inconclusive that the majority are "so
overwhelming as to make all other campaigns exceptions to the rule."
Thus history provided few precedents from which they could derive a
prescription for total victory.

For a decisive campaign Clausewitz and Jomini agreed that the "forces must be adequate," "proportioned in magnitude to the end to be attained and to the obstacles to be overcome." But neither prescribed a specific ratio. They both felt that the size of the enemy's territory was perhaps as important as the size of the defender's armed forces. Clausewitz, who had participated in Napoleon's ill-fated 1812 invasion of Russia, gave this variable the most attention. This experience doubtless had helped him conclude that "a fairly constant ratio exists between the size of a force and the area it can occupy" and "the relationship between these two is permanent and fundamental."

Although Clausewitz did not establish this relationship, he did give a specific example of the forces he considered sufficient for a campaign against France. He hypothesized a war against France by Great Britain, Holland, Belgium, the Austrian Empire, Prussia, and all the other German states. Their population would outnumber France's by two and a half to one, and they would place 725,000 men in the field. He assigned 50,000 Austrian troops to northern Italy and 25,000 British troops to coastal raids to immobilize about 60,000 French troops in coast defense. Deducting garrisons, 600,000 men were allowed for the principal campaign on the front from Switzerland to the English Channel.

He did not assign any force to France, but, considering that the French regular army of that period numbered only 150,000 men, Clausewitz would hardly have expected that the French could manage to have more than 200,000, regulars and militia, to face triple their number on France's northeastern frontier.

He anticipated "one or more major battles," which, "with such superiority of numbers," would promise "decisive victory," the fall of Paris, and the advance of the allied armies to the Loire. At this point France would accept the peace conditions imposed by the allies. He did not define these conditions, but they clearly did not envision taking away French independence. A similar military defeat in 1871 compelled France to agree to a peace in which she lost the Alsace-Lorraine territory and paid an indemnity of five billion francs. Obviously Clausewitz had described a victorious campaign made possible by great superiority and an adequate ratio of the size of the force to the area it had to occupy. But he hypothesized political objectives more limited than those of the Union. He said nothing about what the military situation would have been if the allies had to advance south of the Loire, or if they desired to extinguish French independence. A three-to-one superiority and the immense force of

600,000 sufficed only to occupy about one-third of France; the campaign would have won only limited political objectives.

This hypothetical campaign has instructive parallels with the Civil War. The frontier from Switzerland to the sea approximates the width of the state of Tennessee. The distance from the French frontiers to the Loire is about the same as that state's depth. Tennessee, Mississippi, Alabama, and Georgia together equal the size of France. The number of men Clausewitz proposed for this territory exceeds all Union forces in the field until 1865 and at least triple the number ever used in this area. In addition, he hypothesized a numerical superiority of three to one, more than the Union had until 1865. Further, he implicitly assumed French qualitative inferiority because they would use some militia whereas the invaders could rely exclusively on regulars and well-trained reserves.

Surely Clausewitz's example shows that, had he lived until 1861 and studied the situation, he would not have believed the Union could wage a decisive campaign or that the Union could conquer a country as large as the South: the Confederacy east of the Mississippi, alone, had nearly twice the area of France. One Confederate leader, Secretary of War George Wythe Randolph, believed such a conquest impossible. "There is no instance in history," he wrote at the beginning of the war, "of a people as numerous as we are inhabiting a country so extensive as ours being subjected if true to themselves."

With some understanding of the power of the defense, the usefulness of turning movements, and other European ideas of warfare, Civil War generals went out to fight a war in which battles with significant results proved as elusive as Clausewitz and Jomini would have expected. But Civil War planners had more to consider than the role their armies would play. Logistics, the supply of armies, would prove a particular problem because the Union blockade prevented the South's usual large-scale export of cotton and other staples in exchange for fabricated imports. Even though equipping the armies was relatively simple, coping with the blockade and other supply problems was not.

Chapter Two

The Confederacy's
Logistical Problems

IN RECOGNIZING THE impossibility of waging a decisive campaign against the Confederacy, Union General in Chief Winfield Scott had proposed a strategy proportioned both to the military resources available and to the actual political objective. He chose to take advantage of the western rivers, employing "twelve to twenty steam gunboats" and enough steam transports to carry sixty thousand men. With this combination he intended to drive down the Mississippi, expecting to have a small detachment on the river and another, larger force inland cooperating so as to "turn and capture" the rebel river forts. He then envisioned "a cordon of posts on the Mississippi to its mouth from its junction with the Ohio" and "blockading ships of war on the seaboard." By keeping open the "great line of communication" of the Mississippi "in connection with the strict blockade of the seaboard," he would "envelop the insurgent States and bring them to terms with less bloodshed than by any other plan." Thus Scott's plan embodied a logistic strategy of depriving Confederate armies of the imported resources needed to equip them and of weakening the forces on each side of the Mississippi by preventing the interchange of horses, manufactures, and other products needed by the armies. Probably more important in the general's initial concept was the strategy's political element, that the economic effects of the blockade and control of the Mississippi would cause the seceded states to abandon their Confederacy without bloody and divisive fighting.

Scott's ideas illustrated that, in the Civil War, military and naval strategy went hand in hand. Communications often relied upon naval cooperation, and of course foreign supplies for both sides depended on the seas.

Whether as blockaders or runners of the blockade, merchantmen or raiders, transports or river gunboats, ships had a key role to play.

In 1950 the venerable southern historian E. Merton Coulter wrote in *The Confederate States of America, 1861–1865*, that "without a doubt the blockade was one of the outstanding causes of the strangulation and ultimate collapse of the Confederacy," and in 1962 Rear Admiral Bern Anderson, in the best one-volume naval history of the war, stated that "without the relentless pressure of Union sea power . . . [economic disintegration] could not have been achieved." Charles P. Roland agreed. "The silent grip of the Federal navy," he wrote, "grew ever tighter and the number of captures among blockade-runners steadily mounted. Still more significant, Southern ports were avoided altogether by the major cargo vessels of the world. By 1864 the blockade was strangling the Southern economy."

Yet other studies have indicated that the blockade was not a major factor in Confederate defeat. Was it an ineffective, "leaky and ramshackled affair," as Frank L. Owsley contended? Some fifty years ago Owsley published his monumental study *King Cotton Diplomacy*. In a chapter entitled "The Ineffectiveness of the Blockade," Owsley evaluated the Union blockade in terms of the number of ships that eluded the blockaders, the increase in Confederate cotton exports, and the successful delivery of huge cargoes to the South. Although historians generally did not accept Owsley's conclusions, in later years other studies appeared that substantiated his work.

Marcus W. Price's series of articles published during the 1940s and 1950s in *American Neptune* have been by far the most important in this regard. In his study "Ships That Tested the Blockade of the Carolina Ports, 1861–1865," he estimated that out of 2,054 attempts to run past the blockading vessels off Wilmington, North Carolina, 1,735 succeeded, or an average of 1.5 efforts per day, with 84 percent of them getting through. In a second article he analyzed the blockade of the Gulf ports. Between April 20, 1861, and June 4, 1865, according to his calculations, 2,960 vessels tried to slip through the blockade, a daily average of two. As with the Carolina ports, in 1861 very few vessels were taken. But in 1862 and 1863 the Union tightened the blockade. During that period the proportion of successful runs into and out of these ports amounted to 65 percent and 62 percent, respectively. He attributes the higher percentage of failures to the larger number of sailing vessels used to run the blockade in the Gulf. In 1864 and 1865, the picture changed dramatically, particularly in the number of steamers challenging the blockade; in 1864, 87 percent, and in 1865, 94 percent of the ships that challenged the Gulf blockade got through.

Thus the excellent Union navy failed in spite of a steady numerical increase in the number of warships on blockade duty during the course of the war. One recent study shows that, although the number of blockaders on the Wilmington station steadily grew, the number of blockade-runners captured or destroyed remained approximately the same. Union squadron commanders encountered extremely difficult logistical problems that hindered their efforts to enforce a tight blockade. The use of steam-powered vessels theoretically increased efficiency, but vexatious problems of maintenance and supply largely offset the advantages. As early as 1862 the four blockade squadrons required approximately three thousand tons of coal per week, and the amount needed grew as the number of blockaders increased. A recent study by Robert Browning of the blockade off Wilmington clearly demonstrates that the inefficiency of the vessels deployed at Wilmington frequently and seriously weakened the naval force on that station, by 1863 considered the most important. Many blockaders had inadequate speed or poor seagoing qualities, especially in heavy weather. Blockading squadrons included many converted ships that could not operate at sea for long periods or carry their heavy ordnance without impairment of their performance. Too often they suffered breakdowns in machinery and had to leave their stations for long periods when the navy had no replacements to send. Repair time kept from one-third to two-fifths of the vessels constantly away from their stations. Reflecting the always pressing need to conserve coal, in September 1863 Rear Admiral Samuel P. Lee, in command of the North Atlantic Blockading Squadron, wrote to the force commander off Wilmington: "You may find it expedient not to keep more than one of the little vessels moving about at a time, even at night."

Although the Confederate government nationalized much industry, until early in 1864 it generally allowed blockade-running free reign. The evidence strongly suggests that during the first years of the war those involved in the blockade-running business were more concerned with bringing in goods that sold well than in meeting the needs of the war effort. In November 1864, only a few months before the final collapse, an official of a Wilmington, North Carolina, firm wrote to his agent in

Nassau not to send any more chloroform because he was having difficulty selling it. The businessman requested perfume, "Essence of Cognac," because it would sell "quite high."

Even in 1864, when the Confederate government finally established laws to regulate blockade-running, it required ships to reserve only one-half of their cargo space for government shipments. The enabling legislation became effective on February 6, 1864. Davis interpreted this law with utmost latitude. Far from inhibiting foreign trade—except for a brief period when shippers tried to force relaxation of the regulations by curtailing their activities—these regulations seem to have had little or no effect upon the volume of trade, for in December 1864 Davis and Christopher G. Memminger, the secretary of the treasury, both maintained that the number of blockade-runners was still growing.

That the Confederacy never gave priority to breaking the blockade provides a convincing argument, on its face, that the South did not find the blockade excessively damaging to its war effort. Nevertheless, Secretary of the Navy Stephen Mallory did want to challenge the blockade. The Confederacy used cruisers such as the *Alabama* and *Florida* to assail Union shipping in order to force the federal navy to weaken the blockade by diverting ships to protect the commercial lanes. And early in the war the secretary also ordered the construction of armored vessels, both at home and abroad, to attack blockaders. But neither effort proved successful.

Therefore, historians generally regard the Confederate naval effort, particularly the ironclad program, as a failure. They base this assessment on the erroneous assumption that the Confederates built ironclads to challenge the blockade and commissioned only a scant few. The South laid down approximately fifty armored vessels but completed and placed in operation less than half that number. With the exception of the five initial vessels, however, Confederates intended the ironclads only for harbor and river defense, in part because Union capture of ports did constitute an absolutely effective blockade.

Confederate officials wrote surprisingly little about the blockade in their correspondence and exhibited more concern over its international implications than over the blockade itself or its effects on the Confederacy. President Davis did not show much interest in naval affairs and generally left them in the capable hands of Secretary Mallory. Davis's few references to the blockade indicate concern for the international point of view; he considered it a paper blockade, clearly illegal, and thought other nations should ignore it. In January 1865 he issued one of his few directives concerning naval operations when he ordered the Confederate naval squadron at Charleston to attack Union forces off the harbor—not because of the blockade but to try to prevent linkage between the warships and the approaching army of Major General William T. Sherman.

Even Mallory rarely mentioned the blockade in his reports and correspondence, and Secretary of War James A. Seddon premised his recommendations for foreign trade in strategic goods with the matter-of-fact observation that "our staples can be exported and supplies introduced with reasonable exemption from capture." Confederate officials were well aware that the South broke the blockade more frequently in 1864–65 than at any time previously. As late as March 1865, one newspaper editor yawned over the capture of Wilmington, the last open port, and told his readers that "we shall, no doubt, suffer considerable inconvenience," but denied that it would cause the Confederacy to succumb. "Our inventive faculties and mechanical skill will be quickened and developed, by necessity, to the supply of all our wants." The editor's prediction of the future was a more accurate description of the recent past.

So, clearly Confederates could get whatever they wanted or needed through the blockade, if they wanted it badly enough. The Union navy failed to interdict the flow of commerce in goods which market forces and the Confederate government deemed most valuable; the South did not lose the Civil War because of the blockade.

The dramatic development of war-related industries provided the most significant, probably indispensable, way in which the Confederacy survived in spite of the serious impediment of the blockade. Under government and private auspices, the Confederacy expanded existing and created new industrial facilities, which ultimately met the needs for many essential military items. For example, by the end of 1862 the output of eight government-owned armories reached 170,000 cartridges and 1,000 field-artillery rounds of ammunition daily and 155,000 pounds of lead monthly. Altogether the Augusta works turned out 2,750,000 pounds of powder during the conflict. By the end of 1864 the Niter and Mining Bureau had nearly a million cubic feet of niter beds in operation, fulfilling at least the bulk of all saltpeter needs.

Historians were slow in noting the scale and importance of this development, but in 1950 E. Merton Coulter discussed the work of Josiah

Gorgas, head of the Ordnance Bureau, who organized Confederate munitions manufacturing. He also noted the actions of the Confederate Congress and executive, which loaned private contractors money to meet start-up costs and limited the profits these government-sponsored enterprises could make. They required factories producing goods that were needed in both the public and private sectors to sell as much as two-thirds of their output to the government. This regulation and others as well were enforced by Confederate control of required manpower through conscription and exemption laws and by control of necessary rail transport, without which goods could neither be made nor marketed. Using manpower and transport as a club, the government encouraged a widespread development of war industry—sulfur, niter, powder, clothing, shoes, and the like—that was "remarkable for a region which had long frowned on manufactories."

Despite Coulter's relatively positive evaluation of Confederate industrialization, in 1954 Clement Eaton contended that although the blockade "should have stimulated the growth of Southern manufacturing plants," it did not do so because too many southerners hoped the North would lift the blockade. Yet Eaton, too, remarked on the efforts of the military to produce its own shoes, other leather goods, and clothes, and of the government to channel industrial expansion by its control over manpower and transportation. The Confederacy, he said, found it necessary to "invade" the economy and abandon laissez-faire. Charles P. Roland also noted the accomplishments of General Gorgas and the Ordnance Bureau, and like Coulter he underlined the importance of the expansion of private industry, the Tredegar Iron Works especially.

This interpretation of Confederate economic change was not widely accepted or discussed until the 1970s. Frank E. Vandiver, for example, pointed to the increasing uniformity (the word is ours) imposed on Confederate industry. With splendid success, Josiah Gorgas took over procurement of munitions: powder, lead, cannon, shot, shell, carbines, rifles, and pistols. The same pattern was repeated elsewhere; quartermaster officers took over textile factories, the Medical Department absorbed laboratories and operated distilleries, and private companies were subjected "to subtle management techniques" as government "supervision came in thin disguise." In May 1863 a new Confederate law permitted "the War Department to seize and manage railroads, regulate freight schedules, and interchange rolling stock." At last the imposition of uniformity on the transportation system gave some chance of logic to railroad management.

One of Vandiver's former students, Emory M. Thomas, has taken a similar position, first in a path-breaking, marvelously provocative, and insightful little book, *The Confederacy as a Revolutionary Experience*, and later in *The Confederate Nation, 1861–1865*. In the latter Thomas discusses the industrial concerns owned by the Confederate government, the ones stimulated by it, and the economic controls it imposed. He emphasizes the centralization involved "because time and the South's laissez-faire heritage precluded the development of a broadly based socialized industrial economy." He agrees that Confederates produced an impressive, indeed "phenomenal," industrial establishment, despite some understandably conspicuous failures in the course of a "military-industrial revolution," "a pragmatic response to the demands of industrial war."

Although no one has told the full story of Confederate industrialization and economic intervention, in 1978 Raimondo Luraghi demonstrated what many students of the Confederacy had observed. Luraghi's *Rise and Fall of the Plantation South* became the first scholarly work to do justice to an amazing, even magnificent, achievement—the major industrial expansion of the Confederate South. He argues more extravagantly than Thomas did, but his work merits close examination. In his chapter titled "Forced Industrialization through State Socialism" Luraghi rightly asserts that "this sector of Confederate history is, indeed, far from being well understood."

Luraghi explains, "The Confederate government acted immediately to nationalize the whole productive power of existing manufactures. . . . [And] following the Tredegar [Iron Works], practically every other existing industry was put under contract by the government." But the government also engendered the formation of new industry by providing help through loans for "50 percent of setting up expenses and advancing as much as one-third of the value of the contemplated output." In addition, "such industries were allowed to produce only for the government," and the profits were limited "to keep prices on a reasonable level." Soon the Confederacy advanced to fixing the prices of goods made by its contractors.

After gaining control of the thirty-nine furnaces in the South, the Confederacy provided money to build more. It created the amazing "giant Augusta Powder Works at Augusta, Georgia. The buildings . . .

were taken and the land around them purchased . . . [to establish] the largest nationally owned factory system in the world to that time." The Augusta factory was the most impressive of the many publicly owned concerns that produced niter, lead, rifles, shoes, buttons, and other items.

Meanwhile, the navy contracted with existing shipyards for shipbuilding and repair and established new yards, most of them government-owned. A shortage of machinery forced the navy to buy foundries to produce engines and parts, propellors and shafts. A large, fully adequate ropewalk was established at Petersburg. But the most extensive naval industry, the Selma Cannon Foundry, which had proved unprofitable to its owners, was purchased and transformed into a naval heavy ordnance works that cast more than a hundred cannon. The navy had almost thirty installations, including shipyards, ordnance plants, machinery works, and a powder mill.

All this government-induced and controlled activity turned the cities where it occurred into large industrial centers. "Among the most remarkable of such industrial cities was Richmond . . . [but] Augusta, Georgia, was truly a 'Confederate city,' " as were Columbus, Atlanta, Macon, and Selma. Very significantly, says Luraghi, "had the Confederacy lasted a little longer, coordination of national productive activities in such centers would have brought more and more planning and centralization."

Yet Confederate logistics suffered from many stresses. In calling into its armies a higher percentage of its population than the North, the South had more serious skilled manpower problems than its adversary. Near the end of 1864 General Gorgas, the chief of ordnance, complained of an abundance of machinery but no one to operate it. And often raw materials, particularly iron ore, proved scarcer than machinery and as critical as manpower.

One of the ironies of the Civil War was that the South, with its overwhelming prewar emphasis on agriculture, sustained itself industrially better than it did agriculturally. Several factors accounted for this anomaly: the antebellum stress on the production of cash crops, the federal occupation of extensive sections of southern cropland by the end of 1862, and, finally, the breakdown in the Confederacy's transportation system. As Emory Thomas has observed: "People went hungry in the midst of full cribs, barns, and smokehouses. A bountiful harvest counted for little if local railroad tracks were destroyed by foes or cannibalized by friends, if the road to town were a quagmire, or if wagons and mules were impressed to serve the army." Although the evidence indicates that bountiful crops were produced during the war years, soldiers and civilians alike, particularly the inhabitants of urban areas, faced a constant shortage of food.

The decline of the railway system seems likely the most important economic factor in Confederate defeat. Catesby ap Roger Jones, while commanding the naval ordnance facility at Selma, Alabama, wrote that "the principal difficulty in coal now arises, not from its scarcity . . . but from the limited means of transportation." Finished products—such as guns, armor plate, and shoes—often were delayed drastically in reaching their destination.

Moreover, as Stanley Lebergott has emphasized, Confederate finance proved a most emphatic failure. Avoidance of taxes together with totally inadequate taxation limited tax revenues to 1 percent of income, a significant contrast with the Union's 23 percent, and poor bond sales increased the reliance on printing money. Both resulted in an extreme inflation. Impressment of needed supplies at low fixed prices resulted in the enmity of producers and hardships to their families, as well as evasion of impressment and reduced production. But Confederate finance had its antecedents in both the American and French revolutions, and, in spite of this obvious handicap, the Confederacy did supply and equip its armies.

So, although economic factors affected the outcome of the war, they did so primarily in an indirect manner. Despite all the problems of manpower, inadequate supplies of raw materials and food, and the deficient railway system, logistic shortcomings did not play a major role in Confederate defeat. No Confederate army lost a crucial battle or campaign because of a lack of ammunition, guns, or even shoes and food, scarce though these latter items became. Economic liabilities played an important role in Confederate fortunes but primarily through the debilitating effect on public morale. These hardships tested the will of the people, a quality that necessarily rested in part on the intensity and extent of Confederate nationalism.

Chapter Three

Southern Nationalism

ARMED FORCES, the resources to sustain them, and a civilian population are not the only components of a military effort. Intangible resources also help a people wage a prolonged armed conflict, not the least of which is will, or morale. We contend that lack of will constituted the decisive deficiency in the Confederate arsenal. By lack of will we mean that the Confederates' desire for the goal they sought was not adequate to the large demands, anticipated by only a few, which the war would place on them. One of the principal reasons for this lack of motivation to pay the high price for independence which the Union demanded was the weakness of the Confederacy's nationalism, that feeling of oneness, almost a mystical sense of nationhood.

The student of Confederate nationalism must make a distinction between two quite different kinds of nationalism. A number of recent historians, most notably Frank E. Vandiver, have emphasized the wartime development of a strong central government, which they consider a sign of Confederate nationalism. Using nationalism to denote a mode of government, usually in opposition to a states'-rights style, these historians correctly point to the strong central government—one at odds with the notion of states' rights, as many Confederates promptly and continually pointed out—that Jefferson Davis and other like-minded Confederates created to fight the war.

By the standards of the 1860s, the Confederates had a highly centralized and extremely powerful government, with a Constitution that had the potential for creating a stronger government than that of the Union in 1861. One need only think of the measures about which Jefferson Davis's opponents so frequently complained: conscription, suspension of the writ of habeas corpus, martial law, impressment, the regulation of trade and commerce, and, at the end, the recruitment of slaves as soldiers.

This form of nationalism is a theme of Vandiver's study of the Confederacy. Davis succeeded, believes Vandiver, who goes so far as to say that the southern president made the Confederate Constitution into a "revolutionary document" and "worked to build a sense in the southern people of a higher loyalty than states' rights—a sense of Confederateness" —which admits that he jettisoned states' rights in the effort to achieve victory. Emory M. Thomas made one of the most forthright statements of this position. Thomas contends that nationalism was always present in the Confederacy but that the experiences of the first year of the war produced a revolutionary nationalism in which "national character grew to become more Confederate than Southern," a trend that continued as the war went on.

Paul D. Escott's recent study of the failure of Confederate nationalism also provokes thought. Escott maintains that nationalism was there but that it failed to bring Confederate success because Jefferson Davis's policies alienated his constituency. Some policies, such as exemptions for overseers and conscription substitution, appeared to favor the rich, thereby antagonizing the middle and lower classes; other policies, such as those aimed at organizing a strong, centralized government, irritated segments of the planter class, which accused Davis "of trampling on the constitution and subverting the nation's purpose." This kind of nationalism, reflected in the powerful Confederate government, constituted a major element in enabling the Confederacy to fight as long and as effectively as it did. It is partly responsible for the prodigious struggle required to attain Union victory.

Another meaning of the word *nationalism*, however, comes closer to explaining the breakdown of Confederate will and the perhaps predictable Confederate defeat. This nationalism does not refer to a style of government policy or economic organization but to the emotional bonds between citizens of the would-be nation. The problem is that the people of the South had no widely accepted mystical sense of distinct nationality. Some historians believe they have discovered such a nationalism, and this doubtless is what Vandiver and Thomas meant when they widened their definition of nationalism to embrace more than a mode of government, including also what they termed a "higher loyalty . . . a sense of Confederateness," and "a growing national character." Steven A. Channing also discerned this feeling when he found "an ideological core sustaining a latent cultural nationalism."

In *The Idea of a Southern Nation*, a newer and more challenging study, John McCardell discusses the development of the concept in the nullification crisis of the 1830s, centering on the problem of slavery but examining also economic, religious, educational, literary, and political issues, and concludes that in each issue a feeling of separateness had developed by 1860. McCardell seems to equate nationalism with separatism. And in his introduction he maintains that despite the growth of an ideology of southern nationalism, "it is incorrect to think of Northerners and Southerners in 1860 as two distinct peoples" and that "the majority of Southerners, probably even in 1861, still hoped that their sectional rights could be maintained within the existing Union." In his conclusion McCardell argues that the strong states'-rights position of the southern nationalists had created tensions "that would produce a new American nationalist ideology." This statement, the most able of the southern nationalist case, seems in the final summation to support the position that southern nationalism was not particularly strong and did not even include a majority of southerners. McCardell's thesis, in its essence, equates southern nationalism with the desire of southerners to legislate for themselves, not the same as a mystical sense of nationhood.

But we part company with the Confederate nationalists. We believe that the Confederacy functioned as a nation only in a technical, organizational sense, not in a mystical or spiritual sense. An inadequately developed sense of nationalism hampered southerners in their quest for independence, as Kenneth M. Stampp points out in his provocative essay "The Southern Road to Appomattox." Only slavery gave the South its distinct identity, despite the efforts of some southern writers before the Civil War to pretend otherwise. Southern nationalism was, in Stampp's words, "that most flimsy and ephemeral of dreams." Many Confederates became Confederates not because they shared a sense of unique nationhood but because they had a mutual fear of a society without slavery and white supremacy. Whatever nationalism these southerners may have felt, it was not as strong as the fear of such a society.

It would be unreasonable to expect Confederates to have developed sufficient distinctiveness from their northern brothers to evolve a separate nationality. Grady McWhiney justifiably complains that too many writers "have tended to magnify the differences between Northerners and Southerners out of all proportion. In 1861 the United States did not contain . . . two civilizations." Any notion that the people of the two sections "were fundamentally different" is, says McWhiney, "one of the great myths of American history." He contends that historians have "ignored or minimized the common elements in the antebellum American experience." As Edward Pessen has pointed out, there were indeed differences between the sections, but "the antebellum North and South were far more alike than the conventional scholarly wisdom has led us to believe." After surveying an extensive literature, he concluded that "for all their distinctiveness, the Old South and North were complementary elements in an American society that was everywhere primarily rural, capitalistic, materialistic, and socially stratified, racially, ethnically and religiously heterogeneous, and stridently chauvinistic and expansionist." We could add more obvious similarities, which are so plain to see that they have become clichés. Very little separated them, not even including, for most people in either section, a greatly different view of their black countrymen. Racism was not much stronger in the South than in the North—its expression merely took different forms. The values the South shared with the North proved to be bonds, not wedges, and they were bonds that neither could escape.

And David M. Potter contends that efforts to find a *separate* culture in the South had been fruitless, although a *distinctive* culture did indeed exist. Much of this distinctiveness lay in the institution of slavery, which was so basic to their existence, most southerners thought, that they would fight to preserve it when it was threatened. As Potter points out, "The readiness with which the South returned to the Union will defy explanation unless it is recognized that Southern loyalties to the Union were never really obliterated but rather were eclipsed by other loyalties with which, for a time, they conflicted."

It confuses the historian who desires to know why southerners lost the Civil War to realize that many Confederates harbored conflicting notions of why they fought. Although often true of countries at war, such ambiguity was especially true of Confederates, perhaps more than of any other fighting people. The federals had a clearer idea; they fought, by definition, for national unity, although they added the goal of emancipation along the way. Southerners, however, experienced more confusion. Once the war came, they fought and mostly for the South. But they had to justify the act. Confederates fought to break away from a prior attachment, but this merely stated a fact and did not provide a justification, a goal, or even a realistic alternative. For some it was not even a desired alternative.

Some southerners supported their section because they had no other choice. Indeed, the strength of Unionism in the South before the war began, and even at its beginning, illustrates clearly that many Confederates fought for their independence as a second choice. Given the alternative of remaining within the Union at peace or joining the Confederacy, people in vast areas of the South preferred the former. But they never had the chance to make that choice. When Lincoln called for troops after the fall of Fort Sumter and the war broke out, the border state Unionists—a large enough group to force their states to remain in the Union after the first wave of secession—felt betrayed. They joined the Confederacy, for now they faced a different choice.

Although southern Unionism was not nearly as strong as Lincoln and other northerners had hoped and believed, the delay of the upper South in joining the Confederacy strongly suggests the lack of one of the key ingredients of Confederate strength—an adequately developed sense of nationalism. A bride who is the groom's second choice will not have a very attentive husband, nor will she make the best of wives. William Alexander Graham of North Carolina, for example, wrote after the war that he and other former Whigs "had ever been sincere & zealous adherents" of the Union, but finally "the only alternative left us, was the choice of the side we should espouse, when a favorable result to either, was to be little short to ruin to us." Ralph Wooster's modern work on the secession movement, to take only one example, indicates that in most southern states Unionism constituted a political force of some consequence until Fort Sumter, and in several states it remained significant even after the war began. The failure of four slave states to join the Confederacy exhibits the strength of Unionism.

And yet, despite internal divisions, southerners created an independent Confederacy. Steven A. Channing attempts to deal with this paradox by agreeing that the mere existence of the Confederacy must prove something. The real question remains whether that "something" constituted a distinctiveness amounting to nationality. Channing contends that Confederates had "an ideological core sustaining a latent cultural nationalism." Explaining this latent core, however, inevitably brings Channing back to the Negro presence.

Our argument does not deny that the black population provided, to paraphrase Ulrich B. Phillips, a central theme of Confederate history. It does deny that southern or Confederate nationalism resulted from anxiety, or even guilt, about the institution of slavery. That even those who trembled when they thought of the unchained slave did not agree on secession as a proper tranquilizer for their anxieties provides one of the strongest proofs of this contention. Some of these, the most practical of men, saw in the Union the bulwark of a stable society, without which any slaveholding community must collapse.

James Chesnut, Sr., for example, understood that for all the noise of the abolitionists, the Union was a great protector of slavery, just as many abolitionists had charged. "Without the aid and countenance of the whole United States," he remarked, "we could not have kept slavery. I always knew that the world was against us. That was one reason why I was a Union man. I wanted all the power the United States gave me—to hold my own." As one member of the Virginia secession convention reminded his colleagues, the civilized world opposed slavery, "and it is nothing but the prestige and power of the General Government now that guarantees to the slaveholder his right."

Others, less pragmatic, had sentimental ties to the Union far more difficult to cut than ties based on expediency or rational calculation. When the final break came, with heavy hearts indeed such people followed their states away from the flag of their fathers. A. H. Kenan of Georgia threw away the pen with which he signed his state's ordinance of secession, and George T. Ward of Florida announced, "When I die I want it inscribed on my tombstone that I was the last man to give up the ship."

Some other southerners, notably in west and north Texas and in the eastern mountains, were coerced into secession right from the beginning. With sympathy for the plight of such people, especially those of the mountains, Philip S. Paludan observes that they made their difficult decision to become secessionists often under the pressure of prosecession neighbors, for "reasonable men not seeking martyrdom might [be wise to] become Southern patriots. For many among all classes there was little pleasure in being citizens of the new republic. . . . In such an environment it is not surprising that devotion to the Confederate cause was often not very deep."

If strong secessionists had been nationalists, those so-called southern nationalists would have looked upon their war as a true revolution—but not many of them did. Howell Cobb said that what was most remarkable about the Confederate revolution was its conservatism, which some students might consider a contradiction in terms. In North Carolina, the Unionists, acquiescing in the inevitable, attempted to get the state to base secession upon the right of revolution, only to be heavily outvoted by the secessionist faction, which denied that secession involved revolution. Indeed, says Robert L. Kerby, the South lost the Civil War precisely because the leadership could not "admit that Southern independence could be achieved only by revolution." Such a paradoxical position provides a good indicator of a lack of nationalistic sentiment. And, of course, many loyal Confederates doubtless felt stronger allegiance to their region, state, locality, comrades-in-arms, or constituents than they ever did to a mystical Confederate nationality.

No matter how one calculates, then, the Confederacy had a small number of true nationalists as a percentage of the total population—certainly not enough to carry the burden of a war in which the North heavily outmatched them. A latent core of true Confederates may have existed, but there was no "widespread determination to forge a Southern nation at all costs." And surely a losing war would not create more loyalty to such an abstract concept, especially when Confederates could look back and see highly desirable aspects in the rejected alternative—peace and Union.

Nor was it remarkable that so many Confederates entered the war reluctantly in view of how much the sections had in common. Most of all, these Americans, North and South, shared history; for the southerners did not have a distinctive sense of history. And shared history, one of the strongest bonds, sometimes overcomes even the powerfully divisive influence of language. Switzerland, with its four languages and numerous dialects, nevertheless is held together by the adhesive of a common history. If one scratches beneath the surface of linguistic diversity in a land of dissension, one will likely find historic diversity. If the history has similarity, however, diversity of language may not have a particularly strong influence in creating separate national feeling.

In the United States, Confederates simply appropriated as their own the history they shared with the Union and recreated it. And so southerners did little to change their polity. They adopted their initial laws en masse from those of the United States, and they wrote their Constitution virtually as a word-for-word copy of the federal Constitution, with only a few significant changes; the Constitution underlined the lack of nationalism by implying the right of secession. The several Confederate flags departed from the design of the United States flag, but all included red, white, and blue colors, with stars and bars in one form or another. Moreover, the great seal also followed the federal tradition, for it portrayed the equestrian statue of George Washington erected before the Virginia legislative buildings in 1857 (can one imagine the great seal of the United States portraying King William or Queen Anne?). The South's postage stamps and its currency, too, indicate to the modern historian the extent to which history was used to create a mythic past for Confederate use. Besides Jefferson Davis, Confederate stamps pictured George Washington, Thomas Jefferson, Andrew Jackson, and John C. Calhoun. A certain irony emerges here, for the inclusion of Jackson blots out the memory of his views in the nullification crisis of 1832, and Calhoun—the one true Confederate precursor—adorned a stamp that the Confederacy never used because rapid inflation rendered its low denomination inadequate. Jackson and Calhoun also appeared on some Confederate treasury notes.

David Potter, in his *Impending Crisis*, well summarized the extent of southern nationalism. Discussing the nature of southern separatism, Potter detected the undeniable "spirit of southernism" and thought of Edmund Ruffin and William Lowndes Yancey as genuine southern nationalists because they "had the vision of a South united by shared distinctive qualities, and both seemed to care more for the South as a whole than for their own states." This provides a key to the question, and the Civil War historian would do well to recall the number of times he has read the phrase "he went with his state," used so often to describe the actions of leading Confederates. Vice-President Alexander H. Stephens thought of Georgia as his country, as Potter points out. The contrast of men such as Ruffin and Yancey with other Confederates led Potter to conclude that southerners did not really desire a "separate destiny" but rather "wanted recognition of the merits of southern society and security for the slave system." The southern movement had "a strong color of nationalism," but the war did more to produce that nationalism than vice versa. Instead, fear united them. In short, by 1860, North and South were, paradoxically, "separated by a common nationalism. Each was devoted to its own image of the Union, and each section was distinctly aware that its image was not shared by the other."

Given the ambiguous nature of nationalism, the ambivalent conclusions that other scholars have reached on the subject, and the fragile nature of Confederate identity, we have little hesitation in expressing our serious doubts that the average Georgia plowman sensed a distinct nationality from the average Ohio plowman, even after the war began. We do not deny that the South was distinctive in a number of significant ways. But it seems clear that different though they might have been, southerners did not diverge so much from northerners as to constitute a different nationality. And the lack of strong national feeling made the Confederacy more vulnerable to the demoralizing effect of heavy casualties and hardships at home and enhanced the morale-sustaining importance of military victories. But at the outset, a majority of southerners did not realize the deficiencies of their nationalism, and most, unaware of the odds they would ultimately face, trusted in God and looked with righteous confidence to the outcome of secession.

Chapter Four

Religion and
the Chosen People

IF WILL, OR MORALE, supplies one of the intangible resources necessary to sustain a prolonged armed conflict, religion often proves a vital resource in maintaining will and morale. Unfortunately for the South, religion not only sustained morale, it also had the effect—eventually—of undermining it.

In constructing a model of southern religion, Samuel S. Hill, Jr., builds upon, and then goes beyond, one posited by Emory Thomas. "It all had to do with race," Hill observed, and "by and large . . . slavery was as much an aspect of southern society as Thomas Jefferson, the city of Charleston, a rural way of life, and evangelical Christianity." Furthermore, as Thomas pointed out, to the degree that southerners developed anything resembling a national ideology, "the corporate Southern mind [became] comfortable with the potential for guilt that pervaded a life style largely grounded in slavery." This process, they both very well show, began in the southern churches. Indeed, as Sydney E. Ahlstrom has asserted, the churches took a crucial part in the political events during at least the two decades preceding secession and Civil War. James E. Wood, Jr., recently echoed this idea when he asserted that "at no time was organized religion in the United States more active politically than in the twenty years prior to the Civil War." All the churches, either de jure or de facto, divided eventually into separate northern and southern institutions. The Presbyterians, Methodists, and Baptists did it officially, but others followed suit, albeit in less formal manner. For example, although the Lutheran, Episcopal, and Roman Catholic churches remained officially undivided, "each contributed vigorous polemicists to both sides."

The divisions were more fundamental than mere surface squabbles; the separate northern and southern versions of Christianity instead reflected differences in their environment and the necessity of one to cope with the fact of slavery.

According to William Warren Sweet, "There are good arguments to support the claim that the split in the churches was not only the first break between the sections, but the chief cause of the final break." He believed, too, that the churches provided a major part of the impetus for sustaining that rift. Once the churches split, religion supplied the glue that gave any internal cohesion to either section (or certainly to the South, Samuel Hill has agreed).

Not unrepresentative in his attitude was Leonidas Polk, the Episcopal bishop of Louisiana, who became a lieutenant general in the Confederate army. Polk, who had tried very hard to help initiate division in the national Episcopal church, declared in June 1861, "I believe most solemnly, that it is for . . . liberty . . . our hearth-stones, and our altars that we strike." His Anglican counterpart in Rhode Island, Bishop Thomas March Clark, however, challenged Polk's sentiments. Bishop Clark asserted that the North's was "a holy and righteous cause . . . God is with us . . . the Lord of hosts is on our side."

Even the Roman Catholic church, in its own particular way, shared in this drama. That church had taken an official position during the antebellum period that slavery was not in itself sinful, and during the war, like all the other denominations, it "provided powerful champions of both causes." All eleven of the Roman Catholic bishops whose sees lay in Confederate states cooperated in behalf of the southern war effort, though, interestingly, none were native southerners.

So in some sense the war was one between the churches of the North and those of the South. "The number of chaplains who volunteered was remarkably high," Ahlstrom found. "The Northern Methodist church alone provid[ed] nearly five hundred chaplains, the Southern Methodist and Episcopal churches about two hundred and one hundred respectively. Other churches, North and South, showed proportionate concern." And the feeling ran strikingly deep: when the Roman Catholic archbishop of New Orleans "called for volunteer Chaplains every Redemptorist and Jesuit in [the city] offered his service."

Because wars typically are uncertain, prudent people enter them only with hesitancy but, as with anything else, the way to diminish hesitancy is

to deny the uncertainty and to proclaim the inevitability of desirable results. Outward appearances of southern confidence sprang from any of
several sources. Given the uncertainties of this war and the well-known
deficiencies in rebel resources, some early Confederates held their
tongues and feared for the future, resolutely understanding the high
probability that catastrophe was waiting in the wings. Others, who might
share the same feelings, nevertheless could not afford to remain so reti-
cent. Leaders such as Davis and Vice-President Alexander H. Stephens
had to put on an optimistic front. Although they understood the possibility of failure, they could hardly admit it publicly. But most Confederates seem to have had less perception of the future and less understanding of what they did, and manifestations of their unrealistic bravado were
not at all rare. The famous problem posed by a Confederate arithmetic
text ("If one Confederate soldier can whip 7 Yankees, how many soldiers
can whip 49 Yankees?") provides merely a single example.

This reaction typifies the behavior patterns of people facing imminent
disaster: they blot it from their minds, refusing to believe anything so
awesome could happen. Thus some Confederates managed to convince
themselves—not merely to assert but truly to believe—of the inevitability
of victory. Leroy P. Walker, the first Confederate secretary of war,
bragged with a not unusual confidence born of ignorance that there
would be no war, that he would "wipe up with his pocket handkerchief all
the blood shed as a result of the South's withdrawal from the Union."
Even if war came, he himself would raise the Confederate flag over
"Faneuil Hall in the City of Boston."

Such bravado was widespread. In his memoirs, Jefferson Davis recalled that many Confederates hoped that secession "would so arouse
the sober thought and better feeling of the Northern people as to compel
their representatives to agree to a Convention of the States. . . . There
were others, and they were the most numerous class, who considered
that the separation would be final, but peaceful." Davis noted in his rec-
ollections that most southerners thought even if war came, it would not
last long.

In spite of the support of religion and confidence about the outcome of
the possible conflict, the institution of slavery still concerned some people.
Mary Boykin Chesnut, for example, in her diary for 1861, has some
strong outbursts against slavery. Although she hated the institution, she
admitted that she enjoyed its benefits. "I wonder," she confessed pri-

vately, "if it be a sin to think slavery a curse to any land. Sumner said not one word of this hated institution which is not true. . . . God forgive us, but ours is a *monstrous* system and wrong and iniquity [sic]." "Slavery has to go," she admitted a few months later. "I hate slavery." Clearly Mary Chesnut felt a sense of guilt. And we suspect that she was far from alone, that this perhaps widespread guilt unconsciously compromised the initial determination of many Confederates and from the outset presaged the eventual defeat.

Like the Catholic church, the other Christian churches had told slaveholders that it was not immoral to hold slaves, but it also told them that slavery could lead to sin. Slaveholders had obligations. Even the Bible had told them that; the master had a master, too, as Colossians 4:1 indicated. "Masters," the Scripture warned, "give unto your servants that which is just and equal; knowing that ye also have a Master in heaven." The master had to take proper care of his slaves, which meant respecting their humanity. Failure to meet Christian standards could subject a master to pangs of guilt, all the more because the church told him that in any event he was guilty of sin, a broad term that could cover everything from the condition of his birth to the sharp words he may have exchanged with a slave only a few minutes before. Church-induced guilt could easily be extended, say, to slavery or to a war to preserve slavery, especially after the Confederacy moved in the direction of emancipation.

Although northern and southern Christians espoused similar forms of institutionalized religion that sprang from common origins steeped in Calvinism, differences between the two had evolved. Samuel S. Hill, Jr., has suggested that the work of Lewis Simpson in the literature of the colonial South reveals the early roots of this divergence, showing that "in contrast to the New England settlers' image of their errand into a wilderness, Southerners viewed their new habitat as a paradise."

Hill sees the churches of the two regions as already "first cousins separated" by the time of the immediate postrevolutionary era, and both were evolving toward even greater separation, which became that of "third cousins alienated" by the post-Jacksonian period. "In the course of this evolution," he says, "the South became not only identifiable, distinctive, and self-aware, it was also on its way toward regarding itself as pure (purer than the North at any rate) and superior." Churches in both sections espoused millennialism in some form (looking toward eschatologic last days as imminent and desirable); indeed, as James F.

Maclear so graphically phrased it, throughout the antebellum United States some form or another of millennialism was "so common as to be almost canonical." But, as Hill quotes William G. McLoughlin, "the white southerner felt that his region of the nation was already closer to millennial perfection than any other part of the country." The North was characterized by debate, turmoil, and schism, whereas in the South increasing religious homogeneity prevailed, which helped affirm the prevalent lifestyle.

Increasingly over time, that lifestyle depended upon the continued existence of slavery, or so antebellum southerners typically thought. Slavery and Christianity were never in full harmony with each other, but religion in the South did much more to firm up the institution than to tear it down. During the seventeenth and eighteenth centuries southerners had considerable misgivings about Christianizing the slaves because traditionally in Western civilization only heathens were enslaved. But once they took that step, a particular form of Christianity for the slaves developed, which inevitably infected the Christianity of the southern whites as well.

Whites in the South gave the slaves a form of Christianity that stressed humility, obedience to one's master, and contented acceptance of one's condition in life and put great emphasis upon reward in the hereafter. In addition, perhaps paradoxically, southern Christianity abounded with Old Testament theology (wherein God is all-powerful, totally just, and vengeful; He makes covenants with His people and rewards them richly but is not—as He would be manifested in the New Testament—particularly merciful). Antebellum northern Protestants had veered away from this interpretation, although the war jolted them back a bit. Thus in a Boston church on a fast-day morning, April 3, 1862, the minister's sermon proclaimed that "the Old Testament, in our current notions and sympathies has been almost outlawed from human affairs. . . . And now the days have come upon us, for which these strong-chorded elder Scriptures have been waiting."

Unlike today, in the mid-nineteenth century Christians adhered to a widespread orthodox belief that had as a basic tenet the notion that God enters and intervenes in human history. It also seemed axiomatic to most Americans that the hand of God shaped all events because they implicitly believed that heavenly intervention in the Christian era occurred not only in the manifested divine person of Jesus Christ two millennia before but also in day-to-day events of their own time.

God rewarded, and He punished, and it behooved people to accept His will. But what was His will? Protestants in both North and South, especially after the war began, became convinced that His will was that their side be victorious. According to James H. Moorhead, the northern Protestant's "conception of history converted the Civil War into a crusade [wherein] the contest had to be pressed with unceasing vigor"; conversely, W. Harrison Daniel, author of articles on southern Protestantism during the Civil War, has found that "in numerous sermons the will of God was made synonymous with the cause of the Confederacy." As one Confederate private fervently prayed, "Oh, Lord, we are having a mighty big fight down here, and a sight of trouble; and we do hope, Lord, that you will take a proper view of this subject, and give us the victory."

During the middle third of the nineteenth century, southern religious feeling was strikingly homogeneous. First, the Confederates in near unanimity were Protestant Christians, mostly Baptist, Methodist, Presbyterian, or Episcopalian, and the differences among these denominations were considerably blurred. Episcopalians, for example, tended overwhelmingly to be of the "low-church" variety and differed little from Methodists, who had only recently broken away from that denomination. Emory Thomas has found that this similarity was reflected in "camp meetings and interdenominational revival services, plus the ease and frequency with which Southerners attended services of various denominations."

Furthermore, most southerners held to pervasive puritanical views. Although they might frequently rail mightily against the Puritanism "of their New England brethren," Thomas observed, still "they themselves had incorporated much of the Puritan heritage into Southern-style evangelical Protestantism." Likewise, "the hellfire-and-damnation emphasis of Southern Protestantism served as a kind of inverse support for the hedonistic aspects of the Southern life style" because "paradoxically . . . [their] deep consciousness of sin in this world and perfection in the next served as a bulwark of the Old South status quo." Thus this brand of Puritanism primarily homogenized and stabilized rather than induced change, and it injected an element of gloominess that mixed uneasily and unpleasantly with the more stereotypical "Southern gaiety."

Theologically, although both northern and southern Protestants agreed that "God's greatest concern was to rescue alienated humanity from the consequences of the fallen state in both this life and the one beyond death," the northerner tended to view this process as operative within a large context, that salvation "would be of all as well as of each." For the northerner, society needed to be perfected; for the southerner, society, if already as perfect as man could make it, needed to remain stable while each individual worked out his own salvation. James H. Moorhead has argued brilliantly that northern mainline Protestants— Baptists, Congregationalists, Methodists, and Presbyterians (Old and New Schools)—believed devoutly that they indeed were seeing "the glory of the coming of the Lord," and further that the Union armies were hastening that coming, because the people of these churches perceived the Civil War as Armageddon.

Reformation-era Protestantism generally had revived millenarianism, and the movement had spurred an eschatological revolution. But "in England this reawakened millennial consciousness acquired [a] peculiar intensity." The Puritans intertwined millenarianism with their beliefs concerning God's plan for America, believing themselves His new Chosen People and their new land His instrument for the ultimate conversion of the world. To be sure, similar thought was present among southern immigrants as well, but "it was from New England that [came] the most articulate statements of America's millennial role." By the time of the Civil War most southern Protestant ministers only weakly adhered to millennialism, and many did not do so at all. The southern brand of this thought tended more toward what theologians call premillennialism (that is, that the return of Christ would occur before the millennium began and hence no particular human action was required to hasten the coming of the Kingdom). The majority of nineteenth-century northern Protestants, however, were postmillennialists, who believed that Christ would return at the end of the millennium and that God's people could do a great deal to hasten the course of history toward its inevitable destiny. Thus northern Protestants, albeit with cacophonic voice, variously articulated that "all was not well within God's new Israel" and that they needed to reform it properly before the Lord's return. Although northern Protestants might differ among themselves, and "the candidate for chief demon varied according to one's preference—Roman Catholicism, the slave power, abolitionism, Mormonism, or freemasonry"—they all displayed an amazingly united evangelical front, which consistently thrusted toward reform to make the country ready for God's final intervention. But the South's religious mind-set, unlike that of the North, induced an ironic, uneasy satisfaction with the present condition.

Thus it should come as no surprise that religious differences also played a crucial role in the course of the Civil War. W. Harrison Daniel's studies reveal that there existed "a close affinity, in the thinking of most Southerners, between patriotism and religious faith and duty." And, indeed, Sydney Ahlstrom believes that "for violence of statement and ultimacy of appeal, the clergy and the religious press seem to have led the multitude."

Even more important, observes Ahlstrom, in this "age of great evangelical fervor, the clergy were the official custodians of the popular conscience. When the cannons roared in Charleston harbor, therefore, two divinely authorized crusades were set in motion. . . . The pulpits resounded with a vehemence and absence of restraint never equalled in American history." It was crucial and relevant to both North and South that God be and remain on their side.

Jefferson Davis's early proclamations of days of humiliation and prayer contained pro forma assumptions that God wore the gray. In May 1862 Davis converted to Anglicanism and was confirmed in Richmond's St. Paul's Episcopal Church, the "National Cathedral of the Confederacy" if ever there was one. In addition to Davis, many other institutions and individuals prescribed days of fasting, prayer, and humiliation from time to time. "The Confederate congress, state governors, ecclesiastical meetings, bishops, and sometimes army generals" either urged or ordered them, and typically, Daniel has found, "for these occasions ministers prepared 'war sermons' which could be used repeatedly, with slight revisions as conditions changed." Mary Chesnut noted in her diary that one such sermon "stirred my blood, my flesh crept and tingled. A red hot glow of patriotism passed over me. There was . . . exhortation to fight and die."

Even with the knowledge that "God moves in a mysterious way, His wonders to perform," it still seemed likely that He favored the side of the righteous. Southerners long had examined themselves and their conduct in the light of Scripture, and most of them had concluded that they were the righteous and that slavery was correct, just as many of their northern counterparts had been persuaded by Scripture and by the preaching of northern abolitionist churchmen and their allies that the peculiar institution was sinful. If the institution was moral, so, too, was its protection, and, if forced upon the South, the resulting war as well.

More recent history also served as a useful guide to God's preference. He did, of course, stand on the side of freedom, as white men interpreted freedom, and thus had given victory to the patriots in 1776. Surely He would not change in 1861; once again He would side with those who fought against despotism and for freedom, an idea that inspired confidence as long as southerners were persuaded, or could persuade themselves, that they and not the northerners represented that side. Southerners constantly saw the war as one for freedom, and they equated defeat with enslavement. "No alternative is left you," Davis warned his army, "but victory or subjugation, slavery, and the utter ruin of yourselves, your families, and your country."

Although a few might doubt, from the beginning it had seemed incomprehensible to southerners that God would not side with the Confederate battalions. On the eve of secession the *Southern Presbyterian,* declaring for Christ, called upon southerners to decide current questions "by principles which depend so directly upon the Word of God." Translated into action, this meant that if the North did not give guarantees, but used force to oppose secession, the South should "throw the sword into the scales, and leave the issue to the God of battles." An Alabama minister concurred: "If we are right, and God is on our side, let us go forth fearlessly to meet the present crisis and conflict." There was no "if" about it, however, for "the Lord is with us," and he congratulated himself that his Christian and sectional duties so completely coincided. "We are . . . fighting not for ourselves alone, but, when the struggle is rightly understood, for the salvation of this whole continent," claimed J. D. B. DeBow. But if Confederates were not right and did not have God on their side, how could they go forth fearlessly? How, indeed, could they go forth at all?

The South's religious views served as a trap for Confederate will. If, as Confederates said, God controlled events (and that would be difficult for most Christian southerners to deny) and victory was a sign of God's favor, then repeated battlefield successes would build morale and will by shoring up any wavering faith in the cause. By the same token, however, if the South began to lose battles, it could only mean that God did not side with the Confederacy, and if God sided with right, it would mean that the South did not have right on its side and God favored the adversary. God, then, had not chosen the Confederates, and it would be wrong for the South to continue to fight. This knowledge would inflict a devastating blow to morale. No one wanted to fight God; the fear that perhaps Confederates were doing so would surely knock out all the remaining props that held up Confederate will. When victories decreased and casualty lists lengthened, doubts about God's favor (never very far beneath the surface) began to arise and southern will weakened accordingly.

Such a confrontation between faith and reality might be avoided if the military power of the Confederacy were supported and supplemented with all the civilian willpower available. Thus southern congregations threw themselves into the war effort with a fervor that seemed to know no bounds in an effort not only to win the war but also to prove to themselves that God really *was* on their side. W. Harrison Daniel found, for example, that frequently Confederates would "manifest their patriotism by removing the carpet from the floor of the church and cutting it into blankets for the soldiers, by donating the church bell to be manufactured into armaments, and by contributing pew cushions for hospital beds." The various denominations pulled together with astounding unity, and for the war's duration "arguments of theology and polity were abandoned." Instead of damning each other, they might damn their northern enemies; and, although it occurred infrequently, some "denominational newspapers referred to Northerners as barbarians—modern-day Vandals, Huns, and Goths—who were seeking to gratify their 'hellish lusts.'"

We have already noted the large number of ordained clergy who accepted combat duties; perhaps even more interesting, a number of chaplains threw themselves into the conflict, either occasionally to fight in a battle or otherwise to do something other than religious service. The subject has not yet received much study, but we know about enough of these men to conclude that their number and involvement could not have been inconsequential. Nicholas Davis, chaplain of Hood's Texas Brigade, had a reputation for his "military eye or prowess." Chaplains Andrew J. Potter and Randolph H. McKim displayed "a lust for battle," and Roman Catholic Chaplain James B. Sheeran deserves particular attention because he became, as Bruce Catton assessed, "one of the most dedicated of Southern patriots," who "detested the Yankee invader as hotly as any Confederate could."

Nor did northerners fail to manifest their share of indications that the war had religious undertones. The Yankees employed a female spy to monitor the movements of Reverend Hoge, the pastor who ran Bibles and tracts through the blockade, acted upon her information to capture some of his religious materials, and fired upon him, knowing full well the nature of his mission. And in 1861, when Jim Lane led a raid through pro-Confederate towns in western Missouri, "his chaplains even plundered furnishings for the churches in Lawrence."

New England troops seem to have been especially vengeful toward Roman Catholics in the South. In Jacksonville, elsewhere in Florida, and in Georgia, they ravaged and set fire to Catholic churches. And "in Savannah, in spite of the bishop's protest, a general occupied a cemetery and did considerable damage when he converted it into a fortification."

"As its greatest social institution," James W. Silver correctly concluded at the end of his important little book *Confederate Morale and Church Propaganda*, "the church in the South constituted the major resource of the Confederacy in the building and maintenance of civilian morale. As no other group, Southern clergymen" contributed to and nurtured "a state of mind which made secession possible, and as no other group they sustained the people in their long, costly and futile war for Southern independence."

But the same held true within the victorious North, for as Ahlstrom concluded, "a fervently pious nation was at war [and] men on both sides hungered for inspiration and peace with God. Dedicated men and women on both sides responded . . . with wide-ranging ministries. On both sides the soldier's sense of duty was deepened, his morale improved, his loyalty intensified."

Thus piety provided an essential source of southern strength in victory and defeat, serving the will of the people in much the same way that factories and mines served the armed forces. Supported by their knowledge of the virtue of their cause, southern churches could strengthen the South's morale and energize its will. Religion played a greater role in the Confederate experience than in that of the Union because the South needed it more, for as military power ebbed away, the will of the people needed more and more reinforcement if the Confederacy was to survive. In a time of defeat, piety could do what military victories did in better times. "Perhaps," Ahlstrom concluded, "piety lengthened the war."

We would not have qualified Ahlstrom's observation that piety lengthened the war, as did he, with "perhaps." Not only did piety lengthen the war, but the piety espoused by nineteenth-century Americans also had much to do with how the war was fought and why the war ended as it did. The difference between mainline Protestantism in the North and in the South contributed to tipping the scales. The churches at first induced many persons on either side to dedicate themselves both vociferously and sacrificially to the struggle, but later in the war the situation changed significantly. Because of how they interpreted the war's course and how they related their perception of God's will to the onflow of events, northerners' religious mind-set spurred their allegiance to the war and its aims, even through the darkest periods of weariness with the struggle; southerners, conversely, became gradually convinced that God willed they should not win. As Charles Reagan Wilson has elaborated in his *Baptized in Blood: The Religion of the Lost Cause,* southern clergymen to the end remained the Confederacy's most important morale-builders, but even before the end some of them began seeking and formulating theological explanations for the South's defeat. The campaigns of the Civil War did not alone produce its outcome.

Chapter Five

Trial by Battle

WITHIN AN AIR OF UNREALITY created by an amalgam of confidence, prayer, and some anxiety, both sides rapidly improvised armies after the fall of Fort Sumter in April 1861. The secession crisis and overconfidence of each assured that neither would think any more clearly about military problems than about political problems. Expecting that enthusiasm would provide the key to quick victory, both sides downplayed the need for military training. Symbols had importance, and national capitals are symbols of enemy power; thus it appeared logical to each adversary that the desired quick decision might be achieved by a prompt capture of the other's capital. Each placed its troops accordingly, concentrating to protect its own symbol while threatening that of the other.

Since the Confederates also sought to protect as much of Virginia as possible, they placed their army very close to Washington, menacingly and insultingly near, thought the Unionists. This situation led to a clamor from northern civilians and political leaders for an immediate offensive. So in July 1861, General Scott allayed his misgivings and agreed to an advance by his green forces against what he knew to be equally untrained Confederates. Thus originated the campaign of First Manassas, the first major action of the war. This campaign contained many elements that proved representative of the Civil War. Both sides deployed on two opposing lines of operations. Outside of Washington, the Union army of Brigadier General Irwin McDowell and the opposing Confederate army, under Brigadier General P. G. T. Beauregard, used the same railroad. To the west, in the Shenandoah Valley, the Union army of Major General Robert Patterson drew its supplies from a spur of the Baltimore and Ohio

Railroad while the opposing Confederate force, under General Joseph E. Johnston, held a position only twenty miles from the railroad in his rear.

Each of the opposing armies had a "line of operations," that is, an axis of advance and retreat usually identical with the army's line of communication. This situation was governed, according to Clausewitz, by "Jomini's 'interior lines,' " "one of the main principles for the conduct of major wars." The employment of interior lines enabled a smaller force to "multiply its strength by rapid movement." Interior lines of operations permitted a general to "concentrate the masses and maneuver with his whole force in a shorter period of time than it would require for the enemy to oppose to them a greater force." The Confederates possessed interior lines of operations because the railroad network provided better communication between the armies of Beauregard and Johnston than it did between the Union armies of Patterson and McDowell. The terminology "interior and exterior" derives from the simplest form of this situation, illustrated in the following diagram:

	Beauregard	
Patterson	and Johnston	McDowell
USA ----> <----	CSA ----> <----	USA
exterior line	interior lines	exterior line

The force in the middle, on the interior lines of operations, had the advantage because it could concentrate against first one and then the other of the opposing armies on the exterior lines.

Like the Confederate leaders, Union General Scott understood interior lines. He also realized that coordinated advances by the exterior armies would nullify the advantage of interior lines. When, in mid-July, he ordered McDowell to move toward Beauregard, he assured McDowell that, should Johnston seek to join Beauregard, there would be a simultaneous advance by the army in the Shenandoah Valley. With Patterson on Johnston's heels, the Confederate general could not aid Beauregard. But as it turned out, Scott did not get the performance he desired of Patterson, an elderly Pennsylvania manufacturer and a militiaman with experience in the Mexican War and War of 1812.

In advancing against Beauregard, McDowell based his plan on an envelopment, or tactical turning movement, such as Scott himself had employed in the Mexican War, a maneuver fully in harmony with the practice of Napoleon. Clausewitz strongly endorsed such attacks, insisting that "envelopment is the most natural form of attack, and should not be disregarded without good cause." McDowell and Beauregard were classmates at West Point, and afterward both had served with credit during the Mexican War and had reached the rank of major by the time the Civil War broke out. Both showed their West Point background in directing their troops to entrench, even though each planned to take the offensive.

McDowell's untrained army and untried organization did enjoy one advantage: its numerical superiority of about thirty thousand to twenty thousand. But McDowell lost this superiority when the Confederates not only made but succeeded in executing the proper decision. Aware on July 16 of McDowell's advance, Beauregard called for reinforcements. President Davis ordered Johnston from the Shenandoah Valley to Beauregard's assistance. Because the telegraph provided prompt communication, Johnston, sending cavalry under J. E. B. Stuart to distract and mislead the already confused and withdrawing Patterson, could march to the railroad, entrain, and join Beauregard with most of his army by July 20, the day before McDowell's attack.

On July 21, McDowell's flanking column of twelve thousand men began its advance. After stumbling around in the underbrush for several hours, they crossed Bull Run Creek and assaulted the Confederate positions astride Henry House Hill. At first the Union attack was successful, and the Confederates retired in some confusion. But reinforcements, including a brigade under Thomas J. Jackson, arrived quickly, and Beauregard and Johnston began to concentrate their forces to halt the Union flanking attack. The fighting below the hill surged back and forth for hours. A newspaper correspondent observing the struggle wrote that the battleground was "a boiling crater of dust and smoke." Late in the afternoon the weary Union troops began to falter. Beauregard ordered a counterattack, the Union ranks broke, and before nightfall thousands of McDowell's troops were in retreat back toward the Potomac.

The campaign and battle of First Manassas were representative of many later operations. The Confederates, with direct connections to Richmond, had employed the telegraph and the railroad to exploit their interior lines and thereby effect a rapid concentration. In the battle itself both sides used entrenchments and had planned tactical turning movements. In spite of achieving surprise and seizing the initiative, McDowell's tactical turning movement failed because of the defensive power of the well-articulated nineteenth-century armies.

Although many of the troops carried smoothbores, the fighting at Manassas took place at a distance and, because horses constituted such conspicuous targets, no cavalry successfully charged the infantry. For these reasons the combatants had no need, as in earlier times, to deploy in order to have a continuous front, heretofore an essential to keep cavalry, or even enemy infantry, from getting through gaps in the line and into the defending infantry's vulnerable rear. Firepower now successfully covered gaps in the line.

Yet this new power of more rapid movement and deployment, which permitted McDowell to catch his opponent and to force an engagement at the enemy's disadvantage, also enabled the Confederates to counter it because their army was equally well articulated. They could not have avoided the battle without a precipitate and, for such raw soldiers, disorganizing retreat. But the Confederates could parry the turning movement and avert disaster because they too could move men rapidly by road, concentrate at the threatened point, and deploy quickly, forming rough defensive lines rendered strong by their firepower.

This battle is typical of the Civil War battles in that similar armies with almost identical capabilities could practically never obtain a decisive advantage. Thus battles were usually as frontal as First Manassas and armies almost always proved resilient and essentially indestructible. The battle resulted in a retreat of Union forces, the opposing armies now assuming essentially the same positions as before the battle. Clausewitz had foreseen the likelihood of such an outcome; in spite of McDowell's attack by a turning movement, First Manassas had essentially been what he termed "a battle fought with parallel fronts." Having noted that a battle with reversed fronts, when each army blocked the communications of the other, would prove decisive, Clausewitz believed that one with parallel fronts could not have an important result. In addition to these, he listed other conditions, each of which he believed would help preclude a decisive victory as well as prevent an effective pursuit. The Battle of First Manassas had all of these conditions. Without significant numerical superiority the victory would be less conclusive, and the pursuit would face serious handicaps unless it possessed a major advantage in cavalry. If, as was the case here, the winning army had vanquished only a part of the losing force, the defeated forces would still have available a large number of relatively fresh and unshaken troops to cover a retreat. Without any of these requisites the Confederates could not expect to accomplish more

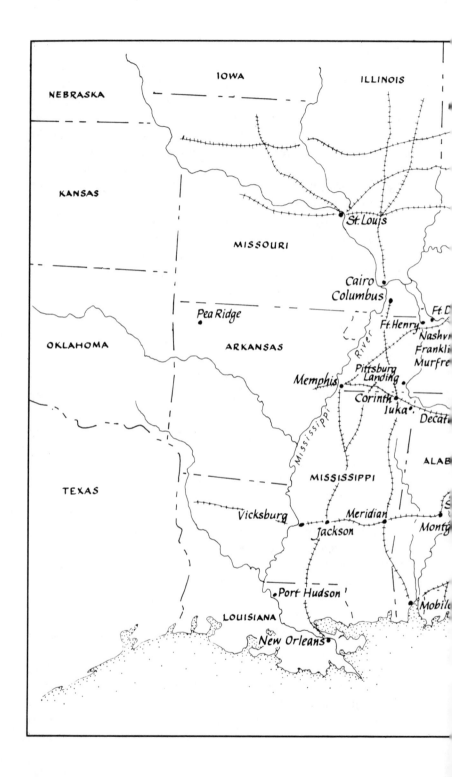

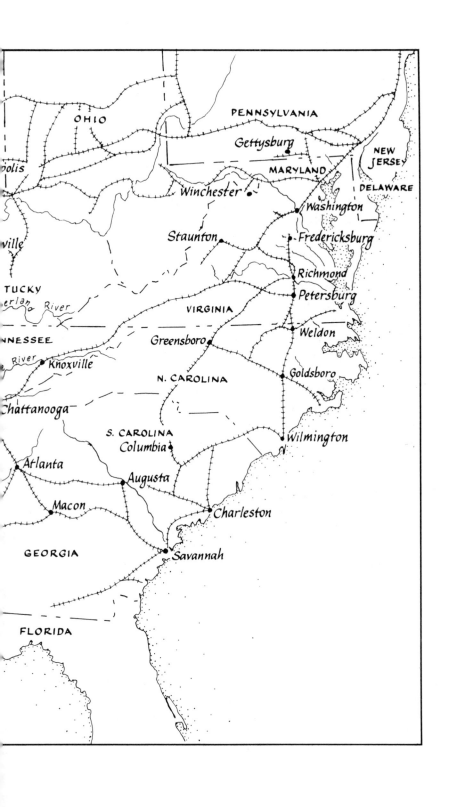

than they achieved. Moreover, since Clausewitz wrote, the rifle had deprived cavalry of most of its mounted tactical value against infantry, thus markedly diminishing its value in pursuit.

"Victory," however, "consists not only in the occupation of the battlefield, but in the destruction of the enemy's physical and psychic forces, which is usually not attained until the enemy is pursued after a victorious battle." Nevertheless, Clausewitz acknowledged the difficulty of pursuit and did not believe it could be effective unless it could begin on the day of battle. He would not have been surprised at the absence of pursuit after First Manassas, realizing as he did that "the winning side is in almost as much disorder and confusion as the losers," a condition that Jefferson Davis, for example, believed existed.

Almost all Civil War battles were characterized by the victor's failure to pursue. Even after the armies later became impressive organizations of well-led veterans, they still fought battles with essentially parallel fronts, and the victors usually lacked adequate cavalry or significant numerical superiority to pursue. Rarely did more than a fraction of the losing army suffer the heavy losses and the demoralization and disorganization of tactical defeat. Clausewitz noted difficult terrain as one more factor that would help prevent a decisive victory and hamper an effective pursuit. Since in the American Civil War the terrain was often rough or wooded, practically no battle ever met any of the conditions Clausewitz deemed essential for a formidable pursuit.

The enemy's physical forces could receive severe blows without pursuit, however, for Clausewitz did perceive one significant achievement that could be gained in a battle without pursuit—attrition, or "a reduction of strength relatively larger than our own." By this reckoning the Confederates gained a very modest victory: the Union forces in this defeat lost 2,708 men, less than 10 percent of McDowell's 28,000 men; but the Confederates, on the defensive, suffered even fewer casualties, barely 6 percent of their 32,000 soldiers. The First Battle of Manassas proved representative, and throughout the war the tactical advantage of the defensive almost invariably resulted in heavier casualties for the attacker than the attacked.

The stalemate in Virginia—established, or at least confirmed, at First Manassas—continued into the spring of 1862, while both sides prepared their armies for the renewal of active operations in that theater. But the Confederate public saw in the victory at the Battle of Manassas and the halting of the Union advance confirmation of their confidence in victory if not of their belief that the war would be short. But as the armies in Virginia faced each other, Confederate morale suffered a grievous blow when the Union attained dramatic successes in the West.

General Scott's plan had envisioned turning the Confederate positions blocking the Mississippi. The most important of these was a well-fortified and strongly garrisoned position at Columbus, where the fort's guns kept ships from going down the river. To carry out a strategic turning movement against that stronghold, Union armies would have to advance along one of the good routes east of the river. For this operation they had the advantage of use of the Tennessee and Cumberland rivers.

Although historians have emphasized the role of railroads in bringing about the Union victory, in the West the rivers, not the rails, provided the key. "We are much obliged to the Tennessee which has favored us most opportunely," wrote Major General William T. Sherman to Rear Admiral David D. Porter. "For I am never easy with a railroad which takes a whole army to guard . . . whereas they can't stop the Tennessee, and each boat can make its own game." There was no practical limit to the capacity of navigable rivers to supply the federal armies so long as the Union had sufficient vessels. One army supply officer calculated that an ordinary western river steamboat with a capacity of five hundred tons could in one trip carry enough supplies to subsist an army of forty thousand men and eighteen thousand horses for nearly two days.

By 1860 nearly one thousand steamboats operated on the western rivers, and several hundred more were constructed during the war. Although an undetermined number fell under Confederate control, the overwhelming majority remained in Union hands. The achievements of Sherman, Grant, and other northern commanders in the West rested upon adequate supplies, and these depended, in turn, upon command of the rivers. The Union could not have established and maintained this control without an inland navy, which it promptly created by building warships and arming existing ships. The Union navy consistently enjoyed supremacy on the rivers just as it did on the oceans. But the ships could not overpower the guns in the Confederate forts along the rivers' banks.

As long as Union armies could depend on secure, efficient water transport, they had success, dramatic in the beginning, steady and dependable later, but when they were beyond the reach of the navy and water transport, the armies encountered severe difficulties. Although naval operations in the West were as difficult as those along the Atlantic seaboard, they were far more important. Whereas the blockade had little effect on the war's outcome, naval control of the western rivers enabled Union armies to gain and maintain control of the heartland of the Confederacy. The Comte de Paris, a French observer with the Union armies, correctly noted after the war, "We shall always find . . . that whenever the Federals were supported by a river, their progress was certain and their conquest decisive." Given this causal relationship, it is clear that the Union navy delivered some important blows to Confederate power and will and provided an ingredient essential to Union success in the western theater of war.

In H. W. Halleck, the Union commander on the Cumberland River and to the west, the navy possessed a good collaborator and a man who grasped the potential of the command of the rivers. Leaving the army as a captain in 1854, he had amassed a fortune in business and law before returning in 1861 as a major general. While Halleck assimilated his command, Confederate General Albert Sidney Johnston, a much esteemed and experienced regular officer, deployed twelve thousand Confederate troops to defend the well-fortified river and rail center of Columbus, where they blocked the Mississippi. He posted his other major force, more than twenty thousand men, at Bowling Green, Kentucky, to oppose any advance by Union General Don Carlos Buell over the railroad from Louisville to Nashville. At Fort Henry, artillery aimed toward the river blocked the Union navy's progress on the Tennessee River, and guns at nearby Fort Donelson controlled the Cumberland River route. But the forts lay vulnerable to attack by land forces, for the combined infantry forces at both of them numbered only five thousand.

Meanwhile, the elderly General Scott had resigned as general in chief, and his ideas no longer dominated western strategy. Instead, the two separate Union western commanders, Halleck and Buell in Kentucky, each received pressure from Washington to advance. But control of the Mississippi no longer remained the only focal point of Union strategic thinking. President Lincoln wished Buell to advance against the feeble Confederate forces in pro-Union East Tennessee.

Major General Halleck had his own plans. In January 1862 he entrusted this river-borne offensive to Brigadier General U. S. Grant, commanding at Paducah, where the Cumberland and Tennessee empty into the Ohio. Grant was an unobtrusive, mild-mannered, colorless officer, yet he was a relentless warrior and far from an ordinary general.

Following Halleck's instructions, Grant with fifteen thousand men and Captain Andrew H. Foote with seven gunboats moved south on the Tennessee, unleashing a combined naval and land attack against Fort Henry. With his own communications secure on the river, Grant followed Halleck's guidance and wisely sent one-half of his army to reach the rear of the fort, interrupt its communications, and trap the twenty-five-hundred-man garrison against the Tennessee River, which he controlled with his gunboats. Understanding the peril presented by this threat to his communications and realizing that his force was too small to attempt to stop Grant or to drive him back, the Confederate commander withdrew his garrison before Grant's overwhelming numbers could trap it. Fort Henry fell to Union forces on February 6, 1862. Again following Halleck's instructions, Grant promptly exploited his success by sending the gunboats upstream to break the Memphis and Ohio Railroad bridge over the river, thus protecting himself by cutting a major route of Confederate troop movements and supply.

Halleck had thus forced open a line of communications that enabled him to turn Columbus. He could not yet use it, however, because the Confederate force at Fort Donelson, whither the Fort Henry garrison had retreated, threatened the communications of an advance south. So immediately after capturing Fort Henry, Grant began marching toward the Cumberland, aiming at Fort Donelson, eleven miles away. While Grant battled roads deep in mud, Halleck frantically rushed him reinforcements of ten thousand men and pleaded for more from Buell, the quiescent commander to his east. Grant's slow and muddy march at last brought him to the river on February 12, near the fort, where the navy met him with reinforcements, gunboats, and supply steamers.

The Confederates responded to Grant's success by strengthening Fort Donelson with some troops moved from Bowling Green. But because the possibility of Grant's further success made the rebel hold upon Bowling Green so tenuous, the southerners also withdrew the remainder of their forces from that position, falling back over the railroad toward Nashville. Advancing on the rear of Fort Donelson, which had its main armament directed toward the river, Grant easily cut off the retreat of its garrison. After an attempt to break through Grant's army, the trapped

Confederates surrendered, giving the Union more than sixteen thousand prisoners.

The Fort Donelson victory portended far-reaching consequences. The Confederates, as Halleck reported, now found themselves "completely turned on both sides of the Mississippi" and thus evacuated Columbus, "the boasted 'Gibraltar of the West.'" Not only were Halleck and Grant giving substance to Scott's strategy, but also Union control of the Cumberland and Tennessee rivers threatened Nashville's communications and forced the Confederates to evacuate the Tennessee capital. So in his operations, Halleck, a thorough student of Jomini and Napoleon, had adhered to the United States Army's 1982 manual, *Operations*, when he attained surprise as he unconsciously followed the injunction "to avoid the enemy's strength and strike at his weaknesses."

These events on the battlefield had immediate consequences on the home front. The Confederacy was one year old, and two forts and an army had surrendered under circumstances that seemed less than honorable, for two political generals had abandoned their commands at Fort Donelson and escaped south, leaving the unfortunate but responsible Simon Buckner to surrender to his old friend, Ulysses Grant. As might be expected, there were numerous recriminations, some expressions of doubt, and occasional confessions of inadequacy. Any northern overconfidence as a result of these actions would soon be dispelled; for the time being, however, there were those in the South who feared that the fate of the two forts presaged that of the Confederacy, especially when considered in the light of recent Union success in taking Roanoke Island on the North Carolina coast.

Still, for most people optimism remained—Union victories had only destroyed overconfidence. Jefferson Davis's proclamation of February 20, 1862, reminded his fellow Confederates that they were "not permitted to furnish an exception to the rule of Divine government, which has prescribed affliction as the discipline of nations as well as of individuals." Faith had to be tested, and "the chastening which seemeth grievous will, if rightly received, bring forth its appropriate fruit." God still wore gray, but He might not always march in the Confederate battalions until they had been punished adequately for their iniquities, and each Confederate could decide for himself what those might be. Governor Joseph E. Brown of Georgia feared that the South's "constant successes" had "filled our hearts with vanity, and caused us to appropriate to ourselves a large portion of the glory that belonged to God alone. . . . The consequence has been that God has, for a time, withdrawn, kept his smiling face from us, and committed our enemies to triumph over us." The Virginia legislature accepted the setbacks calmly and urged Virginians to summon "new energies . . . until, with the blessing of God, we shall conquer an honorable peace, and finally establish our independence."

Thomas Bragg, Jefferson Davis's attorney general, however, never showed much optimism or enthusiasm for the Confederate cause. Like many former Whigs, especially fellow Tar Heels, when the military situation went poorly Bragg always tended to regret having rejected the alternative decision, and in early 1862 recent news from the army indicated that events were going unsatisfactorily indeed. Bragg was not one to throw in the towel; if he now harbored little enthusiasm, he did continue in desperation, the desperation of a cornered animal. He had foreseen the Confederate difficulties in the West and understood their significance; from his insider's position in the cabinet he saw the effect that severance of the line in Kentucky and the losses of Fort Henry and Fort Donelson had upon those who were more knowledgeable about military events than he. He complained in his diary that the Confederate army would be forced out of both Columbus and Bowling Green, and he perceived the Union advantage that derived from control of the Cumberland River. He observed both Secretary of War Judah P. Benjamin and President Davis, assessing them as gloomy and despondent. "It is idle," confessed Bragg, "to disguise the fact that we have latterly been luke warm and not fully alive to our danger." A few days later Bragg lamented that the southern people "cannot be induced to risk all & perhaps lose all, save their honor. The change is going on every day and our people have lost their enthusiasm."

Bragg was prematurely disheartened. Soon after he spoke, Confederate soldiers were concentrating to meet the Union army in Tennessee and to deal it a powerful blow. The resulting conflict, Shiloh or Pittsburg Landing, although bloody, was not decisive. It did, however, unfold under such circumstances that both sides could interpret it as either a victory or a defeat, depending upon their psychological needs at the moment.

In retrospect, clearly the campaigns of the spring and summer of 1862 contributed to the stalemate, for they proved how difficult it was to destroy Civil War—era armies. The question at the time, had anyone known it, was whether stalemate would contribute most to Union victory by prolonging the war to the point that the Confederacy would lose simply because it had run out of resources and will, or whether stalemate would contribute to Confederate victory by proving to the world that the armies could suffer checks and wounds but would always survive to fight again. Decisive victories in this war would be few and far between. No matter how heavy the casualties one army could inflict, the other would always have the strength to survive. Further, the South's great size added to the potency of its defense, and because a stalemate had resulted and promised to continue, the ultimate reliance of both sides would have to be on the will of their people to continue the fight.

Halleck's successful campaign had overwhelmed the Confederate center and deeply penetrated into Confederate territory. Union troops advanced 150 miles in a month, something Clausewitz hardly would have believed possible. Neither Clausewitz nor Jomini envisioned the astounding success made possible by perceptive and energetic use of rivers. Halleck used modern gunboats and steamers to bring about a rapid and decisive Union advance. Concerned about Grant's exposed position so far south and having attained command of all Union troops in the West, Halleck ordered General Buell to march quickly from Nashville to reinforce Grant on the Tennessee.

While Buell's men moved sluggishly on foot, the enemy also relied on products of the industrial revolution by employing the telegraph and the railroad to facilitate counterattack. The Confederates, led by Johnston's second in command, the capable Manassas veteran Beauregard, began concentrating all of the forces of the western department to strike Grant before Buell could join him. Beauregard ordered Major General Earl Van Dorn from Arkansas and Major General Leonidas Polk from Columbus. Johnston himself moved westward, first by road and then by rail, to Corinth, Mississippi, where Beauregard directed the concentration of all the western forces. Seeing the same strategic opportunity, President Davis ordered five thousand men from New Orleans by river and rail and ten thousand from Mobile by rail. He even sought reinforcements from South Carolina. Thus the Confederates implemented a concentration that embraced the length and breadth of the Confederacy—from the Atlantic to Arkansas and from Kentucky to the Gulf.

Only Van Dorn in Arkansas lacked rail or water communications, and his failure to arrive until after the Battle of Shiloh resulted from his being far away in northwestern Arkansas, where he was losing the Battle of Pea Ridge. Despite Beauregard's energy and imperative orders from Richmond, the Confederates did not complete their concentration of forces until after Buell had camped near Grant at the beginning of April. Halleck had won the race to concentrate on the Tennessee, but on the eve of battle Buell's army was seven miles downriver from Grant's, and Grant expected no attack.

Early on the morning of April 6, 1862, Confederates surprised Grant's unprepared army, catching the men at breakfast, unentrenched, with their commander away. In a bloody, two-day battle at Shiloh the Union forces defeated and drove back their assailants, losing a fifth of their men engaged, the Confederates a quarter of theirs. Although Grant had his back to the river and thus risked disaster if defeated, neither Clausewitz nor Jomini would have approved of the frontal attack at Shiloh. But Jomini would surely have been very pleased with the southern strategy. Substituting the railroad and the steamer for marching, the Confederates had sought *"to obtain by free and rapid movements the advantage of bringing the mass of the troops against fractions of the enemy."* They had failed, of course, because Buell arrived.

Assuming personal command of Grant's and Buell's armies, Halleck exploited Grant's victory at Shiloh by pressing the Confederates back until, at the end of May, he had taken Corinth and broken the railroad from Memphis to Charleston. He then consolidated his position in northern Mississippi while sending Buell eastward toward Chattanooga to cut the railroad between Richmond and Atlanta.

General Scott's plan seemingly was succeeding in the West, where Halleck's advances were part of a pattern that included the fall of New Orleans to a combined navy-army expedition in April 1862 and the capture of Memphis and all Confederate positions on the Mississippi north of that important city in June. Only a small segment of the Mississippi remained in Confederate hands. But the other part of Scott's plan was not working. He had relied "greatly on the sure operations of a complete blockade of the Atlantic and Gulf ports." The blockade, however, was proving ineffective.

After combining their efforts to capture a small Confederate coastal position in North Carolina and making a valuable naval base of Port Royal in South Carolina, the navy and the army united to attack Roanoke Island in North Carolina, the fall of which had helped to depress Confederate morale in February 1862. In the fleet's commander, the tall, fat, red-bearded Louis M. Goldsborough, the expedition had an able leader. The army force served under the modest and agreeable Ambrose E. Burnside, who would become well known not just for his fine whiskers but for his limited capacity for military command.

The two made an effective team, however, when, on February 7, 1862, ten thousand troops under Burnside's command joined Goldsborough's seventeen shallow-draft gunboats in assaulting Roanoke Island. Under the protective fire of the Union warships, the troops landed in waves similar to the pattern later employed in the Pacific during World War II. In addition to providing the assaulting troops with fire support, Goldsborough's active vessels defeated a small force of Confederate gunboats and bombarded two forts until they were effectively neutralized. Two days after the initial landing the army had secured the island.

The expedition only partially realized its objectives. The Union occupied a large part of eastern North Carolina but did not break the railroad until William T. Sherman's troops did so in the spring of 1865. Its seizure did, however, contribute a base to the blockade effort, particularly in the North Carolina sounds, and was a factor in the Confederate evacuation of Norfolk. Further, the Union menace to the railroad paralleling the coast gave the Confederates constant anxiety.

Even if the blockade had been very effective, it would not have equaled the task of crippling quickly so large and nearly self-sufficient a country as the Confederacy. More important, the Union had adopted measures inadequate to bring the South "to terms" when these terms were extinction. Thus Scott's strategy would not suffice in view of the Union's war aims and the potency of the South's determination. The Union had, therefore, no choice but to aim at a decisive war, whether or not its resources matched the task. Clausewitz's prescription for a decisive war was to aim at the enemy's "center of gravity," or source of strength. In the case of his own campaign against France, he identified two centers of gravity, Paris and the army. He expected to defeat the French army and in the course of the campaign capture Paris, thus overcoming both. The Confederacy presented no such simple problem: Richmond was in no way analogous to Paris, the Confederacy had several major armies, and the South had many centers of gravity. To seize control of the Mississippi, opening it to Union commerce and dividing the Confederacy, certainly would strike a blow at one source of the enemy's strength, and the necessary attack on the major army defending it would provide another blow. Similarly, the Confederate capital and the army defending it offered two more centers of gravity.

The Union, of course, made no conscious decision to aim at these centers. The traditional importance and prestige of the Mississippi guaranteed that it would be an objective, and the proximity to Washington of a Confederate army and the Confederate capital meant that Richmond and the army defending it would, for domestic political reasons alone, also be a Union objective.

To replace McDowell after the defeat at Manassas and to head Union forces in the important Virginia theater, Lincoln appointed George B. McClellan, who had conducted successful operations in mountainous western Virginia. Like the other generals on both sides, McClellan lacked any previous higher command experience, although he had graduated from West Point and, in addition to his service in the Mexican War, had had the opportunity to observe the French and British armies in the Crimean War. Like Halleck, he had left the army in the 1850s and established a successful business career before returning as a major general in 1861.

Meanwhile, Lincoln had learned much about the art of war. That southern railway lines between Virginia and Tennessee were shorter than comparable northern lines of communication impressed Lincoln and his secretary of war. They became obsessed with the Confederates' ability, using these interior lines, to transfer troops much more quickly from one army to another than the Union possibly could. After thinking about this problem for nearly a year, Lincoln developed a concept identical to Clausewitz's "rule" or "elementary law of war," the "unification of forces in time," which would enable the Union to neutralize the interior lines that permitted Confederates to unify their forces. In the winter of 1862 Lincoln adopted the strategy of simultaneous advances. Though often flawed in execution, this Clausewitzian unification of forces in time, rather than space, remained basic Union strategy throughout the rest of the war.

For the Union situation in Virginia, Clausewitz's recommendation would have been that "if, for instance, the main object is the enemy's capital, and the defender has not taken up a position between it and the attacker, the latter would be making a mistake if he advanced straight on the city. He would do better to strike at the communications of the enemy army and its capital and there seek the victory which will bring him to the city." McClellan proposed exactly this strategy, wishing to use water communications for a surprise turning movement by landing at Urbanna on the Rappahannock River.

As Halleck and Grant moved in the West, Lincoln urged the young and magnetic McClellan to advance against Joseph E. Johnston's entrenched army near Washington. McClellan successfully disputed Lincoln's preference, arguing that victory would give little more than the "line of the upper Potomac" and pointing out that, in a push toward Richmond, the enemy would "dispute our advance, over bad roads, from position to position." As slow and cautious as he was thorough, the general finally implemented his plan to turn Johnston's position. As the advocate of the strategic turning movement, Jomini also surely would have approved McClellan's plan, for he stressed the need *"to strike in the most decisive direction,*—that is to say in the direction where the consequences of his defeat may be most disastrous to the enemy."

When McClellan executed his plan by moving by water to southeastern Virginia and advancing toward Richmond on the Peninsula between the James and York rivers, he there met Johnston's army, which had come from northern Virginia to defend the Confederate capital. Pushing Johnston back by the threat to turn him by using river transports to land men behind him, McClellan soon reached Richmond, where major siege operations loomed as the next step. But seemingly he had only transferred the stalemate from the vicinity of Washington to that of Richmond. This change would, of course, give a significant psychological advantage to the Union, but what other success did it promise? The Union would have to besiege; but such a siege could not starve out the city because its extensive rail network could readily supply both the city and its defending army, a network McClellan could not possibly interdict from his Peninsula position. But the Union forces could conduct a traditional siege, digging diagonal trenches to provide protected approaches, and they could demolish the Confederate defenses systematically with vast quantities of artillery. This form of warfare the engineer-trained West Point graduates understood entirely and McClellan knew perhaps best of all, for he had observed the successful Anglo-French siege of the Crimean city of Sebastopol.

The Union could expect to win such a campaign of matériel, just as the French and British had prevailed over the Russians after an eleven-month siege. Moreover, McClellan correctly believed that the Confederates would feel compelled to respond to this menace to their capital by taking the offensive against his army on the Peninsula. McClellan would then have gained one of the principal advantages of the turning movement, forcing the enemy to assume the tactical offensive against his prudently selected and prepared position. And the Confederates reacted as expected by promptly attacking McClellan's army.

In that first attack, at the end of May in the Battle of Seven Pines, the Confederates attempted to annihilate two exposed corps of McClellan's army. The still inexperienced Johnston and his three subordinates bungled a good plan, though McClellan's absence from the battlefield resulted in the Union army's failure to offer coordinated resistance. The outcome of the essentially frontal battle again demonstrated the relative invulnerability of the contending armies. The Confederates, on the offensive, suffered about six thousand casualties, 15 percent of their force, whereas the Union losses amounted to about five thousand, 12 percent of those engaged.

President Davis, detailing his splendid military chief, R. E. Lee, to succeed the wounded Johnston, still faced the task of preventing the Union from besieging the Confederate capital, an operation he expected would inevitably succeed. While McClellan was approaching Richmond, the Confederates were waging a triumphant campaign in the Shenandoah Valley. This fertile farming region, watered by the Shenandoah River, lay between the main Appalachian range on the west and the single ridge of the Blue Ridge Mountains on the east. Here the Confederates had a small force commanded by the brilliant and combative Thomas J. "Stonewall" Jackson. Skillfully exploiting interior lines, Jackson won four battles in a campaign that had ended by the ninth of June.

Lee and Davis considered sending Jackson additional troops to relieve the pressure on Richmond by having Jackson cross the Potomac, thus further distracting Lincoln's attention and diverting federal troops from the Peninsula. But Lee and Davis decided instead to concentrate against McClellan. As in the Shiloh campaign, the Confederates employed the telegraph and the railroad to take advantage of their interior lines for a counterstroke to drive back the enemy. Reinforcements that Davis had ordered to Richmond arrived from the Carolinas and, at the last moment, Jackson moved stealthily by rail from the Valley. This exploitation of interior lines would have warmed Jomini's heart. Clausewitz, too, would have approved, for "where the weaker side is forced to fight against odds, its lack of numbers must be made up by the inner tension and vigor," which, he wrote, when "combined with a wise limitation in objectives, the result is that combination of brilliant strokes that we admire in the campaigns of Frederick the Great."

In prescribing for the defense, the U.S. Army's 1982 field manual on operations paraphrases Napoleon with approval, saying that "the entire art of war consists of a well-planned and exceptionally circumspect defense followed by a rapid, audacious attack." Joe Johnston's retreat to Richmond had provided the circumspect defense; Lee planned to provide the assault. At Shiloh, Sidney Johnston had effected "concentration," achieved "surprise," and displayed "audacity," all qualities demanded of the offensive by the manual. But in striking an enemy army with its back to a river, he had failed to make one of the manual's desired "well-conceived attacks against weakness," engaging rather in one of the "force-on-force battles of attrition" disparaged by the army's doctrine. Instead, the manual points out that "envelopment avoids the enemy's strength" and that "destruction is most practical after the enemy has been turned out of a position."

Lee, too, knew this, and he planned to force McClellan to retreat by a tactical turning movement that, by threatening McClellan's communications with his base on the York River, would force him either to withdraw or to attack the Confederates. The turning force, Jackson's eighteen thousand men from the Valley, would advance in the rear of McClellan's north flank. Independently of whether Richmond was truly menaced, Clausewitz would have endorsed such a counterattack because "within the limits of his strength a defender must always seek to change over to the attack as soon as he had gained the benefit of the defense." Of course, he realized it was *"a risky business to attack an able opponent in a good position,"* and "it would be stupid to attempt it" if "he can get his way without assaulting" entrenchments. Lee adopted the obvious means of avoiding McClellan's entrenchments, the method indicated by Clausewitz: "Maneuver the defender out by threatening his flank."

When the attack began in late June 1862, however, not only did the inexperienced Lee and his primitive staff bungle almost as badly as had Joe Johnston at Seven Pines, but even the seasoned and usually brilliant Jackson performed badly; the competently conceived and promptly executed concentration and turning movement became a fruitless series of battles consisting of strong frontal attacks against a weak flank of Mc-Clellan's army. The Confederates lost more than twenty thousand men, the Union almost sixteen thousand.

McClellan's strategy had worked in the sense that it had compelled the Confederates to attack him in two battles, resulting in heavier casualties. But Lee's persistent attacks had forced McClellan back, away from the gates of Richmond, a sure indication to the northern and southern publics that he had suffered defeat. Although the Confederates had accomplished their objective of preventing a siege of Richmond, the immense losses involved in his victory made Lee wary of battles and reassured him of the wisdom in his original intent to force McClellan back by threatening his communications. Having graduated from West Point before Professor Mahan's time, Lee and Davis did not share McClellan's respect for the power of the tactical defense. But the Seven Days' Battles educated them rapidly and, like Clausewitz's interpretation of Frederick the Great, "realizing that even victories cost too much," they quickly resolved to avoid battles if possible and to fight on the defensive.

The campaign in Virginia and that of Shiloh exhibited their harmony with that part of Jomini assumed by Clausewitz when the Confederates displayed their mastery of the use of interior lines to concentrate against invading forces. Their exploitation of the railway and the electric telegraph to carry out these concentrations across an unprecedented expanse of territory was a major innovation in warfare. Although Europeans had employed railways for troop movements and supply, they had yet to use them to execute such concentrations as had characterized the campaigns of Frederick the Great and Napoleon. With the aid of the railroad and telegraph the Confederates had magnified greatly the scale of these operations, carrying out concentrations over hundreds of thousands of square miles in North America that marching men had earlier conducted in areas of only tens of thousands of square miles in Europe.

Though the Union had made much less use of these new resources for rapid concentration of troops, federal commanders, especially Halleck when he reinforced Grant before Shiloh, clearly grasped what the Confederates could do and sought to guard against it. The Union innovation consisted of the brilliant use of the strategic and logistic potential of the rivers and the Chesapeake Bay, a potential much augmented by the speed and carrying capacity of the steamer and the combat power of the armorclad gunboat. The Union did not neglect railways nor the Confederates rivers, and both relied on steam power on rivers as well as on rails to supply their huge armies.

In battles the Union forces had the advantage because at Seven Pines, the Seven Days' Battles, and the first days at Fort Donelson and Shiloh they were on the tactical defensive. The Confederates had to rely on the tactical offensive if they were to reap the fruits of their use of the railroad for concentration. Only in this way did it seem possible to defend against the Union's logistic strategy of territorial conquest and recover the matériel and manpower resources lost to Union turning movements. Such a strategy had disadvantages, however. To the extent that Confederates went on the offensive, as they did at Shiloh and the Seven Days, they would suffer more casualties by giving up the advantage of the defensive. But the alternative was permanently to suffer losses to the Union's implicit logistic strategy, which had already driven them from Kentucky, conquered half of Tennessee and Virginia, and occupied parts of most other states. Davis realized the damaging logistical effect, noting that the "evacuation of any portion of territory involves not only the loss of supplies, but in every instance has been attended by a greater or less loss of troops," including prospective recruits as well as men who deserted to be with their families in occupied territory.

The turning movement, Halleck's against the positions on the Mississippi and McClellan's use of the Peninsula, had caused major Confederate losses of territory. Though marked by strategic brilliance in their concentrations, Confederate counteroffensives had won back little territory, in part because they had resulted in essentially frontal battles. Now southern leaders would employ turning movements not only to bring them logistical gains but in hopes of significant political results.

Chapter Six

The Politics of Dreams

THE FREQUENT REPETITION OF Clausewitz's dictum that war is an extension of politics has turned the dictum into a cliché. The repetition of the phrase, however, does not diminish the appropriateness of its application to the campaigns of the fall of 1862, when Confederates attempted to exert military pressure for a political purpose, using military success to undermine Union morale in the hope that another state or two might join the South or go its own way. All wars have at least some political aspects, especially those which Jomini termed "national wars." Civil wars after all often have the character of national wars, too, and in many of them at least one people risks its independence. In a sense the Union as well as the Confederacy risked its independence in 1861–65; one did not have to be particularly foresighted to see that a Confederate victory inevitably would change the Union's character and might even destroy it by encouraging further fragmentation of the truncated remainder.

Indeed, the South hoped for such an outcome, and her early policy aimed toward it. Some historians have speculated that in the beginning many Confederates actually had hoped for a re-creation of the Union—on their terms. Kenneth Stampp discusses this possibility in his thoughtful essay "The Southern Road to Appomattox," suggesting that "for many Southerners secession was not in fact the ultimate goal" but merely a way to negotiate a rearrangement of the old Union. We find some tempting but fragmentary bits of supporting evidence here and there throughout the literature of the secession movement, including the frequently quoted statement of Thomas Reade Rootes Cobb that the South could make better terms for itself under the Confederate Constitution than under the United States Constitution. The Confederate Constitution would have allowed such a reconstruction, for it provided that new states could be admitted into the Confederacy by a two-thirds vote, a provision evidently aimed not only at the slave states still in the Union but also at the states of the old Northwest.

Most likely, however, the Confederates did not hope so much for reconstruction under a new flag and constitution as for a further division of the United States between the Northwest and the East. On February 22, 1861, the Provisional Congress passed "a bill to declare and establish the free navigation of the Mississippi River" in an attempt to calm the fears of Union states bordering that river and to drive a wedge between the interests of New England and the Middle Atlantic states on one hand and those of the old Northwest on the other. Agreeing to this policy, Jefferson Davis signed the bill into law three days later. Only two weeks thereafter, the southern Congress ratified this policy, while acting in its capacity as a constitutional convention, by establishing the process for admission of new states by a two-thirds vote. That this provision was put into the Constitution reflects the anticipated potential and very special meaning it had for the Confederate leadership.

The Confederate strategy in late summer and early fall 1862 therefore comes as no surprise. With one eye cocked toward the Northwest and the other carefully examining the apparently anomalous situation of two Union slave states, Maryland and Kentucky, the Confederate leaders amused themselves by dreaming of a politico-military offensive. The possibility of exploiting northern internal discontent and turning it to southern advantage especially fascinated them. Flushed with successes that began with the Seven Days' Battles and anticipating further victories, the Confederate Senate passed a resolution on September 12, 1862, calling upon President Davis to direct his commanders to reaffirm free trade on the Mississippi River wherever "they approach, or enter, the territory of the United States bordering upon the Mississippi River, or the tributaries thereof."

Both the political aspects of the war and authorized incursions into Union-controlled territory that had clear political implications interested Jefferson Davis. Indeed, Frank Vandiver refers to the 1862 thrust into Maryland as "part of the biggest, most comprehensive political campaign attempted by the Confederate government" and hints that at that late hour some Confederates thought they might yet "detach a Yankee state or two from the Union." Acting upon evidence of northern internal discontent and vague reports of a "Northwest Conspiracy," Davis sought to undermine enemy morale even further by successful advances into both Maryland and Kentucky by Generals Lee, Braxton Bragg, and Edmund Kirby Smith.

Once the armies reached enemy territory, Davis wished these victorious generals to issue proclamations informing the inhabitants that the South fought not for conquest but for self-defense, reaffirming the Confederacy's commitment to free navigation of the Mississippi River, and calling upon individual northern states to "secure immunity from the desolating effects of warfare . . . by a separate treaty of peace." Even if this maneuver did not shake the allegiance of the Northwest, perhaps these military operations, by bringing war to the doorsteps of Union voters for a change, would persuade them to vote for less resolute candidates. The catch, however, was that the operations would have to produce tangible military results.

The most obvious measure of success would be defeat and destruction of a Union army, which would break the stalemate. Such a victory was unlikely under the conditions of the 1860s, although the South could aim for other, more feasible goals. In both the East and the West, Confederate commanders wished to feed their men and animals on the enemy's ground, to tap a new resource of potential recruits, and to afford "the people . . . an opportunity of liberating themselves." Even if these accomplishments proved elusive, Confederates could at least annoy and harass Union forces and spoil their offensive plans.

The pattern of the campaigns in Virginia reflected the geography of the state, for Union control of the Chesapeake Bay and the rivers emptying into it enabled federal naval forces to give the army a source of supplies whenever the soldiers chose, as had McClellan, to move around the eastern flank of the Confederates. Conversely, the geography of the western part of the state favored the southern army because the Shenandoah River flowed northeastward along a fertile valley that led into the rear of any Union army south of Washington. Thus, whereas the Confederate army could exploit the railroad from Richmond into the Shenandoah Valley and the productivity of the region to march northeast in the Valley and turn its Union opponent, any federal advance over the same route would lead southwestward, away from the enemy's rear.

Thus with each contender having one easy route around the other's flank, the campaigns in Virginia consisted of three years of inconclusive seesaws of turning movements in which each side tried, but neither decisively reached the rear of the other. This mutual advantage placed a premium on good generalship. Fortunately for the Confederacy, in assigning Lee to command the army opposing McClellan, Davis selected someone who not only well understood the opportunities presented by the Confederacy's two-sided base in Virginia but who also had the exceptional skill, boldness, and leadership ability to make the most of it.

Just before appointing Halleck general in chief in July 1862 and while McClellan remained immobile on the Peninsula, Lincoln had called another successful general from the West, John Pope, previously one of Halleck's western subordinates. Lincoln now placed Pope in command of the new fifty-thousand-man Army of Virginia, which he had concentrated southwest of Washington.

Immediately seeing that the Confederates had interior lines between McClellan's and Pope's armies, the new general in chief promptly ordered McClellan to evacuate the Peninsula and bring his army north to support Pope. Halleck, realizing that Pope's weaker and unentrenched army constituted the obvious Confederate objective, warned Pope to be cautious and not to advance until McClellan's army was at hand.

Lee analyzed the situation very much as Halleck did but, in addition, saw that Pope's army threatened the Virginia Central Railroad, the Confederate line of communication with the Shenandoah Valley and important for strategic and logistical reasons. Still fearful of being forced back to Richmond and into the siege he dreaded, Lee felt concern for supplies that came from the area south of the Rappahannock. These considerations led Lee to exploit his interior lines again to concentrate quickly against Pope, while McClellan slowly carried out his evacuation of the Peninsula.

Lee's strategy, like that planned for the Seven Days' Battles, called for Jackson to execute a turning movement to threaten the enemy's communications, thus forcing a withdrawal. But this time Lee wished to avoid battle, relying on the menace to Pope's communications to force that general back to the vicinity of Washington, thus liberating northern Virginia without a fight. In late August Lee directed Jackson, with half of his army, to march around Pope's western flank while General James Longstreet, with the other half, fixed Pope's attention on his front. Even though Lee intended Longstreet to follow Jackson's corps promptly once it had passed Pope's flank, Lee necessarily planned to divide his army.

Clausewitz would have seen "hazard" in such a move and would not feel it was justified without significant numerical superiority unless the enemy had exhibited a "loss of impetus," such as McClellan had done on the Peninsula. Jomini would have agreed on disparaging such a division of forces but undoubtedly would have put his finger on part of Lee's inspiration, for he believed that what might be "hazardous in the presence of Frederick, Napoleon, or Wellington might have entire success against a general of limited capacity." Lee counted not only on Pope's limited capacity but also on Jackson's generalship and on the tactical power of the defense, recently exhibited so clearly in the Seven Days' Battles.

Clausewitz explained the hazard involved in splitting Lee's forces: the "danger lies in that division itself, for the enemy has the benefit of his internal lines and can thus bring superior numbers against any individual part of his opponent's force." And Pope tried to do just that, falling back and concentrating against Jackson. But Jackson moved his army into a strong position and, though he did not entrench, arrayed his men behind a railroad embankment. Pope's frontal attack at the end of August had little chance of success against Jackson's ably led veteran corps. When Lee brought up Longstreet's corps to attack Pope's flank, its attack decided the Second Battle of Manassas.

The originally unintended battle contributed to the success of the campaign because Lee's casualties amounted to a little over nine thousand against sixteen thousand sustained by Pope. Since the Confederates had about forty-eight thousand men and the Union seventy-two thousand, Pope suffered losses proportionately, as well as absolutely, higher than Lee's. Compared to total manpower resources, however, the attrition balance stood slightly against the Confederates.

The demoralized Pope fell back to Washington's defenses. Lee, on the other hand, confidently and immediately sought to repeat his triumphant maneuver by again passing west of the main federal army in early September. He could then cross the Potomac River, advance into the slave state of Maryland, and break the Baltimore and Ohio Railroad, threatening vital federal interests and compelling the Army of the Potomac to fall back over that river to conform to his movement.

In this advance Lee relied on the Shenandoah Valley, planning a line of wagon transportation from Winchester, Virginia, through Harpers Ferry into Maryland. He intended, of course, to support his army primarily by living on the Maryland agricultural region during the harvest season while his quartermasters and commissaries gathered the crops in Virginia which would feed his army during the following winter. With such key items as ammunition, salt, and coffee brought by wagon, he could remain in Maryland through most of the fall. But eventually, having exhausted the resources of the region, he would have to return to Virginia and reestablish contact with rail communications for the winter. Clausewitz believed that such an operation could provide "protection for one's own territory" as well as "yield food-supplies." Such pieces of territory "are usually held temporarily, for the duration of the campaign, to be abandoned in the winter." Like Lee, he foresaw that this kind of occupation could "be achieved without major engagements." In expecting to remain so long unmolested north of the Potomac, Lee apparently counted on the reluctance of Union generals to make a frontal attack.

Like other Confederate leaders, Lee saw political advantages in this favorable logistical and strategic position, and they had played a part in his calculations. With his army in Maryland during the Union's fall congressional elections, he believed northern peace candidates would benefit from the resulting impression that the North could not subdue the South, thus undermining the will of the North to continue the war. Successes by Bragg and Kirby Smith in Kentucky would multiply the effect; if they failed, Lee reminded Davis, Bragg's forces could be "advantageously employed" in Virginia.

On September 2, Lincoln, apprehensive over Lee's victory at Second Manassas, so close to Washington, gave McClellan the task of coping with Lee's new movement. Still immensely popular with the army, Little Mac soon absorbed Pope's short-lived Army of Virginia into his own Army of the Potomac and began to conform his movements to those of Lee. Having luckily captured some of Lee's orders, which revealed Confederate plans, McClellan moved his eighty thousand men with unaccustomed speed. McClellan thought surely he could beat "Bobby Lee," knowing his intentions, even though Lee enjoyed the tactical defensive. Hurriedly concentrating his army to cope with McClellan's uncharacteristically rapid movement, Lee had the advantage of the defensive, which, however, he did not augment with entrenchments.

The resulting Battle of Antietam was bloody. One of McClellan's corps commanders reported that "every stalk of corn in the northern and greater part of the field was cut as closely as with a knife, and the slain lay in rows precisely as they had stood in their ranks a few minutes before. It was never my fortune to witness a more bloody, dismal battlefield." It contained so many bodies that, in one veteran's recollection, a man could have walked through it without stepping on the ground.

Without a particularly strong position, Lee's seriously outnumbered and hastily concentrated army of 45,000 beat back McClellan's attacks with difficulty and, though on the defensive, suffered slightly heavier casualties, 13,700 to 12,500. But if the 12,000 federal prisoners taken earlier at Harpers Ferry are also counted, the total losses in the campaign were about proportional to the strengths of each side. In a precarious position, with his immobile army unable either to supply itself by foraging or to obtain supplies by rail, Lee climaxed what was essentially a raid by withdrawing into Virginia. Though Lee had been tactically successful in resisting McClellan's attacks at Antietam, the retreat, foreordained yet premature, proved that the Union had won the battle; thus the benefits in political and public morale redounded to the North.

General Lee had announced to the people of Maryland that he came to enable them to overthrow a "foreign yoke," but he had admitted to Jefferson Davis that he did not "anticipate any general rising of the people in our behalf," although he hoped to gather a few recruits and some subsistence. Nevertheless, Lee had used the opportunity to play the politician, proclaiming to Marylanders as Davis had commanded. He also advised Davis that the time was right to recommend to the United States government that it acknowledge the independence of the Confederacy. Lee thought that, coming at a time of advantage, and before battle, the North could not construe the suggestion as a confession of weakness; Union rejection would prove that it, not the Confederacy, was responsible for continued war. In that event, "the proposal of peace would enable the people of the United States to determine at their coming elections whether they will support those who favor a prolongation of the war, or those who wish to bring it to a termination."

Instead of damaging Union morale by a Confederate victory, Lee withdrew and provided the Union with its first major eastern victory in which the rebels had retreated. Rather than producing a military situation appropriate for the Confederacy to call for peace, Lee's withdrawal had provided Lincoln with the springboard for his preliminary Emancipation

Proclamation, issued September 22, 1862, and seriously dampened any Confederate prospects for diplomatic recognition by European powers. Although the war now completely changed character, Lee had accomplished his strategic aim and part of his logistical objective by halting his withdrawal immediately south of the Potomac. Here he subsisted his army far from central Virginia and still threatened the flank and rear of any Union advances south from Washington.

In the West, meanwhile, Grant's army remained quiescent in northern Mississippi, immobilized by drought and other logistical difficulties, while Buell's army, based at Nashville, aimed to move along the railroad to capture the key junction of Chattanooga. But instead of pushing forward rapidly as Halleck desired, Buell stopped. Already harassed by guerrillas, he halted in August, when cavalry raiders interrupted his communications in the first major application of what became a fundamental and most effective Confederate defensive strategy. Adequately supplemented by the activities of guerrillas, cavalry broke the fragile rail lines in Buell's rear, burning bridges and trestles and tearing up track. Without rail communication and out of reach of the river steamers, Buell refused to advance farther in such sparsely settled country with only primitive roads for supply.

Armies found it almost impossible to resist raiders, who sought to wreck railroads. With such a large and vulnerable target as the long line of a railroad and its easily moved rails and enticingly inflammable wooden trestles across ravines and creeks as well as rivers, raiders, having a broad choice of objectives, could strike anywhere and approach over a confusing variety of routes. Since the Union armies could hardly guard every vulnerable point in substantial strength, the raiders and guerrillas could readily follow the offensive precept of striking against weakness. Almost invincible on the offensive because of the ambiguity of their objective, raiders seemed nearly immune to successful pursuit because they could move as fast as their pursuers and were hard to intercept for they had no need to retreat along the same route over which they had advanced; instead, in withdrawal, they could use the same mystifying array of alternative routes and destinations that made them as hard to head off in retreat as in advance.

Thus, unlike the primacy of the strategic defensive in resisting invading armies seeking to occupy territory, the strategic offensive in the form of raids was stronger than the defense against it. The Confederates could use citizens in occupied territory as well as their numerous and excellent cavalry to employ the intrinsically stronger strategy of raids against vulnerable Union communications while at the same time, with their main armies, exploiting the primacy of the strategic defensive against invading armies seeking to occupy territory.

Although neither Clausewitz nor Jomini explicitly noted the strategic dominance of raiders, they fully understood the substance of their ascendancy. Even though Jomini failed to grasp the ineffectiveness of cavalry on the battlefield, he well understood its role in raiding enemy communications. Also pointing out that militia made "excellent partisan soldiers" for raiding operations, he realized that "it is certain that a numerous cavalry, whether regular or irregular, must have a great influence in giving a turn to the events of a war. It may excite a feeling of apprehension at distant parts of the enemy's country, it can carry off his convoys, it can encircle his army, make his communications very perilous, and destroy the *ensemble* of his operations. In other words it produces nearly the same result as a rising *en masse* of a population, causing trouble on the front, flanks, and rear of an army and reducing a general to a state of entire uncertainty in his calculations." Although Clausewitz did not stress the cavalry's role, he, too, would have realized the significance of raids on communications, the enemy's vulnerability to them, and their effectiveness in "cooperation with disaffected subjects," who, of course, abounded in Buell's rear.

So another factor had helped stop Buell, one which Jomini would have understood and which boded ill for the Union cause. Jomini would have called the Civil War a "national war," which he defined as war "waged against a united people, or a great majority of them, filled with a noble ardor and determined to sustain their independence: then every step is disputed" by guerrillas, "the army holds only its campground, its supplies can only be obtained at the point of a sword, and its convoys are everywhere threatened." The large forces necessarily diverted to protect communications, supplies, and personnel menaced by guerrillas made Jomini very pessimistic. "Under these circumstances" the decisive campaigns of "a war of invasion become very difficult, if not impossible." The tasks to attain victory increased for not only must the invaders destroy the defending armies, but "the country should be occupied and subjugated."

Clausewitz agreed with Jomini about the difficulties of winning a national war, and he also saw that guerrillas needed the support of regulars, which the cavalry raiders provided. He listed other conditions important for guerrilla success:

1. The war must be fought in the interior of the country.
2. It must not be decided by a single stroke.
3. The theatre of operations must be fairly large.
4. The national character must be suited to that type of war.
5. The country must be rough and inaccessible, because of mountains, or forests, marshes, or the local methods of cultivation.

The South possessed all of these characteristics for successful guerrilla warfare as well as men "used to hard, strenuous work." Clausewitz did not consider population density a factor in such warfare; a "scattered distribution of houses and farms" rather than a population concentrated in villages helped the national resistance, as did poor roads and a "disproportion between the invading army and the size of the country." Thus Clausewitz's assessment was as essentially pessimistic as Jomini's.

Both raiders and a national resistance by guerrillas aggravated what would have posed a serious problem in any case. Jomini had stressed that "deep lines of operations . . . are always dangerous in a hostile country," a situation worsened by the need of Union quartermasters and commissaries to bring large quantities of supplies from the rear, it being "quite impossible" to subsist an army in a country as sparsely populated as the South. Clausewitz emphatically agreed, almost exactly describing Buell's difficult situation "at the end of a victorious campaign," which had conquered West and Middle Tennessee, "when lines of communication have begun to be overstretched. This is especially true when war is conducted in an impoverished, thinly populated and possibly hostile country. . . . Often the finest victory has been robbed of its glory as a consequence of this problem."

The Confederates meanwhile did not realize how successful their guerrillas and cavalry had been in halting the main Union offensive in the West. Therefore, they planned a counteroffensive with their principal western army. With the advice of Beauregard, whom he had replaced, General Braxton Bragg, the abrasive new Confederate commander, undertook in July 1862 to use the railroad to counter Buell's already almost-neutralized menace to Chattanooga. Bragg, who excelled in strategy and management of logistics but proved quite inept in execution, planned to do this by carrying out a strategic turning movement on a vast scale to threaten Buell's communications. This offensive with half of his Mississippi army, also embodying the concept of the concentration of dispersed forces against a weak line, employed, of necessity, the circuitous railway route from northern Mississippi south to Mobile, north to Atlanta, and thence farther north again to Chattanooga. Bragg expedited the transfer by ordering the garrison at Mobile to move immediately to Chattanooga, to be replaced by the last troops to leave northern Mississippi. In this way he established a "pipeline" for moving men from Mississippi to Tennessee.

In Tennessee, Bragg's forces, over half of his original army in Mississippi, joined those of Major General Edmund Kirby Smith's Department of East Tennessee for a march into Kentucky. Moving rapidly, unexpectedly, and in coordination with Kirby Smith's march upon Lexington, Kentucky, Bragg planned to threaten Buell's supply, the railroad to Louisville, and force his retirement. This operation, like Lee's in the East, would be a strategic turning movement of the kind Jomini admired, for Bragg might gain a position athwart Union communications, where he could force Buell to attack him. But Bragg did not initially intend this outcome. Instead he began his advance without any precise strategic plans.

Nevertheless, expectations for the western campaigns of Bragg and Kirby Smith matched the hopes for Lee's simultaneous march into Maryland, and all had the same goals. The Kentucky delegation to the Confederate Congress urged upon Bragg and Davis the need to advance so as to secure the services of the "large proportion of the young men [who] will at once join our army," a question they examined in the light of its "political aspects" of an overthrow of Union government in the state. In August 1862, while Lee fought the Second Battle of Manassas in Virginia, Kirby Smith entered Kentucky and, at Richmond, surprised and captured a large party of Union recruits. By the beginning of September he had occupied Lexington and the rich Blue Grass region.

In a separate advance Bragg moved north on a route parallel to Kirby Smith's but west of him and close to Buell's army, which used the Louisville and Nashville Railway for its communications. "Kentuckians," proclaimed Bragg on September 14, 1862, "I have entered your state with the Confederate Army of the West, and offer you an opportunity to free yourselves from the tyranny of a despotic ruler."

Reaching Buell's rear but baffled by supply shortages, Bragg marched on to join Kirby Smith while Buell moved to Louisville to receive large reinforcements before advancing against Bragg. The Confederates waited, disappointed that Kentuckians did not rally to the flag. Quite the reverse. Bragg soon realized the futility of his proclamation and his hopes, admitting that now he had arms but no takers and complaining that new recruits did not equal half his losses. "Unless a change occurs soon," he told Richmond, "we must abandon the garden spot of Kentucky to its cupidity."

Although the strategic turning movement by Bragg and Kirby Smith had not forced the enemy to fight at a disadvantage, nor gained much, it had succeeded magnificently in relieving the apparent threat to Chattanooga, and it had turned Buell all the way back to Louisville. This achievement was short-lived, however, for Buell immediately moved out of Louisville with a strongly reinforced army, and Bragg, after mismanaging an inconclusive battle at Perryville, October 8–9, 1862, withdrew from Kentucky and ultimately based himself at Murfreesboro, Tennessee, on the railroad south of Nashville. Here the Union army, based on the same railroad running southeast from Nashville, stymied him.

In both East and West, therefore, the Confederacy's grand designs of the August to October 1862 campaigns failed, except for the temporary gain of subsisting in enemy territory. Although having, as raids, little prospect of more than a transitory occupation of hostile territory, these advances could have had momentous consequences had the raiding armies remained until after the November elections in the North. As James M. McPherson points out in his *Battle Cry of Freedom: The Civil War Era*, the early retreats "forestalled European mediation and recognition of the Confederacy, perhaps prevented a Democratic victory in the Northern elections of 1862 that might have inhibited the government's ability to carry on the war, and set the stage for the Emancipation Proclamation which enlarged the scope and purpose of the conflict."

Yet the eventual, late-fall withdrawal of the raiding armies would have disconcerted pessimists about Union prospects and provided Lincoln with a political opportunity. Even so the federal elections of 1862 were a setback to the Republican party, but not decisively so; for example, Ohio and Indiana gave only slim majorities to Democrats, and, though the Democratic margin of victory was greater in Illinois, it became clear that the Northwest had no idea of detaching itself from the Union. In the long run, therefore, the political benefits of these campaigns redounded to the

Union. Most important, Lincoln's issuance of the preliminary Emancipation Proclamation changed the character of the war. Conversely, it upset many Unionists, especially in the border states, and encouraged some Confederates to fight with more determination than before.

The proclamation, however, actually stood the war on its head. The Confederates no longer appeared before the world, and themselves, as champions of national self-determination; instead, they were forced to assume the character of suppressors of individual self-determination. Southerners now appeared to the Western world as quintessentially espousing an institution that most of the rest of Western civilization had come to despise and had renounced. They were on the moral defensive; the guilt over slavery and war which some had felt in 1861 now afflicted more southern consciences than before and forced profound reexamination of southern war goals, with consequences that became apparent toward the end of the war.

In their military aspects the campaigns in Kentucky and Virginia and two battles in northern Mississippi had confirmed Clausewitz's forecast that Civil War battles would have no more than the very limited significance they did in fact have. Lacking ability to win total victory in battle or to conduct an effective pursuit, Union forces had to occupy the enemy's country. This meant that the Union had expanded its implicit logistic strategy, moving from Scott's objective of only interdicting Confederate communications overseas and across the Mississippi to conquering territory to deprive the Confederate armies of their human and physical resources. Thus Union forces had to contend with the nearly insurmountable problems of operating over long lines of communication in a thinly populated but hostile and huge country as they conducted a national war without decisive numerical superiority against adequately armed and competently led Confederate armies. Accordingly, they had to devote large numbers of troops to defending their communications in conquered territory against Confederate raiders, both guerrillas and regular cavalry. So, lacking sufficient numerical preponderance or an adequate ratio of force to the Confederacy's large area, the Union, though aiming at Confederate centers of gravity, had to follow Clausewitz's proposal for pursuing less ambitious objectives. Although most campaigns were limited, thought Clausewitz, in truth they fell "between the two poles." For such restricted campaigns Clausewitz recommended conquering territory, just as the Union was doing.

In the first year and a half of the conflict Union forces had aimed at many of the objectives Clausewitz prescribed, including "the occupation of important towns, fertile agricultural areas, or disaffected districts," such as East Tennessee, "which can be seduced into revolt," and of course Scott's plan and Union campaigns aimed to "disrupt communications." The Confederate forces also unconsciously followed Clausewitz's recommendations, adhering to his prescriptions for the defense, taking advantage of the obstacles presented by terrain, employing fortifications, and making the most of the support of the public in a national war. Initially, the inexperience of both armies aided the Confederates, for, as Clausewitz noted, ill-trained troops were "better suited to the defense than to attack."

Clausewitz had listed four alternatives for the defender: (1) deep retreat, (2) passive defense and "direct cover," (3) active defense, including counterattack, and (4) use of the strategic turning movement. In the West, for example, Halleck's offensive had forced the Confederates to make a deep retreat into the interior of the country. But Clausewitz thought a deep retreat should be a last resort, and, of course, the Confederates agreed.

Actually, the Confederate use of the strategic turning movement as a means of defense fully vindicated Clausewitz's view. Lee, explicitly, and Bragg, as his strategy evolved, planned to use the turning movement to force the enemy back without conflict. As it worked out, both fought essentially defensive battles and returned to positions at least as far advanced as their starting points. Each campaign had enabled them to subsist briefly in the enemy's country, and each occupied the enemy throughout much of the excellent fall campaigning season.

Clausewitz's recommendation for resisting a campaign such as the Union's to occupy southern territory would have intended that the Confederates should "draw the utmost benefit from waiting." He would have advised that the defender "cover the country by spreading out forces" and "interpose his force quickly by means of flank marches wherever his extension is not wide enough." The Confederates followed this plan successfully in Virginia, and Sidney Johnston had attempted it with less success in the West. If the attacker pierced this defense, Clausewitz would have advised that "there would still be time for the defender to concentrate his forces." But Sidney Johnston did not concentrate adequately at Fort Donelson, for Grant and Halleck were not to be "stopped by a moderate sized but strong post" as vulnerable as that which Johnston established at Fort Donelson. Only at Shiloh did the Confederates concentrate in a futile effort to recover their lost defensive line.

An alternative to this system of defense by "direct cover" was, Clausewitz explained, "additional reliance on mobility, active defense, and even offensive measures," including "attacking the enemy in flank or threatening his rear." Lee and Bragg followed this style of defense with their strategic turning movements in September and October 1862. But earlier the Confederates had failed to honor Clausewitz's injunction to avoid "any unfavorable engagements." In spite of the surprise attained, the frontal attack at Shiloh does not fit Clausewitz nor does Joe Johnston's attack at Seven Pines. Lee's effort to turn McClellan during the Seven Days' Battles was laudable in intent if bungled in execution, and, of course, the defensive battle of First Manassas turned out well. Beauregard's retreat before Halleck and Bragg's avoidance of battle in Kentucky, especially his withdrawal from the field at Perryville, met Clausewitz's warning to avoid battle; Lee's intent only to turn Pope back and his successful attrition at Second Manassas also conform to Clausewitz's model. The results at Antietam might have been better if Lee's orders to his troops had followed Clausewitz's injunction that "the art of intrenchment must come to their assistance." By the fall of 1862 the Confederates were more often trying to avoid battle or remain on the defensive and thus their strategy harmonized much more with Clausewitz's ideas.

Even though he stressed the defensive and prescribed economical methods for its conduct, Clausewitz always looked to the offensive, and it animated all his ideas. Confederate strategy followed these prescriptions, for the Confederates were, as Clausewitz would have desired, also "on the alert *for a chance to strike a favorable blow*" as "a necessary complement to the defense as a whole, to be used at times when the attacker takes things a little too easily and lays himself wide open at some points." Particularly in Middle Tennessee, the Confederates had followed Clausewitz's second offensive injunction, "action against the enemy's lines of communication." In both the East and the West the Confederates employed "raids and diversions into enemy territory." Thus the Confederates, like their adversaries, substantially adhered to the ideas of Clausewitz and Jomini for prosecuting defensive war under very favorable conditions, the attacker coping with long lines of communications, the huge spaces in relation to the forces available, and an inadequate numerical superiority to achieve a decisive victory.

Confederate generals in the West came to rely on raids. This method of defense, one Clausewitz would have prescribed and Jomini would have regarded as virtually invincible, forced Union commanders to allocate a third, and more, of their forces to defending their communications. So it is hard to criticize either contestant for failing to wage the war according to the recommendations of the authorities.

But the successful exploitation of their advantages of geography and national resistance did not produce sufficient achievements to sustain Confederate morale and determination to fight on to victory, nor was skillful handling of Confederate troops successful enough to prevent the course of military events from sapping Confederate strength and testing Confederate will more than that of the Union. Although momentarily elated by the dramatic advances of Lee and Bragg, the Confederate public received no permanent lift from the early fall campaigns, for the Confederate people perceived as defeats the retreats that Clausewitz and Jomini could have foretold. Few grasped the strategic and logistic benefits of these raids—for that is all they amounted to—seeing them rather as failed invasions.

The Union army owed much to the navy. Halleck and Grant's victories at Fort Henry and Fort Donelson and subsequent advance far up the Tennessee River depended on the river for supplies and the navy for critical support, as did McClellan's Peninsula campaign; conversely, General Buell's advance in Tennessee, deprived of rivers for supply, succumbed to Confederate cavalry raids. Gunboats guarded the transports and even provided artillery support for Grant's army at Shiloh. Union warships contributed less, however, on the Atlantic and the Gulf, waters with which navies usually had more identification. The fleets did impede Confederate trade, but to do more, they needed the help of the army. But on the coasts the army did not give as much help as it might have, and the leaders of coastal operations rarely displayed either the vision or cooperation that had characterized operations on the inland waters.

So command of sea and rivers could not give the Union victory any more than could the army's preponderance on land. Despite northern military and naval superiority, therefore, Confederates by fall 1862 were still not convinced that time was against them. Most southerners agreed that their situation was difficult, and some thought desperate, but they agreed also that the question over which they fought was still an open one. Lincoln's Emancipation Proclamation, which had the eventual effect of increasing northern manpower because it logically led to the use of black soldiers, seriously concerned southerners. Many Confederates considered it an open invitation to the slaves to slay their masters, which it was not; others welcomed the proclamation, for they believed the threat of a new society that it contained would convince Confederates of the need for a more determined resistance, and, for a time, it probably did.

More significant, the proclamation opened the way for the use of black soldiers and more effective use of black labor. Further Union advances permitted and encouraged the disaffection of the black third of the Confederate population and allowed its employment in a military capacity. The flight of the slaves provided tangible military benefits to the Union, while depriving the Confederacy of much of its labor and sapping its morale and will.

Chapter Seven

The Union Navy
and Combined Operations

THE UNION NAVY supplied indispensable aid in moving and supplying the armies along the rivers. But the army proved equally or even more essential in assisting fleet operations against land defenses. Nothing illustrates this cooperation better than the Mississippi activities of David G. Farragut, perhaps the most capable naval officer on either side. A sixty-year-old veteran of forty-nine years in the navy, Farragut used the innovative tactic of lashing his weaker vessels to the more powerful to bring wooden ships past the Confederate river batteries protecting New Orleans on the south. Having received the surrender of the city and the cooperating army force having occupied it in the spring of 1862, Farragut then steamed up the Mississippi to make two attempts to capture the Confederate river bastion of Vicksburg. Each time his contingent of troops proved to be too small to take the town and its strong batteries commanding the river.

These early operations were representative of Union successes and failures along the coast. Beginning well in 1862 with the capture of Norfolk and Galveston as well as New Orleans, the Union failed until almost the end of the war to capture the other ports, Mobile, Savannah, Wilmington, and Charleston.

Leaders on both sides regarded Charleston, the "Cradle of the Rebellion," as dear because of its symbolic importance, and as such it was a major point of contention. Both Union Secretary of the Navy Gideon Welles and his capable assistant Gustavus V. Fox felt confident that a sufficiently powerful naval force, even without army assistance, could capture the port. Earlier successes at Port Royal, Hatteras, and in the

West had convinced both of them that a naval bombardment could overcome land fortifications. They were also certain that ironclads, particularly monitor types, could run past the forts and intimidate the city into surrendering by threatening bombardment.

Rear Admiral Samuel F. Du Pont, in command of the South Atlantic Blockading Squadron, had strong reservations about such action, however, and favored instead a combined operation. Nevertheless, under pressure from Washington he reluctantly agreed. On April 15, 1863, seven monitors, along with the ironclads *New Ironsides* and *Keokuk*, attacked Charleston's Forts Sumter and Moultrie. After an engagement of slightly less than two hours' duration, Du Pont's battered vessels had to withdraw. The attack's failure illustrated to Du Pont and other naval officers that monitor-type vessels, with their small gun batteries, lacked adequate firepower for bombarding well-situated land fortifications.

After this the navy grudgingly accepted Du Pont's conviction of the tactical necessity of combined operations to take Charleston. The navy worked out a plan with the army whereby troops under the protection of naval vessels would occupy Morris Island, a small sand spit within firing range of Fort Sumter. From this position Union artillery might destroy the fort, allowing the warships to enter the harbor and force a surrender. During the months that followed the Union took Morris Island and reduced Fort Sumter to rubble but for various reasons was unable to secure the port until 1865.

Like Charleston, Savannah held out against joint Union army and navy operations for more than two years. As early as the fall of 1861 plans existed for combined forces to attack Savannah, but that assault never materialized. Union troops did occupy Tybee Island, capture Fort Pulaski, and make unopposed reconnaissance forays along the coast and inland streams in the port's vicinity, but the army never provided enough troops to mount a serious effort against the city. Naval vessels assigned to the Savannah station blockaded the inlets leading to the Savannah River, occasionally patrolled the maze of streams that connected the inlets, and bombarded Confederate positions. In turn the Confederates built a series of fortifications and established a small naval force with ironclads to guard the port, but Union forces rarely challenged them. Admiral Du Pont regarded combined operations against Savannah as too risky, and his successor never even considered the idea. Savannah fell to Sherman's troops on Christmas Day 1864.

As at Charleston and Savannah, Sherman's pressure from inland was a major factor in the fall of Wilmington, North Carolina, the last major Confederate port on the eastern seaboard. Wilmington had enormous value to the Confederacy; after the capture of Norfolk early in 1862, it was the closest port of any size to Richmond and the Army of Northern Virginia. By the summer of 1863 it had become the single most important center for blockade-running.

Rear Admiral Samuel P. Lee was the first commander of the North Atlantic Blockading Squadron to emphasize the port's importance. His predecessors, flag officers Silas Stringham and L. M. Goldsborough, had considered the capture of the principal forts and towns in the sounds region of North Carolina more important. Commenting upon this policy, in 1863 Lee lamented to Welles: "Loadstones instead of stepping stones to progress. . . . The easy capture of Fort Macon gave us the possession of Beaufort Harbor; thus we had all the seacoast of North Carolina, except Wilmington, the capture of which was as easy then as difficult now. . . . But the complete acquisition of the seacoast was abandoned in the favor of the sound towns."

One of his subordinates described Lee, a Virginian, as courteous, modest, retiring, careful, and conservative; another, on his staff, called him solemn and serious. He never believed that he had enough ships or the cooperation of a military force powerful enough to attack the forts guarding the river.

Although more than once the navy urged seizure of the forts by amphibious assault, until late in the fall of 1864 the War Department showed little interest. The army was far more desirous of taking Goldsboro and cutting the railroad through there or seizing Charleston as a base from which to move inland. Finally, in late 1864 the army contributed an adequate force, but an inadequate general, to a combined operation that failed. In January 1865 the navy and army made another effort, the sea forces again under the command of the able and experienced Rear Admiral David D. Porter and the soldiers capably led by Major General Alfred H. Terry. On January 12, 1865, Porter's fleet again loomed off Fort Fisher. Forty-four warships, including several ironclads that closed to within seven hundred yards of the fort, opened a devastating and deliberate fire on selected targets. On the thirteenth and fourteenth under the fire of Porter's guns Terry's eight thousand troops landed. On Sunday, January 15, two thousand sailors and marines waded ashore and attacked the seaward face of the fort while Terry's troops assaulted from the land. Although the seaward strike failed, it diverted attention from Terry's columns, which broke inside and captured the fort. Within a few days the Union also captured Fort Caswell, and Confederate troops evacuated Wilmington.

Authorities generally agree that this second Fort Fisher operation was one of the most brilliant, if not the most brilliant, amphibious operation carried out during the war. It surely constitutes the best performance by a naval force in such an operation. From the navy's point of view the Fort Fisher operation had real significance. Its capture and that of Caswell finally closed Cape Fear to blockade-runners.

On April 12, 1865, three months after the fall of Wilmington, Mobile, Alabama, the last major port east of the Mississippi, surrendered to Union forces. Yet nine months earlier the port had ceased to have importance. In August 1864 Admiral Farragut had led a fleet of four monitors and fourteen wooden vessels into Mobile Bay. The fleet had successfully passed the forts defending the bay and then had defeated the small Confederate squadron therein. Farragut's victory effectively sealed the port. If adequate troops had accompanied this naval force, the Union could have taken Mobile after the surrender of the forts guarding the bay's entrance.

Naval operations, especially on the western rivers, contributed directly and greatly to the destruction of Confederate military power and conquest of important territory. Although residents of the Confederate interior might ignore the naval presence unless their homes were located along important navigable streams, in coastal and adjacent river areas Union warships caused considerable anxiety because their unexpected arrival might cause the capture of a town or the closure of a port. Even when its operations were unsuccessful, the existence of the Union navy created tensions for citizens within proximity of navigable water. The naval power thereby contributed to the dissolution of Confederate power and will. Even threats that had little intrinsic military significance had an impact on the morale of the people directly affected. In the West the arrival of the Union fleet, or only a single ship, often created an umbrella under which lukewarm or needy Confederates could engage in an illegal cotton trade with the North, send money back and forth across the lines, or even provide for their individual safety by seeking the protection of Union forces. More often, Confederates fled from the Union presence and went deeper into the interior. In either event, the movement of refugees was demoralizing to the refugees themselves and to those around them. Moreover, both the rivers and the enclaves established along the coast with naval support served as objectives for runaway slaves and, when blacks were admitted into the Union army, they served also as recruiting depots. In short, the navy placed on the doorstep of many southern communities a reminder that the war could affect them personally, not just the soldiers on distant battlefields. Once the war began to turn against the South, the naval presence could be a deadening, morale-sapping reminder of what might lie in store for the entire South.

Although Union land forces made relatively little use of their positions in Atlantic ports or inlets to raid the railroad that paralleled the seaboard between Richmond and Savannah, their ability to threaten the railroad, together with the actual or implied menace to Wilmington, Charleston, and Savannah, also caused the Confederates much anxiety. To protect the ports and the railroad Confederates applied their pipeline concept and used the railroad to transfer forces along the coast. If, for example, they believed Charleston threatened, they could order troops south to the city from a point farther north, while simultaneously ordering other troops to that point from a location even farther north. In this way, Charleston would receive reinforcements from Wilmington, while men from farther north replaced those at Wilmington—and so on up the line to Richmond, which had actually given up some troops. Charleston thus gained forces far more quickly than if it had to await the arrival of reinforcements directly from Richmond.

When the Confederates augmented these defending troops with local forces raised by the states, they further integrated local defense with national. Adequate local defense along the coast played an important part both in sustaining civilian morale in these regions and in defending nationally important ports and the railway along the Atlantic coast. State forces and Confederate regulars long had cooperated in this effort, and in 1863 the Confederacy systematized this joint effort and sought to strengthen it by requiring states to provide such troops. By 1864 they became partly national forces, called reserves, with an experienced Confederate general officer to command them in each state. Composed of men in exempt occupations and those too young or too old to take the field, these troops proved effective at manning fortifications, thus releasing regular soldiers to join the main armies. Thus coast defense came to depend even more than before on local resources, and these local defense forces made a more significant national contribution than heretofore.

It seems that the Union missed valuable chances to deal severe blows to the Confederate war effort. But in 1861 neither side had well-organized land forces available and the Union navy had expanded little from its peacetime strength. The Union had greater opportunities because the Confederates had not erected the fortifications that later protected their ports. But at this stage of the war the Confederates posted a higher proportion of their forces to guard the coast than they did later.

A Union concentration against the coast, earlier or later, would have brought a rapid response, especially along the Atlantic, where the security of the coastal railroad always caused the Confederates much anxiety. But this same railroad would have facilitated rapid concentration of troops to contest the Union landing force; and just as the Union would have diverted forces from the main armies to the coast, so also would the Confederates. In a contest against such landings, the Confederates would have had the advantage of more rapid concentration because their ports all had telegraph communication whereas the Union squadrons, lacking wireless, would have had to depend on dispatch boats for communication. By 1864, when the Union concentrated most of its soldiers to support the simultaneous land advances, the Confederacy could do likewise because the newly organized reserves assumed a greater role in coast defense.

Thus it is not easy to predict what outcome a greater Union effort would have had, and it is clearly presumptuous to assume the easy capture of many ports. If, however, the Union had succeeded early in eliminating ports captured or closed later, the blockade would have been strengthened significantly; but in view of the Confederate ability to improvise, the quantity of consumer goods brought in throughout the war, and the relative Confederate independence of imports in the latter part of the war, it seems unlikely that a more effective blockade would have broken the military stalemate or seriously affected the capabilities of the Confederate armies.

Even so, Union combined operations played an important role. Despite poor cooperation between the services, the wrong kind of ironclads, and the failure to exploit initial advantages, the soldiers and sailors together did what neither could do alone—they successfully brought the war to the coastal areas of the South long before the major Union armies were able to do so. They tied up Confederate troops, diverted scarce resources to building and equipping fortifications, and caused Confederates a great deal of anxiety. And the naval victories and threats had unexpected political consequences, helping to ignite tempers and deepen differences on issues.

Chapter Eight

States' Rights and
the Confederate War Effort

THE RELATIONSHIP OF naval operations to local defense, and specifically of local defense to the problem of Confederate-state interactions, requires special attention; and we also need to give some consideration to the historian most responsible for the states'-rights interpretation of Confederate defeat. If the South lost the Civil War because it did not have the will to win, one reason, surely, was the internal dissension caused by the states'-rights controversy. So thought many historians of an earlier generation, following a thesis demonstrated most prominently by Frank L. Owsley, who contended that the Confederacy "Died of State Rights."

No one would deny the disruptive effect of the conflict generated by differing notions of how best to preserve liberty and to organize southern society for the war effort. Many Confederates became upset over the controversy between the Confederate government and the states on the question of local defense. Owsley asserted, for example, that in the fall of 1861 Georgia's Governor Joseph E. Brown danced "a frantic jig up and down Georgia . . . accusing the Confederate government of gross neglect" because of "the exposed condition of Georgia's coast." Owsley maintained that during the following spring North Carolina kept a large force of state troops to meet the threat of seaborne attack and that by the fall of 1862 North Carolinians resented the conscription of state troops, which the Tar Heels believed had "left the state in the lurch in the matter of coast defense."

Thus Owsley viewed local defense as one of the principal ways in which states' assertion of their rights contributed to Confederate defeat.

Seeing a "veritable tug of war between the central and local governments," he believed that "if the individual states had immediately placed the arms in their possession in the hands of the Confederate armies . . . the Confederate government would have been able to put a much larger army in the field in 1861." Yet, because the states were organizing and equipping troops for the Confederate service, these weapons, imported by the states or seized by them from federal arsenals, did go to equip Confederate troops. Realizing this, Owsley believed the main harm done in 1861 by the states' emphasis on coastal defense was to ensure that the Confederacy's "initial advantages of better trained soldiery and better generals were lost and the popular enthusiasm for the war was dissipated." But it is difficult to see any particular Confederate qualitative superiority in 1861 or what generals could have done with it had it existed. Still, as Jefferson Davis acknowledged after the fall of Forts Henry and Donelson, in 1861 the Confederacy had committed too many men to coast defense, causing Davis briefly to resolve on the drastic overreaction of "abandoning the seaboard." Yet, even insofar as coastal-state concerns had contributed to this faulty distribution of forces, it is difficult to see much long-range harm to the southern prosecution of the war.

Owsley sees local defense, by inspiriting states'-rights opposition to the Confederate government, as harming the war effort by depriving the Confederacy of resources it could have used better than the states. Owsley cites the example of Governor Zebulon B. Vance of North Carolina, who at the end of the war "had on hand in warehouses 92,000 uniforms, thousands of blankets, shoes, and tents. But at the same time Lee's men in Virginia were barefooted, almost without blankets, tents, and clothing. Vance had enough uniforms to give every man in Lee's army two apiece." Although it is doubtful that Vance accurately recalled an accumulation so much in excess of the state's needs, the existence of such stores indicates how states added to rather than subtracted from the war effort. After 1861, when the states almost completely ceased raising and equipping men for Confederate service, they nevertheless continued to look after their men in the army by sending them clothing and other supplies. In addition, they organized and maintained their own militias. North Carolina's supplies thus augmented those of the Confederacy because state funds and state initiative had caused their manufacture or importation.

The same perspective applies to state forces, which Owsley felt had "grown up and multiplied until, like the barnacles on the hulk of a foundering ship, they threatened to drag the Confederacy down to destruction." In tending to see only evil in local defense, Owsley often overlooked the importance of defending ports from capture as well as preventing the Union from breaking the vital railroad that ran along the Atlantic seaboard. Moreover, local forces protected coastal saltworks, whose mundane product was important to diets as well as essential for preserving meat. For this reason Confederate military authorities viewed state forces as an essential supplement to national forces. By 1863 the Confederate government began to support state forces and in 1864 relied almost exclusively on local forces to defend the coast, thus concentrating more men against the Union's 1864 offensives.

If some of the forces engaged in such tasks as protecting the coast or guarding salt production may have been redundant, the number of Confederate troops shielding against menaces to rear areas was minuscule compared with the Union's commitment to similar tasks. The federal armies, on the average, devoted about one-third of their forces to safeguarding communications from guerrillas and cavalry raiders. And for the most part the Union had to commit its regular forces to these tasks of guarding railways and the like for it found too much difficulty organizing a reliable militia in essentially hostile territory. Union local defense for these purposes absorbed far more troops, relatively as well as absolutely, than the Confederacy ever devoted to its local defense responsibilities. And the governors took meaningful steps to meet the difficulties involved in protecting their exposed coasts, and the joint effort of the central government and the states helped to prevent the Union navy from continuing the successful expeditions it had conducted in the first part of the war. This was only one way local defense aided the Confederacy.

When Union armies entered Georgia in late 1863 and conducted an offensive south to Atlanta in 1864, Georgia state troops showed that they were useful for more than coast defense. Though low in military effectiveness because of the predominance of the very young and the overage as well as their lack of experience, Georgia's division-size organization proved formidable when defending the elaborate entrenchments which both sides had learned to dig by 1864. When the secretary of war wanted to keep these men in continuous service, Governor Brown explained why they must remain militia, available for duty in emergencies only. "We must," he wrote, "retain a producing class at home to furnish supplies to the Army, or it becomes a mere question of time when we must submit to the enemy on account of our inability longer to support our armies." Brown explained that "the Home Guards are composed of this reserved producing class, and their services in the agricultural fields are absolutely indispensable for the continuance of our troops in the military field." Governor Brown reminded the president that such men "are willing to do military service for short periods in sudden emergencies, but they cannot leave their homes for regular service without ruin to themselves and their country."

The governor furloughed his home guards for agricultural work in 1864, when the fall of Atlanta indicated a pause in the campaign and a momentary diminution in the peril to his own state, which clearly indicates that he had not filled his militia with men who could, as Owsley believed, readily have served far away in the Confederate army. Thus the energy and resources of the state government did augment Confederate military strength beyond what it would have been without the manpower resources enlisted by Governor Brown and his legislature. Although Georgia made a particularly strong war effort, its exertions were typical of those of all states. The thesis that local defense handicapped the Confederacy's war effort rests on three mistaken assumptions: that coast defense had little importance; that states misused their forces and resources; and that the states' military efforts subtracted from rather than added to the Confederate war effort.

The governors' altercations with the Richmond government over local defense were a symptom of the states' intimate involvement with the war effort. But this was only one of the many problems the states faced and, on the whole, grappled with effectively. Further, many of the actions of the powerful and vigorous Confederate government, as well as its inactions, caused anxiety among the people, who looked to their state government for relief or protection.

Governor Vance, for example, faced a difficult problem in maintaining morale in North Carolina. Individual liberty was very important in the minds of white North Carolinians. "They believed," Marc W. Kruman wrote, "that the white man who was deprived of his liberties was just as much a slave as the black bondsman. Black slavery was only the most extreme example of the condition of slavery." "If checks were not placed on the power of rulers," Kruman continued, "they would concentrate power in their hands and use it to destroy the liberties of the people. Therefore, the people needed specific safeguards for their liberties. First, they demanded that civil power always be supreme over military power. . . . The strength of the military necessarily increased during wartime. . . . Therefore, Conservatives argued that it was 'necessary to hold in check that propensity which war is always likely to bring forth.' " "A strong state government," North Carolinians believed, constituted "the second safeguard of the people's liberties. It could serve as a buffer."

Regardless of their political persuasion, North Carolinians resisted conscription, Kruman noted, because they rightly believed that their state already had provided more than its share of soldiers. But "more important . . . was the fear that conscription represented the first step toward military despotism," a fear the Confederate Congress also aroused when it authorized the suspension of habeas corpus and Davis issued a series of implementing proclamations. With the subsequent arrest of some North Carolinians, Tar Heels developed "apprehension about the independence of the state's judiciary."

These fears, plus the cumbersome and unpopular substitute laws, also contributed to a growing uneasiness on the part of North Carolinians that led many of them to issue calls for a convention to allow the state to "act in her sovereign capacity to defend herself." But the crux of Kruman's case stresses that historians have been incorrect in seeing the movement as an effort to achieve a reconstruction of the Union. The evidence, he says, indicates the contrary, that "many Conservatives were trying to extricate themselves from an almost inextricable situation. They wanted to protect their freedom and seek an honorable peace, *but in the Confederacy.*"

In his essay "Jefferson Davis and the Political Factors in Confederate Defeat," in *Why the North Won,* David Potter pointed out the significance of an important political difference between the problems of Lincoln and Davis. Supposing that long years in a sectional minority protecting slavery with "legalistic safeguards . . . may have impaired the capacity for affirmative and imaginative action on the part of the Southern leaders generally," Potter suggests "that the Confederacy may have suffered real and direct damage from the fact that its political organization lacked a two-party system" to give legitimacy to opposition. Political parties channeled discontent and new ideas in the American system, but without parties the Confederacy lacked an institutionalized way to influence policy from outside the government. Not surprisingly, men such as Governor Vance resorted to states'-rights tactics—what other avenues of protest lay open to them?

Arthur Schlesinger, Sr., long ago pointed out that almost every state had used state sovereignty at one time or another to protect its interests, employing the theory as a political shelter; nevertheless, he believed the argument "artificial," somewhat like the shelter "that a Western pioneer seeks . . . when a tornado is raging." Lewis O. Saum observed that "as is the case with aspirin for a headache, a state rights position is taken at need, and a shelter makes sense when a tornado threatens." In the same way, states' rights made sense to Vance and others facing similar problems.

Time and again the Confederate government overruled state objections to violation of states'-rights principles; if the states had been getting their way, they would not have had so much complaint to voice. States'-rights protesters had very little success, which caused controversy unless their immediate goals coincided with those of the Confederacy. The frequency of their objections indicated frustration rather than disruption. For example, except for the coastal areas, North Carolina was relatively safe and undisturbed for most of the war. It was, however, "more susceptible to the demands of the Confederate government than other states." Thus three states, including North Carolina, paid two-thirds of the levy under the tax-in-kind and made other contributions in like measure. And though Vance and Governor Joseph Brown of Georgia appear to be the most notable obstructionists in Owsley's reckoning, we should remember that their states nevertheless gave generously to the Confederate war effort. The *Official Records* indicate, for example, that Georgia and North Carolina together furnished about 42 percent of the conscripts and volunteers from east of the Mississippi River after the passage of the original draft law of April 1862.

The negotiations and the revealing manpower figures may provide a key to the proper understanding of the Confederate war effort. How can one accuse Georgia and North Carolina of damaging the war effort when they contributed so much to it? Indeed, there is good reason to believe that the states'-rights controversy did not constitute a net loss to the Confederacy and that it was, on balance, an asset. Far from damaging Confederate staying power or subtracting from Confederate will, states' rights put into action was very likely an important reason why power and will lasted as long as they did.

Governor Vance stands out as a good example of the positive aspects of states'-rights theory and practice, for he interposed himself between the state and central governments in an effort to mitigate the more dire re-calcitrance that might otherwise have resulted in North Carolina. A well-liked pro-Union politician before the war, Vance was elected governor of North Carolina in September 1862 while serving as a colonel in the army. The Confederate party, which he ousted, had proved unpopular because of the early reverses at Hatteras and Roanoke Island and wide-spread objections to secession in the first place. Vance received his nomi-nation from the Conservatives, mostly former Union Whigs, led by William W. Holden, a Raleigh newspaper editor who had remained a Unionist until the Fort Sumter incident and who then had become a secessionist. But by 1862 Holden had lost his enthusiasm for the cause. He apparently hoped to achieve control of the North Carolina govern-ment through Vance and then move toward a separate peace. But Holden clearly misjudged Colonel Vance. To the great surprise of some of his supporters, Vance not only promised to support the war but actually did so.

The circumstances of his election as a protest candidate, however, plus his contentious nature, labeled Vance as an obstructionist through the remainder of the war—and much of the historiography that followed. To the extent that Vance did not willingly follow Davis's lead, he was indeed an obstructionist, at least from the point of view of the Confederate gov-ernment. But, as Clement Eaton has pointed out, Vance, and Joseph E. Brown as well, was under tremendous pressures from constituents, most of whom in Vance's case had not been original secessionists and many of whom were thoroughly tired of the war and the hardships it brought them. One constituent asserted his confidence that Vance would defend the state, "that is, that you will do all in your *power to cause the Confederate Govemt* to do it, for it is the duty of the *Confederate Govemt* to do it—We have done our duty as a State—and as a State we should be equally defended."

In recent investigations of the specific issues of conscription, exemp-tion, salt production, impressment, and shipping regulations as matters of dispute between the governor of North Carolina and President Davis,

David Scarboro discovered that time and again "the Confederacy made concessions when Governor Vance was able to persuade the administration that to do so would either be of practical advantage to the war effort or would be politically expedient. Where he failed to do this, the state's claim usually received short shrift." And whenever "Davis refused to offer any concessions the governor backed down."

If Jefferson Davis thought Vance was a problem, he should have paused to consider what William W. Holden or someone like him would have done to the relationship between the president and the governor. Thus governors like Vance headed off and to some extent pacified more serious internal discontent than they created. The proof came, in Vance's case, when the man who originally had promoted his candidacy became so dissatisfied with Vance that he ran against him in 1864 as leader of a faction of antiwar activists within the Conservative party. Vance beat Holden and his peace platform by a four-to-one majority, saving Davis much greater trouble.

Paul D. Escott recently looked afresh at the states'-rights thesis, among other issues, in his *After Secession: Jefferson Davis and the Failure of Southern Nationalism.* Confederates wrestled mightily over the definition and form of their political values and goals. Davis, though undoubtedly a states'-rightist, did not believe his position was incompatible with support of an operative federalism or with the existence of a strong central government. Although Davis had to struggle against those who disagreed, Escott contends that "on the whole he won," but "the victory was not without cost." For example, Davis lost some of the support he previously enjoyed from states'-rights advocates among the planter class, and these became opponents.

But the significant point is that the war effort forced Davis and his government to face problems that transcended any that even the United States had dealt with in the past. There never had existed the "unified national army under central direction" that the South needed and created. Not unnaturally, the state governors balked from time to time at some of the centrally directed military operations and maneuvers. But did they thereby necessarily undermine the war effort? Escott thinks not and proceeds to argue his case by explaining just how much revolutionary centralization did take place despite protests.

Richard D. Brown has addressed the problem of states' rights in his provocative work on modernization. He noted that "secessionists rejected the idea of national uniformity, celebrating instead state and local sovereignty. In their rhetoric, uniformity became a monster." They looked backward "to an earlier, more traditional republicanism." In the North, on the other hand, men believed that "national uniformity . . . required enforcement at gunpoint." In the generation before the war, the North was "propelled . . . further toward modernity," while the South moved "toward a fuller commitment to a traditional outlook." And yet, as Brown explains, "the war was a modernizer of immense proportions for both sides. . . . Both North and South took long steps toward integrating local and supralocal experience." One of these steps, in the Confederacy, led to changes in the labor system, as southerners hired slaves for use in newly developing industries. Indeed, the entire course of Confederate economic change illustrates Brown's point. The government industrial establishments and the control over private producers, which did so much to support the Confederate war effort, so impressed Louise B. Hill in the 1930s that she labeled the result "state socialism."

Even though this industrialization had a narrow base and depended on the Confederate war effort for its market, it reflects a vigor and resource much at variance with the traditional image of a government trammeled by states' rights. Although it would be extreme to claim that the Confederacy developed the value system and habits of mind of northern industrialization, it would not be too much to say that some individual southerners did and that further industrial development and modernization would have occurred if the South had won the war.

With the tremendous growth of control over the economy, nationalization of industry took place in conjunction with exploitation of free and slave labor and with the practice, when necessary, of impressing needed supplies from farmers, producers, or owners. A special bureaucracy reached into each state to regulate the process. This system, too, caused discontent among the governors and citizens. Manufactured goods such as wagons or harnesses, slave labor, and food and forage were the items most frequently impressed. Farmers always claimed they received too little for the goods government agents forced them to give up, and the agents suspected each farmer of being a speculator who thought more of his pocketbook than of the welfare of the army. Protests were voiced in Georgia and North Carolina, as one might expect, but also in other states.

Despite his troubles with Governors Brown and Vance, Davis managed to win most of his struggles with the internal governmental structure on both the national and state levels. Conscription is a major case in point: a revolutionary principle, it met test after test in many of the state courts. Although Davis doubtless felt much apprehension while the deliberations proceeded, even the Georgia supreme court ruled that the draft was constitutional, whereas the Pennsylvania supreme court rejected the Union draft as unconstitutional. But not only "as he predicted" did Davis win "all his court tests," the decisions also met with hearty popular approval, indicating, Escott correctly perceived, that "Davis did not stand alone against his critics."

In his chapter "The Debate over Centralization," Escott also claimed that states' rights constitute something of a red herring. As Thomas B. Alexander and Richard E. Beringer have shown with respect to Confederate congressmen, Escott asserts even more broadly that typically officials at any level of government "took many limitations of states' rights in stride and reacted strongly only when many constituents were involved." Rather than being a malignant disease that brought about the Confederacy's downfall, states' rights, Escott concludes, "became a useful tool for any politician who wanted to rise on the falling fortunes of the South." Manifestations of opposition to the Confederacy on the grounds of violated states' rights thus constituted a safety valve for anger fed by resentment, discontent, and fear of ultimate failure by the government. We are reminded of Lewis O. Saum's argument that just as storm cellars and aspirin have their proper emergency uses, so, too, does states' rights.

Clearly, states' rights failed substantially to inhibit Confederate development of "organizational" nationalism, that is, centralized control and uniformity. State's rights did not hamper economic control and mobilization any more than it restrained such military nationalism as conscription. And state action in raising troops, throughout the war as well as initially, contributed more to the Confederate war effort than it subtracted.

In his chapter "Leadership and Loyalty—Jefferson Davis, Joseph E. Brown, and the Common People," Escott builds part of his argument for *After Secession* upon the excellent doctoral dissertation by a former Frank Vandiver student, John Brawner Robbins. Indeed, Escott proclaims Robbins's dissertation as "a necessary corrective to the view that states' rights caused the defeat of the Confederacy." Escott reasons that "for the first time in their experience," during the Civil War "the yeomen became dependent upon government," and, "although strident opposition to

Davis' policies arose, on the whole people accepted his leadership and the government's assumption of major new powers"; moreover, "many southerners [even] wanted the central government to go further and undertake more responsibilities than it already had."

Owsley attempted to underpin his states'-rights thesis with allusions both to the Confederacy's halfhearted and intermittent suspension of the writ of habeas corpus and to the resistance and resentment manifested when it was suspended. Robbins devotes an entire chapter to the subject. At the outset it is necessary, Robbins observes, to realize how zealously southerners "guarded against any undue intrusion in their life by the national government." Davis "framed his program of Confederate nationalism in consideration of . . . [the] traditions" highly valued by southerners, "constitutional guarantees of law and liberty," which induced them "to be extremely sensitive to any threat of arbitrary arrests or martial law."

The debates of September 1862 "demonstrated that the opposition to suspension of habeas corpus sprang from a concern to maintain civil authority and from a desire to subordinate the military to civilian government." "As a constitutionalist, Davis naturally sought a constitutional solution" and thus believed that he should ask Congress for each specific granting of suspension. Congress failed to grant Davis as much power to suspend the writ as he had requested, but the contention that the reason for this denial was congressional respect for states' rights, as Owsley testified, "is even more questionable" than the idea "that the failure to gain this power substantially altered the course of the war." Owsley argued this point in *State Rights*, but as Robbins noted, quoting from William M. Robinson, *Justice in Grey: A History of the Judicial System of the Confederate States of America,* "There is ample evidence that the army did not permit itself to be wholly checkmated in the handling of disloyal and suspect cases simply because it was denied the more effective modes of dealing with them under martial law."

Even members of Congress who so firmly espoused states'-rights doctrines that they hesitated to allow measures to pass that unduly strengthened the central government often tended to see the necessity of conscription and reasoned it to be "within Congress' constitutional power to pass the law." Most states'-rights congressmen objected to the conscript law primarily because of the form it took; rather than rejecting the idea of compulsory service out of hand, they made alternate proposals.

That the Union long delayed conscription, continuing instead to rely on states to raise troops, seriously diminished the effectiveness of her armies. Whereas Confederate conscripts usually reinforced existing veteran units, most northern states formed their recently enlisted soldiers into new companies, so their veteran units shrank in size and freshly raised regiments, often composed almost exclusively of green men, were sent into battle. A year or more was needed for these novices to acquire the effectiveness of the comparable Confederate organization in which veterans and conscripts were integrated. Thus state prerogatives in the North reduced the Union army's combat effectiveness while national action in the South maintained the quality of the Confederate land forces. But Congress's provision assigning draftees to companies from their own state undoubtedly eased the conscripts' integration into their units.

Giving serious consideration to the common folk's support of the Confederacy, Paul Escott states that, although "ideology meant less" to the masses, it does not follow that they felt markedly different from either their elected leaders or the upper classes. "Their prime need," Escott continued, "was immediate economic assistance, and they did not hesitate to seek or accept it whenever it was offered. Indeed," he asserts, "a majority of the common people may have welcomed and even desired an aggressive expansion of the central government's role."

The masses complained variously about shortages, the substitute law, the law exempting the overseers of twenty or more slaves, and inflation. Davis was not unaware of nor insensitive to these problems, but he took no action to solve them because, as Escott pointed out, of "the continual atmosphere of military crisis. Often . . . the pressing needs of the army . . . aggravated the problems of the poor." But "without the support of the common people the Confederacy could not survive," and as the war went on, the central government failed to fulfill their requirements.

Many families throughout the South were left destitute by the enlistment or conscription of their menfolk. Certainly the soldier's pay did not suffice, with inflation escalating prices, particularly for salt, an absolute necessity in that era. But the Confederate government did a great deal to solve or at least to alleviate its salt-supply problems. A vast array of supportive officials evolved to help with coordination and distribution, and through government efforts salt was often "parceled out to the families according to need, with preference given to indigent soldiers' families."

Escott found much support in North Carolina for the effects of destitution on the morale and will of the people. In that state 20 to 40 percent of the home-front population needed food and poor relief. "Eventually," wrote Escott, "both state government and the Confederacy became involved in relief efforts, but the evidence leaves little doubt that they were not equal to the challenge."

Frank Owsley observed that the operation of the conscription act and its exemptions also caused hard feelings and reinforced the discontent fostered by enemy action and economic deprivation. He stressed the effect of hardship on the home front on soldiers, believing that men deserted when they "received letters from home, depicting such terrible conditions and at the same time telling of able-bodied speculators who should have been in the army." The results, as he poignantly put it, were that "the morning sun often shown upon an empty tent, the former occupant of which was far on his way back home, presenting his cocked musket as a furlough, to any who questioned his going."

Stanley Lebergott agrees with Owsley's interpretation and quotes with approval General Joseph E. Johnston's belief that in "the last year of the war a soldier's pay 'would scarcely buy one meal for his family. . . . Soldiers of the laboring class were compelled to choose between their military service and . . . their duties to their wives and children. They . . . left the army and returned . . . to support their families.'" Impressment of supplies, Lebergott adds, "concentrated on the easiest targets—farms run by soldiers' wives, who," Johnston argued, "'wrote that it was necessary that he [the soldier] return to save them from suffering and starvation. Such summons . . . was never unheeded.'"

The privation and sense of injustice on the home front exercised a tremendous attraction to draw men from the ranks. But for the first three years of the war, soldiers resisted this call surprisingly well. The activities of the state governments must have provided one cause for their persistence with the colors.

In the absence of sufficient aid from the Confederate government, the states were the logical agencies to step into the gap and provide succor to the suffering families of private soldiers and poor folk. Charles W. Ramsdell's classic study *Behind the Lines in the Southern Confederacy* provides a thumbnail sketch of the myriad activities that the states undertook to relieve the trying condition of their people. These steps "involved an unprecedented extension of political authority and control," Ramsdell believed, and he pointed to the record. In 1863, for example, Mississippi appropriated $.5 million to relieve the families of poor soldiers, and

North Carolina spent $1.5 million. Georgia allocated $2.5 million for direct relief, $.5 million for salt, $100,000 for cotton and wool cards, and $6 million for "indigent dependents." Louisiana set aside $5 million for pensions, and Alabama appropriated $4 million for destitute families of soldiers. Early relief efforts had often been under local control, but by 1864 the states had taken over most of the task "in the interest of greater efficiency and a more equal distribution of the burden," and both taxes and grants made from those taxes began to be levied and distributed in kind instead of in cash because of the difficulties with the currency.

In all of this activity, no state stood ahead of Georgia. Her governor, Joseph E. Brown, was in the forefront of governors resisting policies of the Richmond government, and he led his state to a similar premier position in its activities related to the war effort. Much of the state's energy went to aid the poor, especially those dependent on the fighting men, as Paul Escott has clearly shown in his 1979 Southern Historical Association paper, "Serving Two Masters: The Political Acumen of Georgia's Joseph E. Brown."

Governor Brown also deplored the raising of large quantities of cotton, a misallocation of resources, as Stanley Lebergott has shown, resulting from planters looking to their own pecuniary gain rather than the needs of a war economy. The governor tried to restrict the growing of cotton to concentrate production on the foodstuffs needed by the common people. With the same objective he "waged a relentless war on distilleries" to conserve grain for human consumption.

The state of Georgia, for example, arranged for its own stocks of salt, which it supplied free or at low cost to the poor. But "soldiers' wives and widows and the parents of dead soldiers" had priority in this distribution. Governor Brown also advocated many other measures to aid the fighting men, including tax exemptions for the poorer soldiers and a one-hundred-dollar payment for the family of each of these men in the armed forces. The state also provided food to the indigent, including more than one hundred thousand bushels of corn in 1864.

In turning the "state government into an effective relief agency," Brown and the legislature raised taxes and enlarged the budget tremendously, spending in 1863 an amount in excess of all state appropriations for the decade of the 1850s. Inflation accounted for some, but far from all, of this increase. Most of the budget went for welfare and military expenses.

In addition to raising armed forces to protect the state, Georgia did much for the war effort by assisting its men in the Confederate army. To meet their needs the state purchased at home and abroad such necessities as blankets, clothing, and medicine, eventually chartering ships that ran the blockade with state-owned cotton and returned with goods for the state. The governor could point with pride in 1864 to the appropriation of "$10,000,000 to feed and clothe the suffering wives, and widows, and orphans, and soldiers, and to put shoes upon the feet and clothes upon the backs of soldiers themselves, who are often destitute."

By 1864 Georgia's military expenses accounted for over 43 percent of state expenditures and welfare activities for over 51 percent. Although counties equipped volunteers, the bulk of their increased outlays went for welfare. The motive behind this public spending and support of soldiers' families was the desire to diminish desertion. Fearing that if the soldiers became "demoralized," defeat would result, Governor Brown said: "Let our soldiers know that their loved ones at home are provided for." Thus more than half of the state's war-related expenditures went for welfare and even more of the counties' outlays. Of course, soldiers also received direct aid from the state government.

Georgia helped pay for these expenditures by borrowing, reducing nonmilitary costs, and levying a progressive income tax that helped shift the tax base from proportional to progressive and redistributed purchasing power. Brown believed that because the "poor have generally paid their part of the cost of this war in military service, exposure, fatigue and blood, the rich, who have been in a much greater degree exempt from these, should meet the money demands of the Government." Brown intended that Georgia's wealth would be taxed as heavily as necessary to provide for the needs of the soldiers and their families.

On balance, Georgia's contributions toward winning the war seem to have greatly exceeded the losses resulting from obstruction and keeping more men out of Confederate service than necessity probably warranted. And if Georgia's attempts, like its obstruction, surpassed the norm for the other Confederate states, still its contributions show what other states did in a lesser degree to support the home front as well as local defense and the armies. Meanwhile, the central government was not without a share of compassionate and sensitive officials who did their individual bits to provide relief for some segments of the populace.

Thus the common folk, the backbone of the South, felt tremendous deprivation, and, though the Confederate government tried at several levels to alleviate the situation, its efforts proved inadequate to meet their needs. Georgia's spectacular example of state aid endeared the governor to the common folk, for the "southern yeomen were not as ideological as the planter class and they supported Brown not because he was fighting for states' rights but because he was standing up for their interests." As Escott notes elsewhere, "Many states rights controversies in the latter part of the war actually had their origin in welfare." In their "simple desire to relieve their hard-pressed citizens," he concluded, "state leaders found themselves opposing the programs of the central government." Because Brown, Vance, and some other governors achieved a measure of success in meeting the welfare needs of their constituents, the war effort was strengthened, not undermined, and the positive aspects of states' rights became more apparent.

Meanwhile, conscription, adopted by the Confederacy more than a year before the Union enacted a comparable measure, proved effective. This policy helps explain why the Confederacy mobilized a higher percentage of its total population, slave and free, than did the North and, unlike the North, maintained its strength in a way that did not dilute its combat effectiveness. The Confederacy supplied and equipped these large armies and kept its railroads going, albeit with steadily declining efficiency. The Confederate Constitution was strong enough to sanction these effective war measures. And even when there were manifestations of states'-rights-motivated resistance to government practices, their impact was not serious, much less devastating. Though the national military effort circumscribed state activity, it did not impair the vigor of the state governments, which still could and did make many valuable contributions that directly and indirectly aided the war effort.

Chapter Nine

Union Concentration
in Time and Space

CONFEDERATE MORALE, helped by the efforts of the states but not sustained by a deep nationalism, demanded the support of victories in battles and full success in repelling Yankee invasions. And, with its morale more beset than the Union's by the hardships of inflation and, uniquely, by those induced by blockade and impaired railways, the Confederate home front depended more on military success.

In the spring of 1862 the Union armies of Halleck and McClellan had made simultaneous advances (concentration of forces in time, as Clausewitz called them). After repelling the fortuitously concurrent diversions of Lee into Maryland and of Bragg and Kirby Smith in the West in the fall of 1862, Halleck and Lincoln planned a new coordinated offensive. Simultaneous advances seemed particularly important because Halleck and the president were convinced that Confederate use of interior lines had caused Union defeats. Many Union soldiers falsely believed, for example, that reinforcements from Beauregard in Mississippi had fought with Lee in the Seven Days' Battles. But the South did not need to have interior lines of operations, that is, to have better railroad interconnections than the North had, to move troops from a quiet theater to reinforce a menaced army. Surprise could substitute for interior lines. The Confederates had already made vigorous and intelligent use of their railroads in the First Manassas, Seven Days', Shiloh, and Kentucky campaigns.

Lincoln and Halleck again wisely applied the principle of concentration in time, that is, simultaneous advances, in the fall of 1862. But the excellent fall campaigning season had almost passed before any army marched. In late October McClellan finally began to move his Army of the Potomac forward. But immediately after the fall elections of 1862, Lincoln replaced McClellan, the cautious Democratic idol, with the experienced and successful but inept Ambrose E. Burnside. Burnside at once began for the first time the straightforward fighting advance so ardently desired by such combative civilians as Secretary of War Edwin M. Stanton. Lee originally had surmised that the federals again would use McClellan's Peninsular strategy and advance south of the James River. By early November the shape of events was becoming clearer. Soon Lee became certain that the Union objective was Fredericksburg, and on November 22 he informed Richmond that Burnside's forces had arrived on the opposite side of the Rappahannock at Fredericksburg.

Attempting to continue his direct advance on Richmond, Burnside met Lee's army on December 13, 1862, in a most disadvantageous position for Union fortunes. Apparently believing he faced only one wing of Lee's forces, he actually attacked all of Lee's army, head-on. Burnside lost about 12,500 men compared to only 5,300 for the Confederates. This Union frontal attack, like that of Pope against Jackson's corps at Second Manassas, failed utterly.

Burnside's attack was the first conflict in the Union's simultaneous advances scheduled for December 1862. The second took place in Tennessee. Here, too, Lincoln had changed generals, replacing Don Carlos Buell because the victor of Perryville, like McClellan, seemed addicted to overly thorough preparations. The new commander was the competent William S. Rosecrans, who, like Burnside, had achieved success in an independent command. Rosecrans also believed in thorough preparation, but he had ample justification in taking such pains in view of the interruption of the Louisville and Nashville Railroad by Confederate raiders and guerrillas.

Like Burnside, Rosecrans believed in the possibility of a decisive, essentially frontal battle. At the end of December he advanced directly on Bragg's army at Murfreesboro. The Confederates were expecting the move and the impending battle. Bragg attacked first, pushing back Rosecrans's men but not driving the army from its position. After several days with the armies facing each other, Bragg lost his nerve, concluded that he had lost the battle, and retreated. The armies remained unshaken by the immense losses in this hard-fought battle, proving again—as if proof were still needed—that Civil War armies could not be destroyed. Each side lost about twelve thousand men, 31 percent of the Union army and 33 percent of the Confederate. Bragg fell back thirty-six miles to the next town on the railroad, where he took up a position he would hold for the next half year. Rosencrans made no effort to pursue Bragg's unshaken, veteran army.

Of Lincoln and Halleck's three concentrated, simultaneous advances planned for December 1862, one had failed completely in Virginia, a second had only accidental and dubious success in Middle Tennessee, and the third, along the Mississippi River, seemed to be as unrewarding as the campaign in Virginia, though less bloody. Grant's campaign against Vicksburg had preceded Rosecrans's costly but modest victory, and it seemed to lead to no positive results. Strongly reinforced for a push down the Mississippi to capture the Confederate stronghold, Grant determined on dual advances. One force, under William T. Sherman, would move on the river; the other, under Grant, would advance along the railroad toward the rear of Vicksburg's river-oriented defense. Grant thought these two forces would support each other and that his own would turn Vicksburg's defense by cutting the railroad to Jackson.

The offensive proved a dismal failure. Grant had to abandon his advance in mid-December when a raid by Confederate cavalry destroyed his depot at Holly Springs, even capturing Mrs. Grant's horses and burning her carriage; another raiding force had broken his railroad farther north at Jackson, Tennessee. Cut off from reliable communication with his base, Grant fell back. Sherman also retreated, for his waterborne attack failed in the rugged and fortified terrain north of Vicksburg, when, on December 29, 1862, his force of 25,000 lost 1,776 men in an unsuccessful assault at Chickasaw Bluffs.

The events of late 1862 and early 1863 caused a temporary rise in Confederate morale, and Bragg initially had reported the Battle of Murfreesboro as a victory. Early in the new year, Secretary of War James A. Seddon reported to Davis that the army was "fully equal, if not superior, in all the elements of strength to what it has been at any previous period in the war." Pointing to the disasters of early 1862, Seddon summed up the year as one in which the armies were "not conquered, or repelled, but diminished by their own successes"; the salvation of the Confederacy lay in the valor of its army and more particularly in the Conscription Act. The results, said Seddon, could be seen in the victory at Fredericksburg, from which the Union army had "slunk away amid storm and darkness"; the "gallant repulse" of the Union's combined action at Vicksburg; and, writing before he learned of Bragg's retreat, the "decided victory" of General Bragg at Murfreesboro.

John Beauchamp Jones, the rebel war clerk, gloated over the recent news and purred to his diary that it affected "the spirits of the people . . . and we have a merrier Christmas than the last one." The initial news of a victory at Murfreesboro was so good, said Jones, it "caused even enemies to pause and shake hands in the street." This resurgence of Confederate will was even visible to the North. William T. Sherman, once again before Vicksburg in March 1863, informed the governor of Ohio that "the South to-day is more formidable and arrogant than she was two years ago."

In their response to the Union drives, the Confederates, except in Bragg's offensive battle, had adhered to Clausewitz's prescription for the defense. Lee had not avoided conflict, but his very strong position at Fredericksburg had made the attrition of his victory favorable to the Confederacy. Sherman's defeat at Chickasaw Bluffs had the same effect, and the Confederate commanders had stopped Grant's advance exclusively with raids against rail communications and Grant's "great depot of provisions and munitions," as Jomini would have called it.

Confederate communications ran through friendly country, and their forces were not usually short of supplies because, as Clausewitz would have anticipated, they had "been able to stockpile in advance." The larger size of the Union armies proved a handicap, for "an army's dependence on its base increases in intensity and scale with any increase in the army's size." But again this condition bore more heavily on the larger Union army, which, being "in enemy territory," had fewer communication routes and was able to rely only on the "roads on which it advanced in the first place." It must improve its "essential lines of communication" by installing "its own administration and must do this by the authority of its arms." This meant establishing garrisons throughout occupied territory to enforce its authority against the hostile populace and protect its communications, "everywhere exposed to attacks by an insurgent population." Jomini agreed, noting that in his rear the invader "holds scarcely any ground but that upon which he encamps; outside the limits of his camp everything is hostile and multiplies a thousandfold the difficulties he meets at every step of the way."

General William T. Sherman experienced in West Tennessee and northern Mississippi exactly what Jomini described, and in many other occupied areas the situation was comparable. Sherman found, in a land where "every house is a nest of secret, bitter enemies," that, though Union "armies pass across and through the land, the war closes in behind and leaves the same enemy behind."

The effect of the activities of Confederate cavalry and guerrillas, exploiting the offensive superiority of raiders, is well exhibited in the distribution of Union forces in the early spring of 1863, just as Grant was ready for another advance. His army before Vicksburg numbered thirty-six thousand men; that of his rear area commander, headquartered at Memphis, numbered sixty-two thousand.

Such a commitment of force to protecting the rear further diminished the Union's chances of waging a decisive war, for which Clausewitz had placed exclusive stress on battles: "Battle is the one and only means that warfare can employ" against the enemy for "destroying his armed forces." He did envision the fall of a capital as possibly decisive but only if the capital were very significant and the enemy's armed forces quite weak. As a rule, however, and certainly in the case of the Confederacy, "total victory" over the enemy required the "destruction of his armed forces" with "the occupation of his territory only a consequence."

Yet Clausewitz realized that total conquest attained in this way required sufficient superiority in numbers, skill, and morale and an adequate ratio of force to space. If these were not available, Clausewitz would have expounded no means of attaining any victory adequate to the Union's total political objective. Nevertheless, he did occasionally allude to another method of winning, and this method the Union implicitly pursued. He realized that "the fighting forces are meant to protect their own territory and to seize the enemy's: it is the territory, on the other hand, that sustains them and keeps restoring their strength." He thus recognized the Union's implicit logistic strategy in which an invading army's capture of part of the enemy's "territory and resources" would "reduce his national resources" and place time on the invader's side. "If the conquered areas are important enough, and if there are places in them vital to the areas still in enemy hands, the rot will spread, like a cancer, by itself; and if only that and nothing else happens, the conqueror may well enjoy the net advantage. Time alone will then complete the work" because the enemy's armed forces gradually would weaken.

In pursuit of their strategy, Lincoln and Halleck gave priority to the

West, reinforcing Kentucky with a corps from Virginia but stressing the Mississippi by increasing Grant's strength and also directing an expedition from New Orleans up the river. Just as Lincoln had early grasped the significance of concentration in space and time, so the president soon understood the other elements of strategy and comprehended the constraints of logistics. After he had abandoned the popular notion that big battles which destroyed armies typically decided wars, his views fully harmonized with those of Halleck and other professional soldiers. He and Halleck made an excellent team, with the general in chief able to draw on a good headquarters staff to coordinate the operations of the many armies and departments. Lincoln was left with the task of keeping at bay the less sophisticated public and the strident critics of the administration and of generals educated at West Point. This he did with skill, as well as seeking to reconcile the often-conflicting military and political requirements.

Lincoln and Halleck also devoted much of their intellectual energy to solving the problem of operations in Virginia. They did not believe that a siege of Richmond would inevitably succeed; rather, they saw a siege as presenting the well-entrenched Confederates with an opportunity to economize on men in the defensive, enabling them to spare troops to reinforce other armies or to use the Shenandoah Valley to threaten a raid across the Potomac.

Thus Lincoln and Halleck decided to change their objective. They would no longer attempt to reach Richmond but would use the Army of the Potomac to keep Lee well away from Washington and wait for him to make a mistake that would permit the Army of the Potomac to attack him with advantage and hurt his army. They looked to the West, particularly to Grant, for their important achievements.

Davis, lacking a general in chief or a strong headquarters staff, wisely decentralized through four regional commands: Lee in Virginia and North Carolina; Beauregard in South Carolina, Georgia, and Florida; Joseph E. Johnston in Tennessee, Alabama, and Mississippi; and Kirby Smith in the trans-Mississippi. This command organization gave these senior and experienced generals substantial forces coupled with maximum autonomy in their employment and placed on Davis and his headquarters minimal demands for strategic intervention from Richmond. After November 1862 Davis relied heavily on his capable new secretary of war, James A. Seddon, a planter and former congressman, who had quickly acquired a firm grasp of the essentials of strategy and logistics.

Because of his diversified military background, Davis started far ahead of Lincoln in military understanding and always took a more active part in directing military operations. He did not give political questions and public opinion the same attention as did the Union president, in part because he lacked the same talent and inclination. He also had less time for nonmilitary duties because, except for Lee's brief period in Richmond in charge of military operations, Davis had no collaborator who matched Halleck in stature and as a strategist and manager.

In Virginia a new man headed the Army of the Potomac, Joseph Hooker, one of Burnside's subordinates and a capable corps commander who had actively sought the post. Joe Hooker has been aptly characterized as a hard-boiled soldier. In the last few days of April 1863, Hooker took the offensive against Lee, trying to turn his left flank, reach his rear, and compel him to attack to recover his communications. Hooker picked an opportune time to attack, when a major part of Lee's army was in southeastern Virginia, principally to relieve Lee's critical supply situation along the Rappahannock. Lee, concerned to preserve his communications with the fertile Shenandoah Valley, posted himself to protect the Virginia Central Railroad, also covering as much of the subsistence area north of Richmond as possible. These same considerations made him decide to fight rather than retreat.

Hooker employed his two-to-one numerical superiority to force his way across the Rappahannock on April 28–29, 1863, and pierce Lee's defensive line in an advance that turned the Confederate army on the west. Lee, instead of falling back to the North Anna, the next river line, made a determined, skillful, and costly, but successful, effort to hold the line of the Rappahannock. "In such a battle," Clausewitz explained, "the attacker's turning movement, intended to give his attack a better chance and his victory a greater scale, is countered by a subordinate turning movement, which is aimed at that part of the enemy's force that has executed the original envelopment." Lee attempted precisely this maneuver and succeeded in turning Hooker, attacking the turning force in the flank. The demoralized Hooker's retreat back across the river on May 5 signified that he had lost the Battle of Chancellorsville. Lee had held the river line but at frightful cost—12,700 casualties compared to 16,800 for the Union army, 21 percent of his army against 15 percent of Hooker's. Again the armies proved indestructible, and again the stalemate continued.

Meanwhile, to the West, Grant, moving at the same time, at last succeeded in turning Vicksburg and reaching its rear, where he could cut the city's rail communications to Jackson. Abandoning his effort to turn Vicksburg on its northern flank, he had improvised a road and water line of communications on the west bank of the Mississippi and moved south of the city. The navy provided the key to Grant's campaign because on the night of April 16, 1863, it succeeded in conveying quartermaster transports safely below the Vicksburg batteries. The navy thus not only allowed supplies to be moved south of Vicksburg but also provided protection to the transports that ferried Grant's army to the east bank and brought other supplies across from the west bank.

Grant had marched his army southward past Vicksburg on the west side of the river, and the navy had ferried him across, completing the process by April 30. Pushing away the small Confederate force resisting him, Grant then proceeded northeastward. He next moved against Vicksburg's communications, relying on wagon transport from the river for some supplies and on the abundance of that fertile, unforaged region where he campaigned. In the words of the United States Army's 1982 operations manual, which uses this campaign as an example, Grant had "turned the Confederate defenses and put the Union army within reach of the enemy's rear area."

But the Confederates were rushing troops to the scene by rail, and Joseph E. Johnston, the department commander, arrived to assume personal direction of these forces accumulating at Jackson. Faced now by two armies, the far larger one under John C. Pemberton near Vicksburg and a small but growing force under Johnston at Jackson, Grant took advantage of his interior lines. Concentrating against the smaller threat, Grant sent two corps to attack Johnston while he kept the third corps west of Jackson to hold back Pemberton should he advance. The two attacking corps easily took Jackson and pushed Johnston's little force away to the north. Grant then capitalized on his interior line of operations, concentrating two of his corps against Pemberton, while the third, under Sherman, remained temporarily near the Mississippi capital to keep Johnston at bay.

Meanwhile, Grant moved against the inactive Pemberton, defeated and drove him into Vicksburg, and reestablished his connections with his river communications as he surrounded the city. Though President Davis reinforced Johnston with troops from Tennessee and South Carolina, Grant, likewise heavily reinforced by Halleck and Lincoln, remained on the defensive except for one abortive assault on Vicksburg's powerful fortifications. Johnston, too, remained relatively inert, thwarted by lack of a railroad and of enough wagons and daunted by Sherman with a big force on the defensive between him and Vicksburg. Grant had only to wait until Pemberton, trapped against the river obstacle and exhausting his supplies, surrendered thirty thousand men on July 4, 1863.

Grant's turning movement illustrated "the system of rapid and continuous marches," which, Jomini said, "multiplies the effect of an army" and, in seizing interior lines and concentrating his forces first against Johnston and then Pemberton, Grant brilliantly embodied their "successive employment upon points where it may be important to act, to bring superior force to bear upon fractions of the hostile army." Grant had succeeded in his aim "to throw by strategic movements the mass of an army successively upon the decisive points of the theatre of war and also upon the communications of the enemy as much as possible without exposing one's own."

In his analysis of Civil War military operations T. Harry Williams clearly overlooked how closely Grant's Vicksburg masterpiece conformed to Jomini's vision of the strategic turning movement, a concept he had drawn from Napoleon's campaigns. In accord with Clausewitz's judgment as to the rarity of such maneuvers, the Civil War witnessed only two of Jomini's favorites, but Grant executed both of them, at Vicksburg and at Appomattox at the end of the war.

Following the fall of Vicksburg and the withdrawal of Johnston's army east of Jackson, Halleck removed troops from Grant to conquer more of the trans-Mississippi. The concentration against this region, though sound in that Halleck intended for it ultimately to release additional troops for operations in the East, had the effect of presenting the Confederates with no threat on the Mississippi line. The Confederates took advantage of this Union inactivity to give active consideration to a plan long advocated by General Beauregard for concentration against Rosecrans's army, the weakest of the three main Union armies east of the Mississippi. Lincoln and Halleck did not, however, perceive Rosecrans's army as weak. They threatened him with removal from command if he did not make a simultaneous advance against Bragg.

But it was not until the end of June 1863 that Rosecrans at last began his offensive against the weakened Bragg at Tullahoma. Although the federal commander had been obstinate about moving, he proved optimistic once in motion. "Old Rosy" was popular with his troops and, undeceived as to the possibility of a decisive frontal battle, he had an excellent plan to spare them the casualties of another Murfreesboro. Distracting Bragg by a feint to the west, Rosecrans carried all his supplies and marched rapidly, moving his entire army around Bragg's right. Bragg, his communications threatened and facing the likelihood that Rosecrans's army actually might reach his rear, did not attack Rosecrans; instead, he retreated rapidly all the way back to Chattanooga on the south bank of the Tennessee River, where he settled on July 7, 1863. Through his turning movement and without a battle, Rosecrans had, in a little over a week, advanced four times as far as he had after his victory at Murfreesboro. The Union army now stood very close to Chattanooga, where lay heavy industry and railroad connections to Atlanta and Virginia.

Confederates in the East still stood on the defensive, but not for long. Lee's belief that the enemy Army of the Potomac would soon advance again conditioned his planning. Preferring not to defend the Rappahannock line again, apprehensive about being pushed back to a siege at Richmond, and anxious to feed his army at the enemy's expense, Lee decided to anticipate the enemy by employing a defensive turning movement. Although he certainly expected to have to fight a battle if he crossed the Potomac, unconstrained to defend a particular line, he could select a strong position and let Hooker come to attack him. And so in early June 1863, Lee moved into the Shenandoah Valley and northward in a raid that by month's end had carried him across the Potomac and into Pennsylvania.

Lincoln, adhering after Chancellorsville to his and Halleck's belief that the best strategy in Virginia was to wait for an opportunity to catch Lee at a disadvantage, had been content for Hooker to "keep the enemy at bay, and out of other mischief, by menaces and cavalry raids." With Lee crossing into Pennsylvania, they now saw a chance as Hooker followed, keeping east of his adversary. Doubtful of Hooker's ability to take advantage of the opportunity to hurt Lee, Lincoln and Halleck selected a new commander, George G. Meade. Against the wily and cautious Meade, Lee would have to attack or withdraw because he could not remain concentrated in the immediate presence of Meade's army and still forage enough to feed his men and animals. Lee could not tarry; Meade, close to a railroad and in friendly territory, could.

Lee anticipated this necessity by concentrating against and assailing a fragment of Meade's army. Each side then rushed men to Gettysburg until both armies were fully concentrated by the end of the second day of battle. Lee had more than seventy thousand and Meade at least eighty-five thousand effectives. On the offensive, the Confederates had pushed back the Union forces, but the federals did not retreat far. On the third day the two armies faced each other when Lee, uncharacteristically, made a frontal attack that failed disastrously.

The Battle of Gettysburg, July 1–3, 1863, cost the Confederates twenty-eight thousand men, more in three days than in all of Lee's previous purely offensive conflicts, the Seven Days' campaign. His losses amounted to 33 percent of the men available at the outset of the operation. Meade also suffered enormous losses, twenty-three thousand men, but these numbered only 20 percent of the larger body of Unionists available at the beginning of the campaign. On the fourth day, though neither side moved, Lee perceived no choice but to withdraw.

Lee's army was seriously hurt, but it was by no means destroyed. Lincoln, who had regarded the Gettysburg campaign as the long-awaited opportunity to hurt Lee's army, felt terrible frustration at Lee's escape. In his disappointment the president overlooked the successful aspects of the campaign—Lee's army had suffered very serious losses and the strategy of waiting for Lee to make a mistake had worked. Nevertheless, from Lee's point of view the campaign also had enjoyed considerable success. Believing that he would have faced a determined Union effort to cross the Rappahannock, he thought that his Pennsylvania raid had disrupted that campaign. Although he had not remained in Union territory as long as he had hoped, he had for some time supplied his army at the enemy's expense, although not to the degree he had hoped. At least in some measure he had met both of the objectives of the campaign.

If Lincoln was chagrined over the results of the Gettysburg campaign, he felt great satisfaction at the outcome of the concentration on the Mississippi that he and Halleck had engineered. But the Union gains from the opening of the Mississippi were more symbolic and political than militarily substantial. The stalemate only appeared to be broken. The loss of transit between East and West hurt Confederate supply not at all; the two parts of the Confederacy long had been logistically separate.

To Confederates, then, the loss of the Mississippi was largely limited to diminished prestige and a psychological defeat; the enemy had cut their country in half and badly damaged military and civilian morale. True, the Union gained in substance the use of the river for commercial navigation and easy access to the Red River for a possible advance into Louisiana; but the Union also acquired a liability—more territory to be guarded. Instead of Confederate troops protecting Vicksburg, Union troops now had to stand duty there. The Union army had to defend a long frontier between Memphis and Baton Rouge against raiders, and individual snipers could fire on passing steamboats.

The fate of Vicksburg was perhaps inevitable, given Grant's skill and Pemberton's ineptitude. In any event, at Vicksburg and Tullahoma, trouble went out looking for the Confederates. The distressing setback at Gettysburg, however, occurred because Confederates themselves sought trouble, and found it. Passive in Mississippi and Tennessee, they were the active architects of their fate in Pennsylvania. Although in turning Hooker back rather than awaiting his expected advance Lee adopted a shrewd defensive strategy, he overlooked its potential adverse impact on morale. Once Lee reached Pennsylvania, to withdraw without battle would look like a defeat; to give battle and then withdraw would still look like a defeat. Either way, Lee's raid was doomed to be perceived as a defeat by the Confederate public unless he had been able to destroy the Army of the Potomac—a most unlikely eventuality. And morale was seriously affected by the defeats of July 1863, a fact reflected in the fall 1863 elections to the Confederate Congress, when two-thirds of the freshmen selected had been men who opposed secession in the crisis of 1861.

The South had suffered a serious loss of manpower through Lee's heavy casualties in the Battle of Gettysburg and Pemberton's surrender, even though Grant had paroled Pemberton's army. But between June and December 1863 the total manpower on the Confederate rolls declined less than 9,000, from 473,058 to 464,646, a reduction of less than 2 percent. Conscription and volunteering had brought enough new men to the armies almost to make up the losses sustained in the summer and fall campaigning. But the number of men present with their units had decreased from 307,464 to 277,970, a decline of 30,000. This total reflected an increase in the proportion absent from 35 percent to 40 percent and certainly indicates a rise in desertion. These figures reflect discouragement and diminution of the will to continue the struggle. As one young officer informed his father, "The men can't be prevented from deserting when they think there is no prospect ahead for getting home," and he added soberly that "among the deserters are some of the bravest men of our army. . . . Our leaders do not seem to think that the *morale* is as great a portion of an army, as Napoleon thought." Obviously, defeats in the field had severely taxed the Confederacy's flimsy nationalism.

Moreover, military affairs in July 1863 caused Confederates to approach the question of God's support in a new way. As the success of Confederate arms became more elusive, southerners came to ponder God's role in the war, and they concluded that God was punishing or, at the very least, testing them. In time, Confederates would go further than this, concluding that, since victory depended on God's favor, the deteriorating military situation could mean only that God had not smiled on the cause; if this were so, then defeat was inevitable. It was not a cheering prospect.

Chapter Ten

The Battle Is the Lord's

SOUTHERN ARMIES had suffered serious reverses at Vicksburg, Tulla-homa, and Gettysburg in July of 1863, and these in turn had a decided impact upon Confederate civilians' will to win. The loss of control over more of her territory had no particular consequence for the South, or should not have, except insofar as territory was symbolic of a country's ability to maintain its sovereignty over all of its claimed domain. Unfortunately for the South, her people believed that lost territory was more important than in truth it was; accordingly, its loss had a greater negative impact on the country than it should have had, and fear and foreboding stealthily crept in to take over the corners of Confederate hearts and minds, left vacant as morale and will withered away.

As other people have done in times of disaster and stress, many Confederates turned to religion for guidance. Evangelical Christianity had taught them that God operated in human affairs and had assured them that He was on their side—the side, they claimed, of liberty. Thus piety had lent moral strength to the armies, which, like the patriots of 1776, fought not for slavery but against slavery and for liberty. Religion also sustained and magnified the will of the people to see this struggle through to the end.

When victory eluded one's grasp, however, religion showed another face, and Christians both North and South came to wonder whether the war was a punishment or perhaps a trial to test their worthiness. In either case, they could appease God; but if the course of the war was still un-favorable, it would be a sign that God's will was not what Confederates had hoped it was. Reverses such as Vicksburg, Tullahoma, and Gettysburg forced Confederates to reexamine the war and their own consciences, for in July 1863 it was not difficult to conclude that alternative decisions—Union and peace, for example—had attractive features that a long war with an uncertain outcome did not have. And if the South was fighting for liberty, and the means used to fight that war seemed to subvert liberty, why bother to fight at all?

Thus defeatism crept slowly into the hearts of large numbers of Confederates. As they pondered the mysterious ways of the Lord, some of them looked north and saw the massive resources available to the Union cause and wondered whether they had not been tempting fate when they entered the contest. More efficient use of southern resources and the proper strategies could compensate for northern abundance; nevertheless, many Confederates doubtless compared themselves to David taking on Goliath.

This parallel was instructive and comforting, for it would seem to prove that God did not always side with the strongest battalions; rather, He espoused the cause of those who, like David, served the Lord. And, as we have already noted, Confederates liked to believe that they walked rightly with the Lord. The language of Jefferson Davis's early proclamations asking his fellow southerners to celebrate days of humiliation and prayer suggests widespread presumption that the Heavenly Father unquestionably supported the Confederacy. President Davis noted that "it hath pleased Almighty God, the Sovereign Disposer of events, to protect and defend the Confederate States hitherto in their conflict with their enemies, and to be unto them a shield."

But by the middle of the war one reasonably could question the assumption that God wore gray. Although assuredly He still daily entered into human affairs, the *North Carolina Christian Advocate* found no proof "that God had always been on our side, or that he operates *actively*, in this controversy at all." The *Advocate* suggested that God may even have left both sides "to the control of Satan" because of their failure to appreciate "the great blessings He conferred on us under the first revolution." In reply, another religious paper restated the basic suppositions: God never withdraws from a conflict but always chooses one side or the other; the only exception would be "when, in the origin and progress of the war, *each party to the conflict is equally guilty.*" Fortunately for the South, such a situation did not exist in this instance, for the *Fayetteville Presbyterian* concluded that "if God is not for us the Confederacy is in much worse condition than we had ever imagined it to be."

Events had not gone nearly as well as faithful Confederates thought they should have, and these troubled rebels were determined to understand why that had happened. Religiously oriented southerners, which included most of them, believed that they could turn to their Bibles for answers. David had killed the giant Goliath, but the Lord had chosen David. Throughout, the Old Testament drove home the lesson that when Israel remained faithful to God, she prospered; when calamity came upon her, she suffered proper punishment for sin. The prophets repeatedly had emphasized this lesson; they also promised that when God's people returned to their proper allegiance, He would bless them again. So if God's support of the Confederacy seemed not as certain as it once was, the Bible pointed both to the reason and the remedy. Like Israel, Confederates had gone astray; but like the chosen people of old, all would be well if they returned to the fold with rekindled faith in Him.

History had taught its lessons. The southern clergy, says James W. Silver, and, we should add, the laity as well, had "developed an infallible formula. Every Confederate victory proved that God had shielded His chosen people and every defeat became the merited punishment of the same people for their sins." And when faced with defeat, Confederates had not far to look to discover sins that could serve as a ready explanation, including "violation of the Sabbath, intemperance, demagoguery, corruption, luxury, impiety, murmuring, greed and avarice, lewdness, skepticism, 'Epicurean expedience,' private immorality, ill treatment of slaves, profanity, a proud and haughty spirit, speculation, bribery, boastfulness, and the 'sin of all sins,' covetousness." God had smiled at First Manassas, Second Manassas, Fredericksburg, and Chancellorsville, but He had frowned at Gettysburg, Vicksburg, and Tullahoma. After these battles there flowed forth "an avalanche of sermons stressing the sins of the Confederate people."

Thus the events of July 1863 forced Confederates to reassert some of their basic assumptions. The editor of the *Memphis Daily Appeal* (by then published in Atlanta) saw the fall of Vicksburg as "the heaviest blow of the war," and with the news from Gettysburg he confessed that "it is difficult to discover any escape from the present unpleasant dilemma" unless all the people rose up to drive away the enemy—which, of course, they did not do.

But perhaps the people could appease God. A letter in the *Milledgeville Confederate Union* a month after Vicksburg, Gettysburg, and Tullahoma stated the case simply: "We need the favor of God. Without it, we perish. God is angry with us for our sins. Hence the war itself, and hence the reverses of this summer." President Davis led the way. On July 25 he announced "a day of fasting, humiliation, and prayer," appealing to the public "to take home to our hearts and consciences the lessons" taught by recent reverses. "Our successes on land and sea," he warned, have "made us self-confident and forgetful," and "love of lucre [has] eaten like a gangrene into the very heart of the land, converting too many among us into worshippers of gain and rendering them unmindful of their duty . . . to God." Confederates must "receive in humble thankfulness the lesson which he has taught in our recent reverses."

The following fall, after more defeats, but after more victories as well, the states issued proclamations of similar import. Governor Brown of Georgia led the way, declaring a day of fasting, humiliation, and prayer and asking other states to do likewise, in the belief that if God saw "a whole nation on its knees, fasting, in deep humility, and penitential confessions," He would "strike terror and dismay into the hearts of our enemies."

As defeat approached, and God had not vindicated the cause, such logic could lead to only one conclusion: Confederates had not been true to themselves or God, or else God's support would have brought more positive results. The *Raleigh Daily Progress* agreed and urged that the war must end: "We are for peace, because, with an implicit faith in Divine teaching, we believe that the sins of nations as well as of individuals will overtake them, and that God will avenge himself on this American people, if this unnatural, fratricidal butchery is suffered to go on."

With encouragement from the master class, antebellum southern Christianity, distinctly emphasizing Old Testament themes, had helped slaves to accept their bondage; now the wheel had turned, and the same religion helped southern whites accept the possibility of defeat because the victory that would have signaled God's favorable judgment on the Confederacy had proved elusive. The *Daily Lynchburg Virginian* observed: "We dared a revolution, and provoked a war." Southerners thus easily could conclude that "everything now must be sacrificed to success, because anything is preferable to defeat."

But not everyone agreed with the opinions of this anonymous writer because not everyone thought of defeat as the greatest of horrors, and many who did think so did not believe that any and all sacrifices were necessary, or even helpful, in avoiding it. The price of victory, if they could achieve victory, was going to be infinitely higher than most of the Confederates of 1861 had bargained for. As this realization was driven home, the citizenry showed a natural resentment. A Georgia newspaper set the tone: "We are learning by bitter experience," its editor remarked, "that hotspurs and demagogues are unfit to govern a country. Such men brought us into trouble, and seem to be incapable of taking us out. They were suffered to lead the country in 1861, and none of the blessings which they predicted have been realized, while most of the evils apprehended by more considerate men have come to pass."

Clearly, some Confederates felt betrayed. One of these, Governor Vance of North Carolina, agreed substantially. He remarked early in 1864 that, before they tried secession, the people had understood it "as completely as an abstraction could be understood." Angry because in 1861 he and his fellow Unionists had faced a choice between two undesirable alternatives, he reminded North Carolinians that "we were promised it should be peaceable. What is the result? Fie, it has been anything else. It has involved us in a war that has no parallel upon the pages of history."

And the sufferings abounded, reported almost daily by newspapers, private letters, and personal experience. Sometimes impressment officers took more than the people reasonably could give and left them destitute. Other times Confederate irregulars or even regular soldiers committed such outrages on citizens that many plain folk feared them as much as they feared the Yankees. Inflation created devastating inroads into the standard of living of the middle and lower classes, and some citizens who lacked sufficient daily bread thought their more fortunate neighbors delayed in coming to their assistance. These problems, and others, sketched by Charles W. Ramsdell in his thoughtful commentary about life behind the lines, give evidence that despite faith, or perhaps for lack of it, the costs of war were beyond the ability of many Confederates to pay.

The majority of Confederates had very real needs, as Frank Owsley emphasized in a 1926 article, "Defeatism in the Confederacy." He began his exposition by focusing on the up-country regions, where "hope of an ultimate settlement" and "lack of economic interest in slavery and sectionalism" from the first had induced in the populace there either coolness or outright opposition to the Confederacy. Once the war began, however, many of these people had sided with the South because "they disliked 'Yankees' and feared Negro equality . . . and were stung to great anger" by Lincoln's "invasion." Significantly, Owsley thought that "the up-country people could easily fight a ninety-day war . . . but not a war that lasted over several years. Anger and enthusiasm are too transient to serve as a basis of war."

But in his article Owsley did not stress the uncertain bases of Confederate nationalism. Rather, he examined closely the factors that sapped the will to win, seeing the primary cause of the "defeatist psychology" in "the suffering of the soldiers and their families." He noted that "the raids of the enemy and the occupation of the country also added tremendously to the destitution of the people. These raiders frequently left a trail of "robberies, rapes, arsons, and plundering," as well as "depredations of every description, broken open smokehouses and stables and stolen meat, forage and horses" and the "breaking up of furniture." Often this destitution was made more appalling by the terror-stricken women and children fleeing back into the Confederate territory where they were without homes, food, or any means of support save what the charity of others almost as poor might offer."

Experiencing Union destructiveness, as distinguished from reading and hearing about it, influenced few Confederates, for most lived far from the scene of active campaigning. But Owsley does not rely on the direct or indirect effect of enemy action to explain defeatism. He stresses the economic suffering of many citizens, showing that by mid-1863 speculation and rising prices had severely hurt poorer consumers and turned their minds to thoughts of peace; by this date, there were organized tories even in South Carolina.

The Richmond bread riots of April 1863, repeated that spring in Atlanta, Columbus, Salisbury, and High Point and in September in Mobile, bear testimony to real deprivation in the eastern portions of the Confederacy. Even in the countryside disorders erupted because of a shortage of food; the paradox of an agricultural society able to feed and supply its soldiers but not always its citizens was dramatically apparent.

Disaffection caused by the government's inability to meet the citizens' needs contributed to an organized peace movement in the South. Peace societies, Owsley says, "began to show great strength by 1863." "The 'Peace Society' of Alabama," he writes, even "claimed that information furnished by it to the Federal armies resulted in the surrender of Vicksburg and the defeats around Chattanooga." Owsley sketches the problem convincingly. The suffering caused by disorder, destitution, inflation, and inadequate relief had defeated many of the poor up-country people, some of them at an early date, and caused them to withhold their support for the continuation of the war. This "defeatism," Owsley concluded, "had sapped and mined the moral foundations of the South . . . and by 1865 a complete collapse was impending, even had the Confederate army remained undefeated. . . . The will to war had been broken by causes other than military defeat."

Owsley does not directly address the question of the vigor of Confederate nationalism, although he does note its comparative weakness in the up-country region; instead, he stresses the reasons why it decreased and defeatism and the peace movements emerged. Basically, the hardships of a war economy and the almost inevitable inequality among individual contributions to the conflict depressed home-front morale, and this feeling, communicated to the troops, along with the operation of the Conscription Act, helped foster desertion and loss of morale in the armies.

Hardships depleted a morale no longer so well sustained by religion. If many Confederates began to question whether they deserved victory, religion had ceased to provide the same confidence it had supplied two years before. So military defeat not only depressed morale but, by raising a question about God's favor, sapped the support religion had given to morale. And in the absence of strong nationalism and distinctive differences between southerners and the invaders from the North, the South's will to keep on fighting badly needed the support of religion and military success.

What mechanism translated these very real problems and attitudes into a decisive defeatism? It was not simply that morale was undermined but that despite the insurmountable problems apparent to most Confederates by the end of 1863 or early 1864, the war effort continued. Ironically, even as the people's enthusiasm for war diminished, their commitment to it increased.

North Carolina provides a useful microcosm to examine this paradox for, as Owsley observed, it had become one of the major centers of discontent with the war and the Confederate government. It also supplied an exceedingly large number of men and a great deal of matériel to the Confederate army, and not merely because of demographics or geographical location. Governor Vance, a Unionist in 1861, argued toe-to-toe with Davis and resented the war. But he also fought bravely on the battlefield, then administered his state in such a way as to use states'-rights theory to bolster the war effort. Other North Carolina conservatives felt much the same way. All of them, said the *Raleigh Daily Conservative,* "were opposed to the breaking up of the old government." As late as 1864 such men still thought that "to remain in the old government and labor to restore it" would have provided the best way to correct the errors into which the federal government had fallen. Nevertheless, the newspaper advised Confederates to stay with their new government because it was the only one they had and they were sworn to defend it. But this unenthusiastic endorsement shows an utter lack of Confederate nationalism. The editor concluded that the South must fight on, for the enemy stood at the door: "Look steadily at him and drive him from our soil, but never forget that our rulers at home need watching at the same time." What held true for North Carolina, by extension, also held true for any part of the Confederacy afflicted by defeatism.

To most modern Americans these attitudes may not seem paradoxical, but they seemed so to many Confederates. Perhaps the social psychological theory of cognitive dissonance can help to make sense of this strange behavior. The theory sheds some light on the ways people make decisions, why they cling to inappropriate choices, how they reduce tension between urgent courses of action and contradictory reality, and the obstacles they must overcome before eventually they can change decisions. The conservative North Carolinians, for example, provide examples of "the frequent observation that the less rational a reason you had for doing something, the more you will defend and justify the fact that you did it." The theory explains, further, why people act in ways that may seem irrational or self-defeating to today's historians. This approach may help us to understand why Confederates fought to preserve an institution that bothered the consciences of many of them, how casualty lists increased psychological tension, and the way an unsuccessful war and the change of war goals combined with religious views to undermine fatally the Confederate war effort.

Sometimes contradictory or self-defeating behavior results from cognitive dissonance, which we may summarily define as the perception of contradictory information. Dissonant perceptions lead to "psychological discomfort" in decision making, just as hunger leads to physical discomfort. In both instances an individual seeks to reduce discomfort by whatever action he deems appropriate. He eats if he feels hungry; he examines and reexamines his information if he suffers from cognitive dissonance. In the latter instance, he evaluates information in such a way as to justify his condition, plans, hopes, activities, or beliefs. In a negative sense, he unconsciously seeks to fool himself and may even attempt to defeat his own goals.

In the words of psychologist Leon Festinger, who developed the theory, cognitive dissonance "centers around the idea that if a person knows various things that are not psychologically consistent with one another, he will, in a variety of ways, try to make them more consistent." Festinger clarifies the concept by the common-sense observation that a person standing in the rain without getting wet would be puzzled because he would receive dissonant information (rain, yet dry), which would motivate him to reduce the resulting discomfort by trying to comprehend how such contradictions could occur. In the absence of a satisfactory and logical explanation, such as a raincoat or an umbrella, the victim of dissonance may need to resort to an unsatisfactory and illogical solution, although, if that explanation effectively reduces dissonance, it will not seem bizarre or illogical to him.

An individual's knowledge of some alternative information or course of action does not ordinarily create a dissonance problem. The mechanism comes into play to the degree that a given decision contains an emotional investment. The greater the emotional investment, the greater the commitment to the decision; the greater the commitment, the greater the dissonance created when the decision turns sour; the more inappropriate the original decision becomes, the greater the dissonance, and the more effort the victim makes to reduce the discomfort of conflicting knowledge. To justify one's choice of a dress or shirt presents an easy task, but to justify human bondage, rebellion, war, a change in war goals, or death confronts people with severe problems. Such decisions could, and did, create understandably severe postdecision dissonance. Under the pressure of cognitive dissonance, southerners equated bondage for slaves with freedom for themselves; rebellion against the nation became loyalty to constitutional ideals; war became a means of achieving honorable peace; changes in a war goal from preservation of slavery to independence became a restatement of an old desire simply to be let alone; and death became life, at least in the hereafter. Such contradictory justifications could cause confusion for outside observers.

The knowledge of the attractive features of rejected alternatives creates such dissonance. Memory of roads not taken and choices not made may cause the decision to frustrate and disturb the individual, especially when he has a strong emotional commitment to it and when rejected alternatives have features that look more attractive than they did at an earlier time. But because he has already made the decision, he must justify it, no matter how desirable the rejected alternatives may seem. Having made a bad bargain, he must hug it all the closer; having made his bed, he must sleep in it. By the middle of the Civil War most Confederates had become fully aware of the advantages of the repudiated choices. Especially among original Unionists, peace and Union looked extremely alluring by 1863; but the South had not taken the road of no war, no casualty lists, and Union. Rather, southerners had decided to protect their autonomy and institutions, by force, as it turned out. The more aware of the attractive features of the rejected alternatives Confederates became, the higher their postdecision dissonance and the greater the necessity for them to justify the choice they had made.

They could accomplish that unconscious task—reducing dissonance and justifying choices—in several ways. Southerners could deal with dissonance by distorting their perceptions, filtering out new and disturbing knowledge so that they could no longer perceive any conflict of dissonant information. The militant secessionist, for example, might convince himself that all Republicans were "Black Republicans" and, like John Brown, wished to see servile insurrection with all the bloodshed and horror that implied. Events actually reinforced this perception, for the Emancipation Proclamation convinced many Confederates that the North sought a servile insurrection. And if one became convinced of that, then certainly he fought on whether or not he originally had favored secession. Such people could not turn back because the threats to their well-being had become even more serious than in 1861. This resolution of cognitive dissonance created a commitment that augmented or substituted for deficient Confederate nationalism in prolonging determination to continue the war.

Southerners could also reduce dissonance a second way, as the discussion at the beginning of this chapter illustrates: they could add new "knowledge," perhaps by emphasizing that the disasters of this unhappy war, and indeed the war itself, were, somehow, the unfolding of the will of an omnipotent God, and they could not, and should not, avoid God's designs; many Confederates would have agreed with the editor who claimed that "the terrible convulsions which have been witnessed in this land for the last two years . . . have been permitted by Him for some wise, it may be inscrutable purpose."

Altering one of the two elements, either by revising one's beliefs or changing one's decision, provided a third way to reduce inconsistency between knowledge and behavior, that is, dissonance. Some amended their knowledge (beliefs) and discovered that the war to preserve slavery actually had become a war for independence, and always had been, a tack that Confederates increasingly adopted as it became apparent that slavery would become a casualty no matter who won. Other Confederates varied their behavior (decisions) by subtly attempting to renounce their decisions. They contended that they had forced the Union to accept constitutional limitations, that they had vindicated southern honor, and hence they could envision an acceptable peace without the military victory that their comrades demanded. These people became the true peace advocates, some even convincing themselves that timely reconstruction could preserve slavery. John A. Orr, congressman from Mississippi, claimed that in the spring of 1864 he and several other representatives and senators drew up a resolution "looking to the reconstruction of the Union, in which the institution of slavery was to be secured by compact with the Government of the U.S."

Group behavior also contributed to reduction of postdecision dissonance. Individuals sharing similar beliefs could control new information. Mutual discomfort brought relief through the social support of one's leaders, followers, or comrades, who, because they had the same beliefs, mitigated doubt and reinforced one's original conclusions by adding the new information that one had companions facing the same difficulties. Doubtful decisions took on new validity because social sharing of attitudes bolstered the legitimacy of the original decision.

In an area where southerners had undertaken secession only with great reluctance, such as North Carolina, for example, people frequently used another way to reduce postdecision dissonance caused by the knowledge that they had opposed secession but had nevertheless accepted it and supported the war that resulted. They asserted, as did M. S. Robins, the editor of the *Daily Conservative*, that the South had to pursue the unwanted war as a matter of principle. Reminding his readers that "many of us battled faithfully against the causes which brought on this war," he washed his hands, or reduced his dissonance, by the Pilate-like remark that "the crime of bringing it on does not rest on our heads."

But he faced a decision already made that he must render acceptable despite the attractive alternatives of peace. "What then," Robins wrote in surprise and shock at the very idea of ending short of independence the war he and his fellows had opposed, "shall we, after having spilt so much blood, sacrificed so many lives and so much treasure, in defence of the eternal principles of right, shall we back down? Never! Never!" He denied that the South had entered into war to maintain the right of secession. Rather than this nonsense, he asserted that "we are fighting for Southern equal rights and Southern property, and nothing else." He not only accepted the unwise decision but glorified it despite his knowledge, indeed his active support, of earlier, more attractive alternatives.

Robins and others with the same view reduced their dissonance in a way that may seem strange to some historians today—they hugged an acknowledged evil all the closer to their hearts because it was their own—but they used their arguments to convince others and in so doing managed to persuade themselves. In this way, groups clung to ideas—slavery, unsuccessful war, the chimera of independence—long after they had become inappropriate. "After being exposed to evidence of one's senses which unequivocally demonstrates a belief system to be wrong," notes Leon Festinger, "people tend to proselyte more vigorously for the belief system." They ignore new and incompatible information: hard-line Confederates, for example, who were firmly committed to the decision for secession and war, reduced dissonance by changing information—claiming that they fought the war for independence, or southern rights, or whatever—rather than by changing behavior and giving up the fight.

Faced with the realization that they might not merit God's favor or, after a prolonged and costly struggle, that they might have made the wrong choice in seceding, many Confederates found ways to resolve the resulting dissonance. But the very fact that many of them faced dissonance indicates the weakness of their original resolution. Moreover, a determination to fight on based on the product of dissonance resolution provided a very feeble substitute for a will based on strong nationalism with deep roots in the past or important cultural or linguistic distinctiveness from the enemy.

Southerners had to add a new element to their mental equations when unwanted by-products of their war efforts accentuated postdecision dissonance. Not only did they have to reckon with God and the northern army, but they were hindered by other Confederates. Many a Confederate might have discovered that he was his own worst enemy. For example, the issues involved in the establishment of centralization, uniformity, and internal control shocked, amazed, disillusioned, and angered significant segments of the southern community. The mobilization of both men and resources necessary to wage war successfully proved a good deal more rigorous than Confederates ever had dreamed, creating postdecision dissonance over and beyond that caused by the mental and spiritual traps of religious fatalism and the increasing size and success of the Union army.

Suspension of the writ of habeas corpus for varying periods of time, martial law with ever-present provost marshals to enforce it, impressment of supplies at less than market prices, and conscription had not been part of the original bargain. No one had expected such unpleasant side effects when the states marched out of the Union. At the end of the war one politician echoed the disillusion of many of his fellow Confederates, remarking with magnificent understatement and sarcasm, "Secession seems not to have produced the results predicted by its sanguine friends. There was to be no war, no taxes worth prating about, but an increase of happiness, boundless prosperity, and entire freedom from all Yankee annoyance." But instead the war brought conscription, destruction, and infringement of civil liberties.

As he often did, Governor Joseph E. Brown of Georgia well articulated the resulting discontent. Brown objected violently to the suspension of the writ of habeas corpus for its alleged infringement upon state sovereignty. More to the point, he said suspension was "not the constitutional liberty which so many Georgians have died to defend," for it gave the president the powers of a monarch. Conscription provoked Brown's displeasure even more. When Georgia entered the "revolution," "we [little] supposed . . . that the person of the free-born citizens of the respective States would be regarded and claimed, while at home in pursuit of their ordinary avocations, as the vassals of the central power, to be like chattels, ordered and disposed of at pleasure." "At one fell swoop," Brown asserted, conscription "strikes down the sovereignty of the State, triumphs upon the constitutional rights and personal liberty of the citizens, and arms the President with imperial power."

Others besides Brown vehemently objected to the conscription law. Texas Senator Williamson S. Oldham declared that the Confederate government had no power to conscript without the consent of the states: "This was not circumlocution; it was the theory of our government." C. C. Herbert, one of the Texans in the House of Representatives, supported Oldham and warned that "it would not do to press the conscription law too far upon the people. If it became necessary to violate the Constitution . . . he would be for raising in his State the 'lone star' flag that had twice been raised before." Reuben Davis of Mississippi (no relation to Jefferson Davis) thought conscription a mark of slavery, telling his colleagues in Congress that "he had rather be a 'naygur' than a victim of the Conscription Law." Vice-President Alexander H. Stephens, resenting conscription, suspension of habeas corpus, and impressment, vented his frustration to Senator Herschel V. Johnson. Stephens did not wish to build up opposition to Jefferson Davis; rather, his feelings for Davis were "akin to suspicion and jealousy." Stephens wrote that his "hostility and wrath (and I have enough of it to burst ten thousand bottles) is not against him, or any man or men, but against the thing—the measure and the policy which I see is leading us to despotism." Stephens's objective was not to inaugurate a counterrevolution but "to keep the present one . . . on the right track." James L. Orr, a South Carolina senator, referring to the suspension of habeas corpus and the vast numbers of provost marshals enforcing martial law on the civilian population, feared that the executive was subverting the civil power and demanded that "the legislature should put a curb on the unbridled will of military power" to avoid "despotism."

In a famous letter to Jefferson Davis, written as the curtain began to fall in October 1864, South Carolina Congressman William W. Boyce urged the president to bolster the fortunes of the peace faction of the Democratic party in the North by indicating a willingness to have all the states convene for the purpose of discussing peace. Not only motivated by a desire to end the war, Boyce also hoped to avoid Confederate despotism. "Well," he wrote Davis,

we have been at war not quite four years, and what is the result? Is not our Federal Government in the exercise of every possible power of a national central military despotism? Suppose there were no States, only provinces, and unlimited power was conferred upon you and Congress, what greater power would you exercise than you now do? . . . Indeed if you were appointed Military Dictator, what greater powers could you exercise than you now do?

If you tell me that they [the powers] are necessary, I reply, that is precisely my argument. My argument assumes and requires that necessity. It is plain that our government exercises the powers of a central despotism. . . . The truth is, that the Government at Washington has not dared to exercise power on the grand scale that our Government has.

The only way to avoid that despotism, thought Boyce, lay in escaping wartime centralization by securing a lasting, harmonious peace.

One of the operating assumptions behind the thinking of these critics and others was the very practical one that if the war inevitably resulted in despotic rule, the reason for fighting was nullified. If one believed in the desirability or inevitability of restrictions upon self-government, he could have had them without leaving the Union. Some southerners had used the fear of subjugation to powerful central authority to justify secession in the first place; to go through a bloody war and come out at the same point hardly seemed worth the effort. Idealistic motivations also affected attitudes. Thus some Confederates apparently believed deeply that unless they could preserve the spirit as well as the letter of their Constitution, they had made a mistake by seceding and fighting. A game won by cheating would bring only a hollow victory. "This is the peoples' revolution," declared Congressman John P. Murray of Tennessee, "and they will tolerate no subversion of their ancient liberties. . . . [I have] never understood that political doctrine that teaches that in order to get liberty you must first lose it, nor the paradox that in order to be healthy you must first ruin your physical constitution."

No longer was it possible to renounce secession itself. Multitudes of Confederates did the next best thing and attempted to resolve their dissonance and seize whatever remained of the rejected alternative by renouncing secessionists. In the 1863 elections many secession Democrats lost their seats to Union Whigs. North Carolina, an extreme example, replaced a delegation in the House of Representatives that was 60 percent Democrats with one composed of 90 percent Union Whigs. In the entire Congress about half the secessionists and half the Unionists won reelection; the new congressmen, however, were two-thirds Unionists, and many of the reelected secessionists won their seats by votes from refugees and the army, for these congressmen represented districts in which normal political process had become impossible because their constituents lay outside effective Confederate control. This election did not reflect a true peace movement, for the winners, with a few exceptions, warmly supported the war effort. But they had opposed the decision of 1861, had consented to it only with reluctance, or had at least warned of the dangers to come, and they represented a desire on the part of many Confederates to "turn instinctively to those old leaders, who foretold their present situation, for counsel and instruction."

The election of 1863 not only reflected an attempt to reduce postdecision dissonance by partially renouncing the decision makers of 1861, it also indicated popular perceptions of Confederate prospects. The people seemed to feel that if the previous leadership had blundered in getting the South into a war and then could not achieve victory, perhaps those who had had sufficient farsightedness to oppose the secession movement might have more success in the conduct of the war.

As military power declined, civilian will, now undermined by the doubts of religion, could no longer supplement the force of arms. As will slowly expired, so too did the military strength of the Confederacy. In spite of the discouraging outlook, however, the Confederacy fought on, some Confederates even retaining hopes of eventual victory. And truly these hopes did not lack a foundation, for northerners also were becoming war weary and southern arms continued to inflict heavy losses upon attacking federal armies. The final question, therefore, still remained in doubt over the winter of 1863–64.

Chapter Eleven

The Last Campaigns

THE IMPORTANT Union victories of July 1863 did not inaugurate a steady decline in Confederate fortunes. Indeed, the fortunes of war turned rapidly in the opposite direction, but first another advance by Rosecrans's army, this time into Georgia, further diminished southern hopes.

After Tullahoma, Rosecrans planned to maneuver Bragg back still farther by turning the Confederate flank once again and threatening the rebel rear. Again distracting Bragg, this time by moving one corps toward Chattanooga and bombarding the city, Rosecrans succeeded in moving his other three corps over the unfordable Tennessee River and around Bragg's west flank. This move so threatened Confederate communications that Bragg forfeited Chattanooga to the federal troops on September 9 and fell back to protect his railroad in north Georgia. Though his inadequate cavalry failed to supply him with information, Rosecrans felt confident that Bragg was withdrawing all the way to Atlanta. Meanwhile, Burnside had advanced from Kentucky and taken Knoxville on September 2, also cutting the railroad from Virginia to Atlanta. Far from retreating, however, Bragg was repeating previous Confederate strategy, when, as Jomini would have expressed it, "the whole theatre of operations may be considered as a single field upon which strategy directs the armies for a definite end."

Though they lacked interior lines because their troops had to move in roundabout fashion over a rickety transportation system, the Confederates achieved strategic surprise when they exploited their railroads and rapidly assembled the most far-flung concentration since Shiloh. When they abandoned the East Tennessee line of operations, the army opposing Burnside there moved to unite with Bragg, and they were joined by most of Johnston's infantry from Mississippi. President Davis earlier had sought a part of Lee's army to reinforce the West but had run into an example of what Clausewitz called a commander's feeling of "proprietary right" over all of his troops and the usual objection "to any part being withdrawn for however short a time." Nevertheless, on September 9 Davis ordered the bulk of Longstreet's corps, nearly a third of Lee's infantry, to join Bragg. The Confederates were making such a powerful response not only because they wished to counteract Rosecrans's success but also because they had become convinced that Tennessee presented a promising opportunity for an offensive.

Turned from his Chattanooga position, Bragg was, as Clausewitz would have analyzed such situations, "forced to fight an offensive battle and to forego the further benefits of *waiting, of a strong position, and of good entrenchments,* etc." As the battle of Chickamauga developed, Rosecrans countered Bragg's plan to overlap his north flank and the Confederates therefore resorted to frontal assaults. One of these assaults, a strong one under Longstreet at midday of September 20, achieved an overwhelming triumph because Rosecrans had inadvertently left a hole in his line. Then Rosecrans withdrew to Chattanooga, September 21–22, 1863.

The tactical victory of the Confederates meant that their relative losses were not as heavy as the tactical offensive typically dictated; they lost fewer than 18,500 to more than 16,000 for the Union army. As a result of winning this encounter, Bragg could take up a position on the south side of the Tennessee River, where he could compel a further Union retreat because his position cut the railroad from Nashville to Chattanooga. Without the railroad, Rosecrans would be unable to bring in enough supplies. Nevertheless, the demoralized Rosecrans clung to Chattanooga and the gains of his second strategic turning movement. He had again demonstrated the defensive power of a Civil War army, not only to resist attack but also to maneuver so as to survive even a major breakthrough in its line of battle.

Confederate strength around Chattanooga soon diminished, when, on November 4, Bragg sent a major part of his army, Longstreet's corps, toward Knoxville in East Tennessee to resist Burnside's army from Kentucky. Meanwhile, Lincoln having placed Grant in command at Chattanooga, the Union forces took the offensive against Bragg's entrenched army, succeeding in one major frontal attack in driving the demoralized

Confederates well back into north Georgia. Grant thus raised Bragg's siege of Chattanooga and consolidated the gains Rosecrans had made by his September turning movement.

When Meade lost two corps in September to reinforce Rosecrans, Lee took the offensive in early October 1863 to prevent the Union from sending more of Meade's men west. But no battle resulted when, after Lee had turned his adversary back to Washington and then withdrawn to find supplies, Meade planned an attack on Lee. Finding the Confederates too well entrenched, the Union general abandoned his plans, and both armies went into winter quarters. In Virginia, as well as in Georgia and Tennessee, the armies had a quiet winter.

But again the lesson was in the ease with which the fortunes of war swung from one side to the other. At Chickamauga Bragg raised Confederate hopes from the bleak outlook of the previous July, only to suffer disappointment again at the battles of Lookout Mountain and Missionary Ridge. So the defeats following the victory at Chickamauga affected morale much as had Lee's inevitable retreats following his two raids into the North, to Antietam in September of 1862 and to Gettysburg in June and July of 1863. Doubtless the withdrawals had depressed morale as least as much as the initial advances had elevated it.

In his message at the opening of the fourth session of the First Congress in December 1863, Jefferson Davis confessed that the South had suffered "grave reverses" over the preceding seven months and that these setbacks had caused considerable discouragement, but he also observed that morale soon stiffened. Despite serious losses in 1863, the Confederacy proved at Chickamauga that the war would not end very soon. Also, in spite of the fortunes of the battlefield, the problems of the blockade, relatively inferior economic development, and some decline in morale, the Confederacy remained strong enough to prevent significant deterioration of its military position. Indeed, southern armies won other victories that year, although less dramatic. Confederates repulsed the federals in Texas, Louisiana, and at Charleston, as well, and otherwise held them at bay in the major theaters of war.

Yet the Confederacy's morale was too dependent on the fortunes of war; and it was bound to suffer repeated blows, even if the great extent of the country in comparison to the size of Union forces meant that the Union victories gained them small increments of territory. Moreover, each Union conquest contributed to the depletion of its forces as it diverted more and more men to garrison hostile country and guard vulnerable communications. Nevertheless, Confederate morale suffered. Although a good public information program might have had value, we cannot expect nineteenth-century men to think in twentieth-century terms.

In two and a half years of warfare Confederates had followed closely Clausewitz's prescription for the defensive, except for the Fort Donelson capitulation and Pemberton's egregious blunder of losing his army at Vicksburg. Each Confederate general had sought "to keep his territory inviolate, and to hold it for as long as possible." In Tennessee the Union had driven back the Confederate armies, conferring on them the benefit of the strategy of withdrawal into the interior, and the Confederates had taken advantage of this situation by striking at "the enemy's lines of communications" and carrying out "raids and diversions" in Bragg's Kentucky campaign. And Lee's position after the Battle of Antietam fulfilled a similar mission for "he did not hope to hold it, still less to make it a base for a further advance, but as a sort of outwork."

The heavy Confederate casualties at Gettysburg, Chickamauga, and Vicksburg meant that the Union had gained much through attrition in 1863. For the 1864 campaign, the Confederacy tried to make good most of these losses by conscripting seventeen-year-old boys and men aged forty-six to fifty. The older men would tend to lack the physical attributes for extended soldiering and were therefore to be used, with the seventeen-year-olds, for local defense.

Union strategy became more sophisticated when Lincoln added a political dimension that Clausewitz and Jomini would have approved. On December 8, 1863, the president announced a plan for reconstruction of the Union that made it easy for separate states to establish governments that Lincoln would recognize and receive back into the Union. Except for abolition of slavery, Lincoln's plan did not penalize the seceding states, although it did punish certain classes of rebels, excluding them from the privilege of taking an oath of loyalty. Further, the provision that loyal state governments could be reestablished when 10 percent of the qualified voters in the state voluntarily took the prescribed oath suggests Lincoln's lenience and political sagacity.

The terms seemed easy enough, yet some northerners opposed them on that very ground. Confederates displayed mixed reactions. Although they were virtually unanimous in rejecting Lincoln's amnesty, the reasons for that rejection varied. Some simply were amazed at Lincoln's presumption of eventual victory, warned that "Lincoln has counted his chickens," and questioned the chance of a "successful hatching" in the face of the three hundred thousand men the Confederacy had under arms. Others thought it would tend to increase the Confederate war effort by stimulating determination to avoid defeat. Robert G. H. Kean, head of the Bureau of War, called Lincoln's proclamation "an able and crafty paper" and thought the 10 percent provision was designed to promote class antagonism by "divid[ing] the lower orders from those in positions of power." Some southerners thought it incredible. "We have only to confess that we are felons needing to be pardoned," protested one editor, "that we are cowards . . . that we are fools . . . to kiss the hand dripping with the blood of our kinsmen." Others held it up to ridicule. William Porcher Miles, a South Carolina congressman, thought it best "to treat Mr. Lincoln and his amnesty manifesto with silent and unmitigated contempt. The whole thing was too weak, so puerile, that it would only meet with the derision of the civilized world."

Lincoln had hoped that his measures would help build Unionist strength in such partially reconquered states as Louisiana and Tennessee. If they succeeded, they would have contributed toward diminishing civilian resistance and guerrilla warfare in occupied areas. Jomini, having served with the French in their struggle against the Spanish national resistance to Napoleon, reached the same conclusions and explicitly prescribed political measures for combating guerrilla warfare. He recommended that the invader "calm the popular passions in every possible way, exhaust them by time and patience, display courtesy, gentleness, and severity united, and, particularly, deal justly." Lincoln's liberal plan of reconstruction certainly met Jomini's prescription fully, and Clausewitz's, too, in his only political suggestion, "treating the population well."

But many Confederates saw Lincoln's amnesty proposal not as a way for uncertain Confederates to get out of a difficult situation as gracefully and as easily as possible, which it clearly was, but as an attempt by Lincoln to impose a despotism. Southerners had resisted change, and rather than allow the attractive features of the rejected alternatives—peace instead of war, Union in place of secession—to dictate their course, they supported their resolve to secede, and, inadvertently, to fight, by interpreting the new information contained in Lincoln's declaration in such a way as to support their original choice or at least to make a change of selection impossible. Thus southerners interpreted Lincoln's 10 percent plan, which might have created severe postdecision dissonance, in such a way as to prove the undesirability of reunion with a government that circumvented the principle of majority rule. From the northern point of view, as few as 10 percent of the voting population of the rebel states would be able to rescue the South and return it to the Union without further penalty save the abandonment of slavery; from the southern point of view, however, that same small 10 percent could dictate the course that the other 90 percent would have to take. Seizing upon this latter as truly indicative of Lincoln's intentions, and viewing it from the standpoint of the republican tradition of majority rule, they refused it.

Lincoln's political program could aid the Union war effort when and if southerners accepted the terms of the amnesty, but the Union's military solution was not working well. The blockade remained only a serious nuisance and the conquest of the Mississippi had conferred no significant military or logistical benefit. The prospects for the conquest of additional territory were bleak because the Union had exhausted its water communications. It had taken about a year and a half to advance the one hundred airline miles from Nashville to Chattanooga and another half year to consolidate the gain. This did not augur well for additional western advances using rail communication. An advance in the East had even bleaker prospects, and Lincoln and Halleck had not planned any serious effort in Virginia for a year.

But upon General Grant devolved the task of determining the strategy for 1864, and he would try a new approach to break the stalemate. Grant's success at Chattanooga confirmed his reputation, not just as the premier Union general but as one of sufficient standing to receive the rank of lieutenant general, previously held only by the revered George Washington. In the winter of 1864 Congress established the rank, and in March Lincoln appointed Grant to the position. As the senior officer he automatically became general in chief. In actual function Grant became chief of staff to Lincoln, and Halleck became Grant's chief of staff, continuing his duties of operating the very effective army headquarters.

In anticipation of his new assignment, Grant already had envisioned a strategy for the 1864 campaigns, conceived out of his experience of the war as well as his collaboration with the brilliant and imaginative William T. Sherman. Like virtually every other Civil War general, Grant by the end of 1863 perceived that the destruction of an enemy army in battle was practically impossible and that a change to a combat strategy was sure to lead to failure. Though he twice had captured entire Confederate armies he remembered the difficulty and how much he owed to the ineptitude of his opponents. Grant also had long been convinced of the almost insuperable obstacles to supplying the Union armies over great distances by railroad. Confederate raiders and guerrillas were too formidable. The strategic consumption caused by the use of troops to guard the railroad eventually would absorb so many men as to stall the advance. The Union armies encountered the same problems in occupying territory. Guerrillas and raiders made it hard to control the country, and occupation required an enormous number of soldiers. The Union already employed a third of its soldiers garrisoning territory and guarding communications. Thus the logistic strategy based on territorial conquest seemed doomed to failure.

Seeing the extent to which motionless, concentrated armies depended on railroads for their food and fodder, Grant realized that severing the South's trunk-line railways could force the breaking up of the main hostile armies. To do this he would use his own armies to carry out raids against the railroads. He planned to aim primarily at the two railroads that passed through Georgia, linking Alabama and Mississippi with South Carolina, and the two lines that joined South Carolina to Virginia. Raids by armies with infantry and engineers could do a more thorough job of destruction than raids by cavalry, if only because they had more manpower. Living on the enemy's country, the raiding army also would consume food and fodder that otherwise would be available for the Confederate armies. In addition, Grant wished to destroy arms works, foundries, textile mills, and other installations that contributed to the Confederate war effort. These raids would deprive the Confederate armies of their support and implement a logistic strategy without the necessity of Union occupation of more Confederate territory.

It is unlikely that either Clausewitz or Jomini, steeped as they were in the Napoleonic tradition, would have approved of Grant's plan of merely raiding the enemy's communications. Actually Grant's strategy had a fortuitous correspondence with the ideas of Heinrich Dietrich von Bülow, an early nineteenth-century thinker from whom Clausewitz and Jomini had taken the concept of the base but had rejected all of his other teachings. Bülow disparaged battles, urged striking at enemy communications, and aimed at conquering territory, ideas much like those T. Harry Williams attributed to Jomini.

This strategy had, of course, something in common with that of the Confederates, who consistently used cavalry to raid Union communications. Clausewitz had recommended counterraids, "sending a force of equal strength to raid an equivalent area of the enemy's country," but Grant's plan differed in that he intended in part to use armies for this task and to substitute these raids for further attempts to conquer territory. Of course, the strategy of raids and the strategy of conquest of territory both had the common objective of attacking the enemy's supplies, thus crippling his armies by means of deprivation. Grant made this strategy clear to Sherman in early April, directing him "to get into the interior of the enemy's country as far as you can, inflicting all the damage you can against their war resources." Grant's strategy had a parallel in the strategic bombing in World War II, in which bombers attacked enemy factories and railroads to deprive enemy armies of the essentials to keep fighting. Strategic bombing also included the element of killing and terrorizing civilians, which Grant did not include in his strategy, although in practice it sometimes had that effect.

Grant's strategy was old-fashioned in the sense that it reverted to that of earlier times, when the ratio of force to space did not suffice for belligerents to aim at the territorial conquest of their enemy. Instead, they raided enemy territory, living at enemy expense, carrying off booty, and thus trying to extort political concessions. The Battle of Poitiers in the Hundred Years' War, for example, occurred when the French overtook a booty-laden, raiding English army and forced it to fight.

Although Sherman saw the potential political impact of such raids, Grant did not plan primarily a political strategy. Rather, he continued the Union's logistic strategy of eliminating the Confederacy's means of supplying its armies. But Grant changed the Union's logistic objective to breaking railroads, abandoning the long-pursued objective of occupying territory to deprive the Confederate armies of recruits, food, and manufactures. Having seen that the Confederacy was too large and too hostile and railroad communications too vulnerable to pursue this strategy successfully, Grant made a fundamental change in method in dropping what one might call a persisting strategy and embracing a raiding strategy.

The Confederates had already demonstrated the offensive primacy of raids and the vulnerability of railroads. So Grant's armies would exploit the ambiguity of the raiders' objective to avoid enemy armies and, instead, strike at them indirectly by breaking the railways that supplied them and secondarily by smashing foundries and mills that supported them. Retaining the same logistic strategy, he had switched from the offensively weaker persisting confrontation with hostile armies so as to occupy territory and adopted the offensively stronger strategy of raiding the same country with the same objective. Before, the Confederates had used the stronger persisting defense to oppose invasion, while employing against the Union rear offensively stronger raids by cavalry and guerrillas.

Although these strategic ideas, like the relative superiority of raiding on the offensive, underlie the strategic concepts of Clausewitz and Jomini, neither explained them systematically nor provided any classification. If one applied the name *combat strategy* to aiming to destroy the enemy army in battle and *persisting strategy* to the antithesis of raiding, territorial conquest, a matrix is available, which presents, simply, the ideas used to present Civil War strategy.

	Persisting	Raiding
Combat		
Logistic		

Classifications of Military Strategy

Operations in Middle Tennessee, for example, early displayed three of the four possible strategies. In the early summer of 1862 General Buell made a persisting advance in an effort to carry out the logistic strategy of conquering Middle Tennessee and breaking the Confederate rail links at Chattanooga. In August the Confederates halted him by a logistic strategy of using raids of guerrillas and regular cavalry to wreck his rail communications. In December Rosecrans, Buell's successor, switched to a combat strategy when he sought to destroy Bragg's Confederate army in battle. Taught the futility of this strategy by the inconclusive Battle of Murfreesboro, in 1863 Rosecrans returned to an essentially logistic strategy when first his June and then his August–September turning movements expelled the enemy army from the state, thus depriving the Confederates of this rich region.

This elementary classification has the advantage of embracing naval operations, a part of warfare neglected by both Clausewitz and Jomini. In stationing blockading squadrons before each Confederate port, Union naval forces clearly used a persisting strategy to implement their logistic objective. The Confederacy, also having the logistic aim of interrupting the enemy's commerce, used the raids of such commerce destroyers as the CSS *Alabama*.

Making his strategic decision without any such classification or explicit choice of alternatives, Grant faced disappointment because he had to limit his initial objective for his 1864 campaign to cutting the railroads in Georgia. Only Sherman's army was left explicitly aiming at the enemy's railroads, and Sherman was to begin his operations with a conventional campaign to capture Atlanta. After that, he intended to carry out a raid against the other east-west railroad by marching to connect with the navy either on the Gulf or the Atlantic at Savannah.

Overall, Grant followed the traditional Union strategy of simultaneous advances, using, in addition to Sherman's, three in Virginia as well as numerous cavalry raids to distract the enemy. Making his headquarters with Meade's army in Virginia, Grant had a dual task in the campaign against Lee. Strategically the Union still was making its main effort in the West, which had implied accepting stalemate in Virginia and not besieging Richmond. But the transfer of Longstreet from Virginia and the South's subsequent victory in the Battle of Chickamauga had been a traumatic experience for the Union. So the Union army in Virginia must occupy Lee so closely and continuously that he could not spare any reinforcements for the West to help Bragg's successor, Joseph E. Johnston, oppose Sherman.

Grant also had a political task in the campaign in Virginia, one which fortunately conformed to this strategic objective. The northern public counted on the new lieutenant general to take on Lee, the South's best general, who had threatened Washington and twice raided north of the Potomac. The public, Lincoln's critics, and many soldiers both expected and demanded such action.

Beginning almost simultaneously with Sherman in north Georgia, in May 1864, Grant moved forward. Grant's basic strategy provided that Meade would turn Lee by marching around his eastern flank. Lee sought to prevent this move, and the armies met in a densely forested region called the Wilderness. The terrain nullified numerical superiority, and Grant's progress was arrested in bloody engagements on May 5–7, 1864. He promptly moved east and south in another effort to get around Lee. But the Confederates headed him off at Spotsylvania, and during the next two weeks the armies dug in opposite each other.

Grant resolved on a frontal attack to push Lee directly backward toward Richmond, to placate the public, and possibly to gain a significant victory in battle. He began a series of assaults against the Confederates at Spotsylvania on May 10. But against entrenched, well-led, rifle-armed veterans, Grant's skill and numerical superiority were of no avail. Repeated strikes in mid-May failed at Spotsylvania. Avoiding another attack, in late May Grant again turned Lee on the east and reached a position at Cold Harbor, east of Richmond, where he could draw his supplies from some of the same sources McClellan had used in 1862.

After making the blunder of a costly frontal attack at Cold Harbor, in the last act of this campaign, Grant skillfully conducted a surprise turning movement against Petersburg, but a determined defense by General Beauregard from June 15 through June 18, 1864, prevented him from capturing the city. Beauregard fended off inept Union attacks until Lee sent reinforcements. Both sides then dug in and a trench-warfare stalemate continued for the next nine months. The rickety Confederate supply organization managed to feed both Lee's army and the Richmond population during this siege, despite Union raids on the railroads.

Grant correctly appreciated that Lee could spare a substantial force. Lee sent an entire corps under the eccentric but talented Jubal A. Early, who moved in the Shenandoah Valley and crossed the Potomac into Maryland, where his raid caused a great commotion, especially when he paused near Washington before falling back to the Valley. Grant diverted two corps to strengthen Washington, but they could not prevent Early later in July from again raiding across the Potomac and reaching Pennsylvania.

Grant then placed the capable and energetic Philip H. Sheridan in command of nearly fifty thousand men assembled at the north end of the Shenandoah Valley to resist Early's scant twenty thousand. In September and October 1864 Sheridan seized the offensive and, winning three battles, which helped to depress already depleted Confederate morale, drove Early far southward. Sheridan's campaign did, however, have a political effect in the North. It ensured the protection of Washington, and it assisted the Republican party in the fall elections.

Sherman's 1864 operations against Johnston paralleled Grant's against Lee but with several important differences. First, Sherman did not have to win battles, for the public had no such expectation of him. Second, he had to move more slowly than Grant because he lacked water communications, possessed only one base, and had to rebuild and fortify the railroad as he advanced. Third, just as Grant feared that Lee might detach troops to reinforce Johnston, Sherman felt a similar but less acute apprehension that Johnston might send men to strengthen Lee.

The careful and thorough Sherman began his campaign on May 7 with a very wide turning movement by about one-fourth of Sherman's consolidated force. That excellent plan, conducted by a competent general, came close to reaching Johnston's communications, but the Confederate general withdrew quickly enough to cover them, though forced to abandon Dalton, Resaca, and other points in the process. The timely arrival on May 13 of a reinforcement of thirteen thousand men from the Mississippi, the bulk of the infantry of the Department of Mississippi and East Louisiana, aided Johnston.

Successively, Sherman faced and turned elaborately entrenched Confederate positions at Allatoona Pass, Marietta, and the Chattahoochee River, against which he deployed his own men in entrenchments similar to those of Johnston; both the astute Sherman and the wary Johnston probed for weakness without finding any. The weather alternated between hot and rainy as Sherman rebuilt his railroad and in a period of less than two months carried out the five major turning movements that forced Johnston back toward Atlanta.

Johnston, undermined by his own corps commanders and by his usual secretiveness about his plans, failed to allay genuine fear in Richmond that he would continue to retreat indefinitely. Moreover, the public had high expectations of Johnston, touted as one of the best generals in the Confederacy, second only to Lee. At the beginning of May the Confederacy had enjoyed no major victories since Bragg's at Chickamauga in September 1863. Thus public expectations were almost as high and demanding of Johnston as they were of Grant, and both commanders were confidently expected to satisfy the needs of their country for a morale-boosting victory. These victories were to have not only the spiritual result of raising each public's morale but also the political effect of influencing the forthcoming federal elections of 1864. In the case of Union victories the connection would be obvious, helping to persuade the voters that the end would not be far off if only they continued to support the war effort.

The effect of a Confederate victory on the Union elections would have been a little more subtle. Larry E. Nelson has pointed out that Davis sought to demonstrate to the Confederate public that the 1864 political campaign would exacerbate the internal problems of the Union. Protests against emancipation, the draft riots, and separatist tendencies in the old Northwest "might result in election of a [presidential] candidate amenable to Confederate independence," although Jefferson Davis tried to prevent southern expectations from becoming unrealistic. Northern war weariness also was applying pressures for peace on Abraham Lincoln, many Confederates thought, and the best way to increase this pressure was to win military victories. All these forces increased pressure on Johnston, just as political necessity had done to Grant. Southern hopes of influencing the election of 1864 rested on Johnston's ability to stop Sherman, but a Confederate force that always retreated could not halt that Union general. "Undoubtedly," says Nelson, "the Federal election was among the welter of considerations that led to the removal of Johnston and the appointment of Hood to command the army." Davis had told his people that "only significant Southern military success could influence Northern sentiment," but in the end the effort was beyond Confederate abilities and Davis was criticized by some Confederates for relying on military success to apply political pressure, instead of using political means to do so. On July 17, 1864, Davis gave the command to John B. Hood, a bold young man, untried in independent command. He proved combative but ultimately recklessly imprudent. He promptly attacked Sherman on July 20, 22, and 28 in the costly battles of Peachtree Creek, Atlanta, and Ezra Church. On each occasion Sherman's well-entrenched veterans repulsed the assault. Sherman's casualties, about six thousand men, numbered much less than half of Hood's, whose much smaller army of fifty-one thousand could ill afford such losses.

After a month of preparation outside of Atlanta, Sherman moved his army south of the city and severed its communications, forcing Hood to evacuate. Sherman occupied Atlanta on September 2, 1864, blocking one of the key east-west rail lines. He gave his men a rest, but Hood, watching from a few miles away, devised a new and more sophisticated offensive. After he and President Davis had conferred, Hood changed from his disastrous policy of attacks to one of emulating Lee's defensive use of the turning movement.

Less than a month after the fall of Atlanta, Hood marched west and north of the city, menacing Union communications and drawing Sherman and the bulk of his army north, back toward Chattanooga. Hood could remain in this area indefinitely because he had a line of communications from Rome, Georgia, southwestward into Alabama. Pehaps more significant than Hood's good base in Alabama was his wise decision to avoid Sherman's army and confine his activities to menacing Sherman's communications.

Drawing on his experience of the French campaign in Russia in 1812, Clausewitz commented that "in a country as immense as Russia, two armies could play a regular game of tag with one another." Although the region in which Sherman and Hood played tag was much smaller than Russia, their armies were puny in size compared with the huge forces used by Napoleon and the Russians in 1812. Hood had ample space in which to keep out of Sherman's way, to keep in touch with his sources of supply, and yet to threaten Sherman's communications. Clausewitz could also have noted a similar disproportion between the size of armies and the space in which they operated in the South in the last years of the American Revolution.

Thus in October 1864 the contending forces found themselves locked in an entrenched stalemate in Virginia and in another deadlock based upon marches and countermarches in north Georgia. West of the Mississippi the situation differed little, the Union having just repulsed a raid by General Sterling Price that went east to the outskirts of St. Louis, Missouri, and as far west as the Kansas border before Union troops defeated him and forced him back to Arkansas. In more than three years of war the Union had divided the Confederacy along the Mississippi River, captured key cities, and operated in every one of the Confederate states, while the Confederacy had captured no Union cities, except temporarily in Kentucky, and had operated only in the border states of the Union, leaving the others totally untouched. And yet the Union had conquered completely only one Confederate state, Tennessee, and had taken two and a half years to do that. It was not until September 1864, forty months after the firing on Fort Sumter, that Union troops had occupied Atlanta, in the heart of the Confederacy. This military stalemate carried a potentially significant impact on political affairs. Well might Confederates expect that the snail's pace of Union conquest would so discourage northerners that they might be willing to turn to a peace candidate in the 1864 elections.

But Confederates did not look upon these signs of defensive strength and gird their loins to continue the battle indefinitely. The political significance of this attitude was clear. Before the fall of Atlanta, it appeared to the weary Union that the war was likely to drag on for several more years, unless by some stroke of good fortune the Confederacy simply collapsed, which did not seem likely. The fall of Atlanta changed the entire complexion of events, for Sherman had provided a needed victory—expected more from Grant than from him—that indicated the beginning of substantial progress. As a result, in 1864 the Union voters reelected the administration.

On the Confederate side the fall of Atlanta produced exactly the opposite effect. Desertion rates, already serious, now multiplied as the needs of destitute families at home were reinforced by a soldier's presumption of the inevitable outcome of the war to persuade him that there was no more point in risking his life for a lost cause. The basic purposes of government are to protect lives and property, but as casualty lists lengthened, the letters from home grew more urgent, and the Union armies seemed more aggressive, it became clear that Confederate armies were doing neither. Why, then, a Confederacy? Thousands of soldiers and civilians asked themselves that question and concluded that "their interests could best be protected by rejoining the Union": accordingly, they waged war with less enthusiasm than heretofore. After Atlanta, the bottom was about to drop out of the Confederate tub. But Confederate victory had never depended on military successes; a national resistance in a vast, thinly settled country would have sufficed. Such a war, however, the South was no longer prepared to wage.

Adventitiously Grant's raiding strategy provided the perfect antidote to Hood's defensive use of the turning movement. In a raid Sherman would no longer have any communications to protect or for Hood to threaten. In the middle of November 1864 Sherman therefore abandoned Atlanta and his northward line of communications and led an army of more than sixty thousand men on the long-projected raid to the coast. He marched to Savannah, Georgia, but he created such ambiguity about his route that he had no difficulty avoiding the meager forces available to oppose him. His army moved rapidly, easily living on the country. It destroyed in its path anything of value to the Confederate war effort but concentrated on the major east-west railroads, accompanied by an engineer regiment specially equipped to destroy them.

Southerners had looked anxiously to the Union presidential election, hoping for Lincoln's defeat as a sign of the failure of the enemy's determination to triumph over the Confederacy. But hardly had the northern electorate disappointed them by reelecting Lincoln when Sherman commenced his campaign, and it further eroded the South's will to continue the struggle. Thus Sherman's Georgia raid was a political as well as a military maneuver, and it was aimed as much at Confederate morale and will as at her railroads and granaries. The object was not only to destroy resources needed for the Confederate military effort but also to "illustrate the vulnerability of the south. They don't know what war means; but when the rich planters of the Oconee and Savannah see their fences, and corn, and hogs, and sheep vanish before their eyes, they will have something more than a mean opinion of the 'Yanks.'" This was a deeper thrust into the heartland of her territory than the Confederacy had yet experienced, and it would mark a complete change from only two months before, when the Confederate interior had seemed virtually invulnerable to large-scale Union operations. It would also have a corresponding effect upon the people's will.

Sherman's march presented the Confederates with a serious dilemma. Hood had his main Confederate force in northern Alabama, far in Sherman's rear, and would have little chance to overtake him. Instead of opposing Sherman, Hood decided to march into Middle Tennessee while Sherman moved toward the coast. This odd spectacle of two armies marching away from each other into the other's territory had occurred during the American Revolution and had more than once characterized operations during earlier times.

But as Hood headed north toward Nashville, he planned not a raid but a reconquest of Middle Tennessee. Clausewitz would have expressed skepticism of such a strategy, asking whether a permanent or temporary occupation would "really be worth the cost of the operation. . . . An offensive of this type is not always appropriate to make up losses elsewhere" because "in general one tends to lose more from occupation by the enemy than one gains from conquering his territory, even if the value of both areas should be identical."

Not only in strategy but in other ways Hood's and Sherman's campaigns differed significantly. As a raider, Sherman had the goal and the opportunity to avoid the enemy's army. But Hood, aiming to conquer territory, had to engage Union forces in his path. The advantage of the defense belonged to the Union, which Sherman counted on when he left in Tennessee a large but motley contingent under command of the careful George H. Thomas. And Hood seemed determined to help the

Union make the most of its advantage. After first turning back the federal army opposing him almost to Nashville, on November 30, 1864, he made a costly frontal attack against his entrenched opponent at Franklin, Tennessee. His capable adversary, the seasoned John M. Schofield, withdrew even though he had resisted Hood's attacks successfully and his casualties numbered barely a third of his opponent's. Schofield fell back to Nashville, where he joined Thomas in well-entrenched positions protected from turning movements by the Cumberland River, patrolled by Union gunboats.

In freezing weather Hood reached the outskirts of Nashville and waited before the city, unable to move against Thomas's superior and amply supplied army. Thomas would normally have done nothing except let the bad weather and inadequate supplies complete the destruction of the enemy army. But Hood's advance to a position not occupied by a Confederate army since early 1862 created a sensation in the North, and it was not counterbalanced by any news from Sherman, whose march cut him off from communication with army headquarters. Lincoln insisted on an attack, and on December 15–16 Thomas, in an essentially frontal battle, easily drove Hood's already demoralized army into northern Mississippi. Superior in numbers, morale, and cavalry, Thomas conducted a damaging pursuit. Discredited and disgraced, Hood resigned as commander; his army had lost so heavily in numbers and morale that it effectively had ceased to exist.

Meanwhile, back in Georgia, Sherman's raid had reached the Atlantic coast near Savannah on December 13, enabling him to make contact with the South Atlantic Blockading Squadron and force Confederates to evacuate Savannah, which permitted him to establish a new supply line. Sherman and Grant now decided on a second raid, north through South Carolina into North Carolina. Sherman's route would allow him to break the Charleston-Atlanta railroad again as well as cut both north-south rail lines between South Carolina and Virginia.

To implement his raiding logistic strategy, Grant did not depend only on Sherman's two raids. A combined army-navy expedition captured Wilmington, closing the port and opening a North Carolina base should Sherman need it. In addition, a Union army of forty thousand men landed, took Mobile, and prepared to raid north in Alabama. Nor did Grant neglect cavalry raids, sending out several small forces and two large ones, operations that depended on the success of the Union effort to improve its cavalry. Both major raids began in March. One, under James H. Wilson, moved from Tennessee into Alabama and captured Selma, an important war industrial center on a rail route connecting Georgia and Mississippi. The success of this maneuver preempted the work of the slow-moving force at Mobile. The other raid, under Sheridan, went from Winchester, Virginia, through Virginia to the army near Richmond. Sheridan's raid successfully disrupted Richmond's rail and canal communications with the western part of Virginia. By the end of March Sheridan had completed his destructive raid and had joined Grant at Petersburg, the army was besieging Mobile, the Selma cavalry raid was in full swing, and Sherman had reached North Carolina after beating off a feeble attack at Bentonville on March 19–21 by a small Confederate army under Johnston. Grant was clearly attaining the object of his raids, to "leave the rebellion nothing to stand upon."

In early April Sheridan's cavalry and two corps of infantry reached the rear of the Petersburg defenses, precipitating Lee's long-contemplated withdrawal from Richmond. His line of retreat lay along the railroad running southwest, but he had to begin by marching due west because Sheridan's detachment moved southeast of him, heading westward. Lee faced a perilous situation, which Grant made the most of by strengthening Sheridan. Grant's continuous turning movement reached its climax at Appomattox Court House, where Sheridan's detachment blocked Lee's withdrawal route, and Lee surrendered his army on April 9, 1865.

Long siege lines, like those around Petersburg, reappeared in future wars and characterized almost all operations on the western front in World War I. The siege lines and Grant's Appomattox campaign provided an opportunity for the elderly Jomini, who studied the Civil War closely, to make a prescient comment. Noting that the long, entrenched lines of the Richmond-Petersburg siege might reappear in the future, he showed his approbation for his favorite maneuver when he asked: "But will they terminate in as brilliant a victory as that obtained by General Grant?"

Thus Grant again carried out the strategic turning movement favored by Jomini, and like that at Vicksburg, it forced the capitulation of the enemy army. Rosecrans had attempted this maneuver, and Lee had used it to drive back Pope, but only Grant had carried out campaigns comparable to Napoleon's of Marengo and Ulm. In formulating his interpretation of Civil War military strategy, T. Harry Williams failed to note both the conformity of Jomini's precepts to Napoleon's practice and how Grant, doubtless unknowingly, had successfully followed Jomini and emulated Napoleon. Williams also did not see how much Grant's greatest successes resembled in concept the practice common to both Union and Confederate generals and thus how much Jomini and Napoleon agreed and how uniformly their essentially identical ideas permeated the campaigns of generals on both sides.

Grant's brilliant campaign, and the strategy of raids, however, did not end the war. The Confederacy had lost long before, when its armies had melted away during the fall and winter. The loss of Atlanta and Sherman's march, combined with Lincoln's reelection, severely crippled the Confederate will to win. Military events had marked and helped to undermine the southerners' commitment to their new nation.

Yet in December 1864, with Sherman's army confined to the Savannah area, Union forces had almost completely evacuated Georgia, holding little or no more of the state than they had when Sherman began his campaign in May. The situation differed little in Alabama, though the Union navy had closed Mobile Harbor; and in Mississippi the Union had not acquired much new territory since the fall of Vicksburg, though Union forces had conducted several raids since the fall of the city on July 4, 1863. In the vast Confederate area west of the Mississippi no substantial territorial changes had occurred in 1864, and Price's raid into Missouri had created a serious commotion in that state.

So, except for broken railroads and the damage done along the path of Sherman's raid and the smaller diversionary spring and summer raids in northern Mississippi, the Union did not leave much evidence of Sherman's crucial campaign and its concomitant operations. Except in Virginia, the Confederacy had lost little territory since May, and even there the Union had added only a small portion of the state to the area it dominated, dramatic evidence of the Union's abandonment of its persisting strategy. But Grant's raiding strategy had not aimed at acquiring more of the Confederacy and, in any event, a raiding strategy could not control territory. But even breaking the key trunk-line railways in Georgia did not have an immediate effect on Confederate logistics, for the main Confederate armies continued to receive needed supplies.

The capitulation of the Confederacy was but a symptom of the triumph of defeatism throughout the South. Few southerners wished to continue the fight. Slavery was gone, states' rights appeared to be gone, soul-searing casualty lists evidenced the loss of many young men, and even God seemed to be against them. The armies had not yet surrendered, but the people were beaten. A Richmond editor correctly pointed out in January 1865 that the disasters suffered by Confederate arms were not worse than earlier setbacks, but he noted that "the people have been more depressed by them than they ever were before" because now they were expecting peace. Statesmen were talking of peace, believing that the people would give up the "chimera of Independence" if they could be "restored to their rights of the Union." The contest was over. "Our people *are* subjugated—they are crushed in spirit—they have not the heart to do anything," wrote one Confederate congressman, "but meet together and recount their losses and suffering." There were still those who felt the Confederacy could not lose if the people made up their minds to accept nothing but independence on their own terms and "to make any sacrifice which may be required." But the days of sacrifice were over.

All that remained was to contemplate the struggle, to ponder the meaning it may have had and the lessons God may have intended to teach, to learn to bear one's burdens, and to consider the attractive features of the alternatives rejected in the great decision of 1861. The Civil War disappeared from the battlefields, except for the monuments that future generations erected. It remained, however, in the hearts and minds of the people, which is the most enduring feature of flimsy and romantic Confederate nationalism.

Chapter Twelve

God, Guilt, and the Confederacy in Collapse

In 1864 the Confederates had halted Grant's persisting advance in Virginia in the trenches of the siege lines of Richmond and Petersburg; in the West, after the fall of Atlanta, Hood applied Lee's successful strategy of the defensive turning movement, forcing Sherman back toward Tennessee but avoiding any battle with the powerful Union force. The Confederates might also have halted Sherman, just as they had stopped Buell and Grant in 1862, by employing the logistic strategy of cavalry raids to break Sherman's vital but vulnerable railroad communications. But Grant's intention to use raids would have defeated either means of breaking Sherman's communications because Sherman was not irrevocably committed to capturing Atlanta before beginning his march to the sea. And Sherman's movement toward the coast caused Hood to counter with his Nashville campaign, giving him the opportunity to wreck his army, first in frontal assaults at Franklin and then in his futile Battle of Nashville and the subsequent debilitating retreat. Thus Grant's raiding strategy had the unintended consequence of countering the defensive turning movement. On the other hand, Sherman had intended and foreseen the additional consequence of the raids, helping materially to deplete Confederate morale and belief in victory. Yet the South gave up before the strategy could have its principal intended effect, breaking up the main Confederate armies by depriving them of supplies.

Grant's way of war, though differing in objective from any envisioned by Clausewitz or Jomini, fit well with the evolution of Union strategy along lines anticipated by Clausewitz. For total defeat of an enemy he had prescribed *"the destruction of his armed forces and the conquest of his territory,*" pointing out that "the destruction of his armed forces is the most appropriate action and the occupation of his territory only a consequence." But Clausewitz would have known as well as the Union commanders that they lacked adequate superiority to destroy the South's armed forces with a combat strategy. Instead, Union leaders adopted as their objective the "necessary evil," to "occupy land" before defeating the hostile armies.

Clausewitz had seen value in ways "to influence the enemy's expenditure of effort; in other words, how to make the war more costly to him." Casualties inflicted in battle and conquest of territory provided two obvious means, but he noted three others all relevant to the Union's pursuit of its logistic strategy: "*the seizure of enemy territory; not with the object of retaining it* but in order to exact financial contributions, or even to lay it waste"; giving "priority to operations that will increase the enemy's suffering" with the essentially political object of increasing his desire for peace; and finally, outlasting him, "using *the duration of the war to bring about a gradual exhaustion of his physical and moral resistance.*" Clearly, in such a war it was unlikely that one army could use a combat strategy to annihilate the adversary's physical existence; it was important to lay siege to his spiritual-moral resources as well as to attack his armies with a logistic strategy.

To this objective all facets of the war had contributed, including everything from deaths in battle to the influence of the blockade's deprivations on civilian morale and the subtle effect of Lincoln's nonpunitive plan of reconstruction. If they had engaged in active operations in the spring, the Confederate armies would have felt the effect of the breaking of the trunk-line railways and the closure of the ports of Wilmington, Charleston, Savannah, and Mobile. To campaign in 1865 the main Confederate forces would have had to withdraw into the interior, closer to their sources of supply, and disperse into smaller groups. This strategy would increase the availability of food and fodder but would not have worked as well to connect with sources of ammunition, weapons, and shoes. Because of the simplicity involved in equipping and sustaining mid-nineteenth-century armies, however, the Confederates still would have remained formidable, having at least as many as the 174,224 men who surrendered to Union forces in the spring of 1865. John Shy notes that "when the Confederacy gave up, its main armies had been destroyed, its people were tired, and its resources depleted." But "continued military resistance . . . was possible and was seriously considered at the time." The Confederacy still possessed important advantages, considering that "the vast spaces, rural economy, and poor transportation system of the South were ideal factors for an effective large-scale resistance movement along guerrilla lines." Under such conditions, Shy contends, "the South could have been made virtually indigestible for a Federal army."

If the Union had had to deal with continued military resistance, it would have faced many seasoned soldiers as well as a hostile population and the great extent of the unoccupied Confederacy. General W. T. Sherman would have fully agreed with John Shy as to the power of guerrilla "bands, a thing more to be feared than organized war." A keen student of history, Sherman did not need to draw on his knowledge of French failures against a national guerrilla resistance in Spain; in commanding in Union-occupied West Tennessee, he had experienced at first hand the weakness of the occupiers, the ascendancy of the hostile inhabitants, and the need to "reconquer the country . . . as we did from the Indians." Clausewitz and Jomini surely would have anticipated that Union armies would feel most acutely that they were engaged in a national war in which "a people enthusiastic in its political opinions" rushed "to meet the enemy in defense of all it holds dear." When, in a national war, the defeated withdrew into the interior, defenders employed the guerrilla warfare of a "general insurrection." In this way they could mobilize new strength, "not otherwise available" until that time. Jomini knew how formidable it could be: "The whole country is the scene of hostilities."

Jomini described a war in which the invader "holds scarcely any ground but that upon which he encamps; outside the limits of his camp every thing is hostile and multiplies a thousandfold the difficulties he meets at every step." The defenders enjoyed an overwhelming advantage because "each armed inhabitant knows the smallest paths and their connections; he finds everywhere a relative or a friend who aids him; the commanders also know the country, and, learning immediately the slightest movement on the part of the invader, can adopt the best measure to defeat his projects." Jomini believed the invader "*must inevitably yield after a time.*"

Jomini called this a "war of extermination" and considered it to be a "last resort," not only because he believed regulars and a national guard would provide an adequate defense but because he saw guerrilla warfare as unnecessarily expensive. Having seen such a war firsthand in Spain, he knew that the invaders retaliated with savagery and "by way of reprisals" committed "murder, pillage, and incendiarism throughout the country." These "consequences are so terrible that for the sake of humanity we ought to hope never to see it." Believing in the sufficiency of his system of regulars and militia, Jomini had written: "I sum up this discussion by asserting that, without being a utopian philanthropist, or a condottieri, a person may desire that wars of extermination may be banished from the code of nations and that the defenses of nations by disciplined militia, with the aid of good political alliances, may be sufficient to insure their independence."

Jomini restated this point in a way that has misled many readers as to his view of warfare: "As a soldier, preferring loyal and chivalrous warfare to organized assassination, if it be necessary to make a choice, I acknowledge my prejudices are in favor of the good old times when French and English guards courteously invited each other to fire first—as at Fontenoy,—preferring them to the frightful epoch when priests, women, and children throughout Spain plotted the murder of isolated soldiers." Readers, failing to note that Jomini wrote of the fate of Napoleon's soldiers in Spain, that he supported the kind of warfare Napoleon waged, and that he was making a choice between two undesirable extremes, have taken this statement to mean that he advocated some species of pre-Napoleonic warfare. But as a soldier he wished to avoid assassination at the hands of "priests, women, and children" and to fight a war he understood rather than a guerrilla war for which he believed the main weapons were political.

Union generals shared Jomini's aversion to guerrilla warfare and feared that the Confederates, who had employed it in Union rear areas, might rely on it even more in 1865. Grant's recurring nightmare in the last days and weeks of the war was that Lee's troops somehow would succeed in eluding his grasp and escape to the mountains to continue the fight by means of guerrilla warfare. Yet the Confederates never reached the time when they had to choose between guerrilla warfare and military surrender—they gave up well before then. Sherman, facing Joe Johnston's small but active army in North Carolina, showed his apprehension that the South would exploit its enormous space to swallow up its opponents when he expressed fear that Johnston "may travel back toward Georgia," requiring Sherman "to follow him again over that long road."

Such futile pursuits of small, elusive Confederate armies clearly showed the limits of military victory in a national war against an enemy with such vast territory.

But the Union did not have to depend on trying to expand its military success. The enemy showed that the federals had won a political victory when, instead of marching back to Georgia, Joe Johnston surrendered his army just as Lee had already done. In thus making such essentially political decisions to end the war, the officers acted in accord with the feelings of their men, the many who had already left the war as well as those who had remained with the colors until the end. And the men reflected the sentiment of the country. The Confederates had already paid as much for independence as they thought it was worth. They declined to continue a conventional war, much less incur the far higher costs of Jomini's "last resort," the guerrilla warfare of a "general insurrection."

Had the Confederates actually resisted long enough to face the choice of more extensive and prolonged guerrilla warfare, they would have confronted the specter of a population of former slaves slipping all remaining bonds of social control and black participation in some form. But, as Kenneth Stampp and Carl N. Degler have reminded us, guerrilla war did indeed break out during the years of Radical Reconstruction, spurred by the government's policy of black equality.

During the war Sherman saw the power in the interaction of political desire and military cost. He stressed prospective cost when he pointed out that "if we can march a well-appointed army right through this territory, it is a demonstration to the world, foreign and domestic, that we have a power which Davis cannot resist. This may not be war but statesmanship." He hoped, as Clausewitz expressed it, "to overcome the enemy's will," because his raid, "operating upon the minds of the sensible men," would convince southerners that "victory was impossible." As prospects for victory dimmed, "the desire for peace on either side will rise and fall with the probability of further successes and the amount of effort these require." But as Clausewitz always stressed, war is not "*something autonomous* but always an *instrument of policy.*" And policy provided the key because, "since war is not an act of senseless passion but is controlled by its political object, the value of the object must determine the sacrifices to be made for it in *magnitude* and also in *duration.*"

In the closing months of the war the military and psychological bases of Confederate defeat became closely intertwined. The fall of Atlanta,

Sheridan's victories, and the impact of the strategy of raids starkly brought home to Confederates that God did not support their side, at least in the ways they previously had believed; clearly, if He had preferred them, the fortunes of war would have favored the South. Facing defeat, southerners felt compelled to reconcile the ways of God and man. They could do this by changing the perception of God, which led to the conclusion that perhaps He was not on the Confederate side after all. They could also manipulate God by appeasement, supplication, and prayer. If these efforts did not work, however, the only way to reconcile man to his God was for man to change his perceptions of himself. This led to self-examination that obliged Confederates to confess that God punished them for not being in step with His ways. "Can we believe in the justice of Providence, or must we conclude that we are after all wrong?" asked Josiah Gorgas. "Such visitations give me to great bitterness of heart, and repinings at His decrees. It is apparent that we are yet sufficiently tried," he confessed, for he saw the hand of God directly punishing the people for not being in step with His ways. His people had the duty to confess their sins, accept His punishment, and invoke His blessing. "If repentance, humiliation and faith were unfeigned," then He would prosper southern arms and the war would go well.

Since the discomfort created by the dissonant knowledge of alternative decisions surely caused great pain, it took much thinking to reduce it and accept new ideas of the Confederate future. Some southerners could not envision and accept even the possibility of defeat, so understandably painful the prospect loomed. At the end of March 1865, one Confederate expressed his "unshaken faith in the ultimate triumph of that cause" and confessed himself "provoked and annoyed that any human being, who had *faith in God*, should doubt." Others felt equally certain of the outcome, even on the brink of defeat. The editor of the *Lynchburg Virginian* thought that the side devoted to "right and justice, against wrong and oppression," inevitably would win, and concluded that, since the Confederacy had right on its side, "if we . . . do not falter, we must succeed."

For most Confederates, however, after the fall of Atlanta and the re-election of Lincoln, and certainly after Sherman's march to the sea, the time had come to face the inevitable. Their religious views made this process easier. Their brand of Christianity and the religious fatalism they espoused allowed them to overcome more easily than otherwise the dissonance created by the knowledge of the attractive features of rejected alternatives. God's will became a psychological bridge to the acceptance of defeat.

Reliance on God meant repentance of sin. Southerners fully realized that they had shortcomings. God had punished them and would continue to do so "until the whole people shall have repented of their sins in sackcloth and ashes," for they "have sinned grievously." Here the clergy had a vital role to play. A Richmond editor called upon the preachers to "preach until every man thinks the Devil has gotten into his pew, and is chasing him up to the corner of it." The clergy, rigidly scrupulous and ambitious, proved only too ready to respond and thundered attacks on such vices as alcohol, sexual pleasure, merrymaking, and gambling, among others. Obviously, some ministers were using the war for complex ends, to promote the church, or their version of it, rather than the Confederacy; nevertheless, most clergymen preached that a "return to Christ" would bring victory. Others pointed to the apparent manifestation of God's wrath and complained that people had not learned the obvious lesson. Rather, they had been "driven away from God's commandments" at a time when they ought to be learning to submit to His will. The Episcopal bishop of Virginia, John Johns, asserted that God's displeasure resulted from the collective guilt of all southerners, and he expressed amazement that God had not punished His people sooner and more drastically.

Psychologists emphasize the role of guilt in shaping behavior. This emotion would have equal importance in any age, for Christians believed, and still do, in the omnipresence of sin. Bishop Johns gave voice to this belief, but what sin or sins so oppressed Confederates as to cause God to spread His wrath over the people? Some thought God might be punishing southerners for extortion (charging high prices) or violation of His commandments. Others looked to other sins. In his study *Confederate Morale and Church Propaganda*, James W. Silver points to the role of slavery and touches upon the two aspects of the institution that caused Confederates to ponder. Many thought the institution inherently wrong; but even if it were right, the people did not administer it according to God's will. The institution itself, plus failure to respect slave marriages, to encourage sabbath worship among slaves, to provide religious instruction to slaves, or to protect them from unkind masters, clearly involved sins that led to God's condemnation. Thus the Roman Catholic bishop of Savannah called upon the South to make slavery "conform to the law of God" because He would not bless "a state of things which would be a flagrant violation of His holy commandments."

More important, as a consequence of this guilt, some southerners even questioned the entire institution. This questioning had a close relation to the problem of morale and to Confederate nationalism, for slavery constituted the major difference between North and South. If Confederates lost confidence in its legitimacy, sooner or later they would lose confidence in their country as well.

The South had seceded because many southerners thought that the Lincoln administration made slavery unsafe within the Union. The Confederates fought for a separate nation based on slavery, their political objective, and the strength of the Confederacy's will to make a long, strong resistance could, Clausewitz would have believed, "only be gauged approximately by the strength of the motive animating it." The motive animating the Confederates determined how much military success the Union must achieve, for "if the enemy is to be coerced you must put him in a situation that is even more unpleasant than the sacrifice you call on him to make."

But Lincoln realized that military success did not constitute the only variable, for he understood Clausewitz's point that "the smaller the penalty you demand from your opponent, the less you can expect him to try to deny it to you." Lincoln's peace terms, in the form of his reconstruction plan, asked nothing from the South except the extinction of slavery. Insisting on no political or economic penalties, he invited the states back into the Union to resume their places as if they had never left it—except that they must give up slavery. He even invited them back with increased strength in the House of Representatives because, with slavery obliterated, the three-fifths compromise would become moot, enabling the South to count its entire population.

"Wars," Clausewitz wrote, "must vary with the nature of their motives and of the situations which gave rise to them," and "the original political objects can greatly alter during the course of the war and many finally change entirely *since they are influenced by events and their probable consequences.*" Just as the Union had added the extinction of slavery to its original war aim of preservation of the Union, so too had the South altered its concept of the political goal of the war. The changed prospects of slavery gave hope to some of its secret opponents and caused second thoughts among many of its unthinking or passive supporters, just as the course of the war must have discouraged those who had not believed that secession would bring war. After all, Clausewitz had realized that "the same political object can elicit *differing* reactions from different peoples, and even from the same people at different times."

Kenneth Stampp has reiterated the close relationship of morale and slavery in a challenging attempt to solve the puzzle of the breakdown of Confederate will. He suggested what he believes to be "a partial explanation of Confederate defeat." In an essay entitled "The Southern Road to Appomattox," Stampp advanced the admittedly controversial thesis that enough slaveholders and other southerners had doubts about the morality of slavery and hence the validity of the Confederate cause to undermine southern commitment and help ensure defeat. Accepting David Potter's argument that Confederate failure resulted largely from the failure of its politicians and political system, Stampp asks why southern politicians—who had shown so much able leadership in the generations before the war—should suddenly prove incapable of providing the leadership necessary for achieving independence. Rejecting Frank L. Owsley's notion that states'-rights doctrine had much to do with the outcome, agreeing with David Donald that the Confederates lacked self-discipline, and nodding toward Bell I. Wiley's thesis of the decisiveness of internal disharmony, Stampp sums up the Confederate problem, correctly, we believe, as "weakness in morale." A country with resources equal to or inferior to those of its adversary can conquer only if it possesses superior morale, but this the Confederacy lacked because of "uncertainty about the South's identity, of the peculiar circumstances that led to secession and the attempt at independence, and of widespread doubts and apprehensions about the validity of the Confederate cause." Stampp believes that the fact of slavery, which had caused secession and war, made Confederates uneasy. Southerners had "to soft-pedal the very *cause* of the war," making it "a considerable disadvantage as far as its moral position was concerned."

Building on these observations, Stampp proposes the hypothesis that many Confederates lacked deep commitment to the cause and that, unconsciously, "the behavior of some suggested that a Union victory was quite an acceptable result." The failure of a true southern nationalism to develop partially caused this paradoxical conduct; only slavery gave Confederates a common and distinct identity, for most of the attributes that southerners shared with each other—language, religious values, and his-tory—they also shared with northerners. Pointing out that some south-erners had favored secession only to force negotiations for a favorable restructuring of the Union (one suspects that Stampp overestimates the number of those who took this ambiguous position), Stampp concluded that these Confederates found themselves "fighting for an independence they had never sought" and "may well have turned now unconsciously to reunion through defeat" to regain their true national identity.

That, in defeat, the South managed to jettison the burden of slavery provides a second, more important reason for its paradoxical behavior. Believing, as we also do, that a significant number of southerners never truly convinced themselves of the positive good of slavery, Stampp agreed with an argument posited by Charles G. Sellers, Jr., that the inconsis-tency between maintaining bondage and at the same time promoting lib-erty bothered them. We would add that the dissonance between Chris-tian precepts and the administration of slavery was also bothersome. Although not universally true, guilt, from whatever variety of sources, tormented enough consciences to influence collective behavior and pro-vide a margin of shattered morale that led to Union victory. Stampp notes one convincing proof of this thesis: "the readiness, if not always good grace, with which most Southerners accepted the abolition of slavery." In doing so, they abandoned the elemental cause of the war and the emblem of their nationalism.

Kenneth Stampp hardly stands alone in detecting an undercurrent of guilt in southern thought on slavery. Thomas Jefferson trembled for his country when he reflected that "God is just . . . [and] his justice cannot sleep forever." Mrs. Chesnut's prayer on the eve of the Civil War, "God forgive us, but ours is a *monstrous* system and wrong and iniquity [sic]," forthrightly confesses her afflicted conscience; her overseer believed that most southern women were abolitionists at heart, "and hot ones, too." And yet, though Jefferson and Chesnut were not alone, at the same time multitudes of southerners seem to have felt no apparent guilt whatever. The writings of modern historians reflect this dichotomy. In 1949, Rollin G. Osterweis remarked that the "guilt complex over slavery . . . is as difficult to prove as it is to establish" and suggested that "this hypothesis of the guilt complex" reflected "some projection of twentieth-century standards."

Charles G. Sellers, Jr., made perhaps the most straightforward statement of the hypothesis when he contended that "the paradox of the slaveholding South's devotion to 'liberty' " provided "the key to the tragedy of southern history." When white southerners demanded freedom for themselves without acknowledging that others had similar rights, they engaged in "a disguised protest against, or perhaps an escape from, the South's daily betrayal of its liberal self." Bell I. Wiley believed that Confederate internal dissension came from feelings of guilt about slavery and that this consciousness of culpability became an ever-heavier burden as Confederate defeat approached. Carl Degler notes that "emancipation was not accompanied by the kind of emotional resistance that a challenge to deeply held values can be expected to call forth." The clear implication is that emotions were shallow because southerners were, on the whole, happy to be rid of slavery.

Perhaps the best discussion of slaveholders' guilt is by James Oakes, who provides a useful discussion of the relationship of religion and slavery that makes some salient points. "Within the context of a slave society," says Oakes, the attack on materialism "served as a psychological medium through which masters expressed their misgivings about bondage. They complained repeatedly about the 'difficulty of serving both God and Mamon.' " Evangelical religion influenced slaveholders "to bring their ethical convictions into line with their daily practices," a difficult task that never was fully accomplished. The resulting psychological tensions, Oakes believes, were mitigated by the notion that slaveholders were responsible only to God. This reasoning had the convenient effect of justifying slavery and denying the arguments of the abolitionists; it also had the disturbing effect of underlining "the masters' fears that they would ultimately be judged by God for their behavior as slaveholders." The result, as one may well imagine, was psychological turmoil in which slaveholders (and, by implication, other evangelicals as well) questioned their beliefs, confessed the weakness of their faith, and made "startlingly frequent declarations that when they died they would go to hell."

On the other hand, James L. Roark thinks few slaveholders felt any sense of remorse about their property, except, perhaps, women, who "may have had special empathy for slaves because they subconsciously recognized the parallels between their positions, one as slave and the other as 'Southern lady.' " Eugene D. Genovese goes even further, expressing surprise at the very notion that planters had such feelings: "Did substantial numbers of slaveholders feel guilty about holding slaves?

There is no evidence that they did . . . and it is difficult to see why they should have." James Brewer Stewart agrees, at least for the nullification-era generation. Instead of "spasms of racial guilt," South Carolina's nullifiers were motivated by a desire "to fend off malevolent forces which eroded patriarchal independence and threatened to destroy white domination and therefore all social order."

Despite these sweeping statements rejecting the guilt thesis of Stampp, Cash, Sellers, Wiley, Oakes, and others, it seems obvious that it existed—not for all planters, certainly, but for many, perhaps even most. One need not prove, and probably could not prove, that either guilt or its absence predominated among southerners, whether slaveholders or not. Stampp's argument, to which we subscribe, simply states that however many slaveholders felt the pangs of conscience, the number was large enough to have a far-reaching effect upon the Confederate war effort.

We discuss Stampp's hypothesis at length because it seems to us to offer much help in understanding why the Confederates abandoned the war when they did. Building on Stampp's suggestion, we offer a more complete and, we hope, more satisfactory explanation for the result of the Civil War. Perhaps we can provide in addition some notion of the psychological mechanisms that operated upon usually unconscious desires among Confederates to produce a fearful yet consoling resolution of their problems.

We argue that many southerners did feel guilt over slavery and thus unconsciously looked to a Union victory and emancipation as desirable outcomes of a disastrous war, as Stampp suggests. We would add further, however, that these Confederates, and many other southerners as well, came to believe that God willed that slavery should end, and from that point they logically progressed to a sense of guilt over the war itself, a guilt that could only increase as both the war and the casualty lists grew longer.

This is not to say that a significant number of southerners consciously desired defeat. But many of them had unconscious inclinations in that direction, and defeat would have its rewards. For some, the loss of slavery would be a favorable outcome, if the collective behavior of the postwar South is any indication. Few southerners ever admitted a desire to restore slavery, but thousands confessed relief that war had destroyed the peculiar institution.

A nationalism based on an institution about which many southerners felt guilt could not sustain the Confederacy past the losses and disappointments of late 1864. And with military reverses inducing many to believe that God did not favor their cause, religion, which had originally buoyed up Confederate confidence, not only no longer supported morale but even inspired in some southerners a fatalism about defeat. When Confederates read in their Bibles the verses that assured them that "there is none righteous, no, not one. . . . For all have sinned, and come short of the Glory of God," they saw the inextricable connection of religion and guilt. So strong was the relationship of the two concepts that both of them must constitute key words in the lexicon of those who would isolate the causes of Confederate defeat.

As defeat came, the dissonance between the supposed knowledge of God's favor and the knowledge of imminent defeat created great psychological discomfort. Like any dissonance, this discomfort would have to be reduced. One could not achieve psychological harmony, at least not in 1865, by maintaining that Confederates actually were winning the war. Only one way led out. Those who concerned themselves with religious matters could finally reduce cognitive dissonance only by the cognition, or "knowledge," that the loss of the war proved that God, if not actually against the South, at least was not acting positively for the South. Thus, one Confederate confessed to his diary the anguish of his heart and the loneliness of an abandoned soul: "I fear that God has ceased to work miracles. He certainly seems now to be on the side of our oppressors."

One sees in the behavior of many Confederates the working of this hopeless struggle to avoid the logical consequences of their beliefs and to reduce dissonance. Thus, in 1864, Governor Vance sincerely proclaimed his belief that it constituted an "impiety to suppose He will let us be conquered by such a cruel and wicked race as the Yankees, if we only prove true to ourselves." A Raleigh newspaper earlier had reflected unease at the thought of the masses of dead and of God's judgment and urged the South to fight on. "To entertain the thought of giving up the struggle in which we are engaged, before the accomplishment of the object which we have in view," it warned, "would be to prove false to ourselves—to our brethren who lie slaughtered on many a gory field, to our country, to the interest of civilization and humanity, and to those who are to come after us." Most important, "it would also indicate a want of faith in God which would merit the severest punishment that could befall us." The writer who composed and accepted this commentary reflected a defeatist mentality. For to stake victory on God's favor, justly conferred, confessed that if victory did not come it would fail because God had not conferred His favor, and, more ominous, would lead to the inevitable conclusion that the South had not merited that favor. In true circular fashion, this logic could only lead back to the further confession that the South did not deserve God's favor, and, if it did not, sin and guilt were the reasons. Guilt over what? Slavery, the war, the long casualty lists, although every orthodox Christian undergoing the punishment of defeat could search his heart and find other reasons as well. With this logic, such individuals eventually would become more than ready to bow their heads to accept the defeat that seemed to be God's will.

Evidently God guided affairs only according to His plan. Feelings of sin and guilt naturally provoked a fear of punishment and provided an obvious and ready answer to those who questioned why God had let such evils occur. The outcome of the war constituted heavenly punishment, which must not be resisted but accepted with Christian humility because God ordained it. And because He ordained it, the punishment—for slavery, for making war, for shedding blood—was fully justified.

Chapter Thirteen

Coming to Terms with Slavery

AS SOME southerners retreated into religious fatalism, many felt surprise and shock and endured severe dissonance at a proposal to arm slaves. Thus a scheme to increase military manpower worked to diminish morale and willingness to sacrifice more for victory. Few had been surprised when the government impressed slaves for use in military construction or mobilized them to serve as cooks, laborers, teamsters, nurses, and the like with the armies; some Confederates, however, were dubious about any military use of the black population for fear that it might lead to their use as soldiers. These doubters were correct.

In January 1864, General Patrick Cleburne proposed to his fellow general officers of the Army of Tennessee that the South employ blacks as soldiers. Cleburne and thirteen of his division officers concluded that the time had come to "commence training a large reserve of the most courageous of our slaves, and further that we guarantee freedom within a reasonable time to every slave in the South who shall remain true to the Confederacy in this war." If he had to choose between slavery and independence, the practical Cleburne preferred to give up the former to save the latter. The plan would work, Cleburne thought, because then slavery no longer would present an obstacle in the path to European recognition and, moreover, it would remove the incentive for slaves to join the Union army.

Shrinking from the possible consequences of public knowledge of Cleburne's recommendation, Jefferson Davis suppressed it. Davis had good reason for anxiety concerning the question of slave soldiers, for, as Cleburne implied, the slave must receive an appropriate incentive for him to perform as an effective soldier. Emancipation was the only suitable reward, and that raised ticklish questions of racial adjustment and the horrifying question of war goals, the reasons so many had gone to war in the first place. That Davis kept Cleburne's memorandum to himself does not mean he did not think about it or that the idea had not already occurred to him. Davis admitted after the war that early in the conflict he would have considered such an idea "preposterous." But he also confessed that when he had suggested the use of blacks as teamsters and laborers, he had thought the experience would be useful in case the South should ever need them under arms.

By the time the last session of the Confederate Congress convened on November 7, 1864, many saw black soldiers as the only possible alternative to capitulation. But for fear of public opinion, the issue had to be soft-pedaled. In his opening message to Congress, Davis stated, "I must dissent from those who advise a general levy and arming of the slaves for the duty of soldiers." He continued, however, with the ominous warning that "should the alternative ever be presented of subjugation or of the employment of the slave as a soldier, there seems to be no reason to doubt what should then be our decision."

Using the moral and popular authority of his office in a way he never had before and never would again, Davis floated trial balloons and encouraged his administration to join him in hinting to other influential people that the country had to consider arming the slaves. In the fall of 1864 many Confederate leaders, editors, clergymen, and army officers agreed with Davis. Immediately a number of congressmen supported the trial balloon with enthusiasm, while official policy, and indeed the secretary of war, was still denying that the administration contemplated the use of black troops.

This issue, then, forced fundamental reconsideration of the entire Confederate position. The arguments of Cleburne, Davis, and their supporters in the leadership took the practical side of the question. Support came from all over the Confederacy. In Mississippi editors split on the question, but as early as April 1863 one of them had urged the people "to make any and every sacrifice which the establishment of our independence may require. . . . Let not slavery prove a barrier to our independence. . . . Let it perish!"

Indeed, by January 1865 General Lee used the same practical argument for the same practical end. "I think," he wrote, "we must decide whether slavery shall be extinguished by our enemies and the slaves be used against us, or use them ourselves at the risk of the effects which may be produced upon our social institutions. My own opinion is that we should employ them without delay." Lee added that "the best means of securing the efficiency and fidelity of this auxiliary force would be to accompany the measure with a well-digested plan of gradual and general emancipation."

Any plan to use slave soldiers clearly must include emancipation, as men on both sides of the question realized. Thus the issue of slave soldiers led inevitably to questions of economic interest and racial adjustment. R. G. H. Kean noted in his diary that congressmen from the occupied areas were more in favor of arming slaves than were those from the rest of the country and that the planter interests strongly opposed it.

Congressman James T. Leach of North Carolina thought arming slaves "would make a San Domingo of our land." Some Confederates were so frightened that a few began to think of returning to the Union as a way of retaining slavery. This notion seemed as strange to some Confederates as it does to us today. In the summer of 1863 an Alabama newspaper editor saw such people as deluded fools, and the next winter Governor Vance viewed as "lost to reason" those who thought reconstruction would save slavery. Yet Senator William A. Graham of North Carolina and others believed that voluntary return to the Union in January 1865 would save the peculiar institution and perhaps secure other concessions as well. Much impressed by the discussions that a peace commission had had with Lincoln and Stanton, Graham began to consider "whether reunion, by which ten States may defeat the proposed [thirteenth] amendment to the Constitution, & retain slavery be not preferable to the triumph of his arms, and the subjugation of every thing to his power."

The issue of slave soldiers and emancipation went beyond the merits of the question, however, for it forced Confederates to evaluate the goals of their war effort. But as they began to consider what they were fighting for, they realized that ideas on the subject varied. Back in 1860–61 the issue had seemed clear. Southerners talked then of slavery and, to a lesser extent, of racial adjustment and states' rights. They had not said very much about independence per se or about honor. Although many advanced different arguments from time to time, and in a complex problem such as this probably no two people thought the same, from the start a large part of the Confederate elite pointed to slavery as the cause of armed conflict. Robert Hardy Smith, a member of the Provisional Congress, wrote in 1861 that "the question of negro slavery has been the apple of discord" and that "we have dissolved the late Union chiefly because of the negro quarrel." Only a few contemporaries would have disagreed—in 1861.

Virginia's Senator R. M. T. Hunter drew the most disturbing conclusion: if slavery caused the war (Hunter had believed in 1860–61 that it did), and if the Confederacy had abandoned the war goal of preservation of slavery, how could it justify the loss of so many lives to save it? How could one justify one's emotional investment and the expenditure of so much blood and treasure? "If this is so," cried Hunter, "who is to answer for the hundreds of thousands of men who had been slain in the war? Who was to answer for them before the bar of heaven?" To answer Hunter's question, to resolve the dissonance, one must justify the bloodshed by inventing a new war goal, else those multitudes in blue and gray had died for nothing.

If the Confederacy needed more soldiers to achieve its goals, if slaves provided the only major source of new soldiers, and if emancipation was necessary to motivate those slaves to fight on the side of the Confederacy, those southerners who believed the states had seceded, established the Confederacy, and gone to war to save slavery would suffer a severe dissonance problem. Not yet able or willing to resolve that psychological conflict by changing their decision, that is, giving up the war effort, some southerners mitigated their dissonance by changing their information instead, claiming that they were not waging the war to protect slavery but to achieve independence. By contending that they had not fought the war to save slavery, such southerners made it easier for their comrades to push for emancipation and the arming of the slaves.

As Robert F. Durden indicates, the question of goals helped force many Confederates to decide what they valued most, slavery or independence. Before 1864 one could fight for both. By the summer and fall of 1864 it became an either-or proposition; Confederates could not achieve both goals but might still achieve one. "We are fighting first for our liberty and independence," a Georgia preacher warned his son, "not for our interests." Not surprisingly, the discovery that the South was not fighting for the purpose that many Confederates originally believed raised resentments and reopened old arguments. Had they not created the Confederacy to save slavery? Who had advocated independence in 1861 without linking it to slavery in some way? No wonder the rejected alternatives began to look more attractive, as some southerners who had not favored secession and war logically asked why, if the South could abolish slavery so it could continue the war, it could not do so to end it?

But if the Confederacy freed its slaves, it would be denying its own history. If not for slavery, why did the South fight? Some Confederates had always contended that states' rights constituted the heart of the problem, and others who asserted that they fought to check the encroachment of an all-powerful central government now joined them. Confederates reached the states'-rights thesis by either of two routes, neither of which excluded the other. First, there were some southerners who had looked to the incompatibility of Yankee centralization and southern autonomy during the secession winter of 1861 and others who had come to that idea later on. Second, there were those who accepted the same issues as the first group but extended the struggle against centralization to include Confederate centralizers as well as those of the North. These true states'-rights men wondered why the South had established its own modern, centralized state if it was waging war to escape centralization.

So, whether one fought for slavery or states' rights seemed to make little difference in 1864 and 1865. The policy of the Confederate government—under the guise of necessity, to be sure—subordinated both of these goals to emancipation and centralization. But war, emancipation, and despotism seemed to be a poor exchange for the privileges that southerners had enjoyed in the Union before the war. Nevertheless, many Confederates had a difficult time trying to avoid posing the question: Why should the fight go on?

The recent work of Bertram Wyatt-Brown should remind us how important honor was to southerners. It involved not the bleating of a braggart so much as a standard for the conduct of life. It comes as no surprise, therefore, that when Confederates talked of honor they did not mean pride so much as moral integrity, personal bravery, Christian graciousness, deference to and respect for others, and self-worth, recognized by their peers. Most southerners held these values as important considerations, not only in the settlement of the war but also in daily life. It was no small thing, therefore, to fight for honor. The impediment was that honor had come to be all there was left to fight for; slavery was about to go, by the action of the Confederacy itself. Independence had become just as precarious by 1865. Some Confederates thought the South itself had destroyed states' rights, and all believed that they would lose it for certain if the Union triumphed. By the process of elimination, therefore, honor became important as never before.

But a second impediment sprang from the particular demands for an honorable peace, by which most Confederates meant a peace that did not entail reunion. By definition, therefore, Confederate defeat must result in a dishonorable peace, the compromise of honor. A peace with reconstruction would have to be rationalized in some way, until it appeared compatible with honor. If surrender and honor could be reconciled, however, southerners could accept defeat more easily. In the long run, honor provided a justification that Confederates thought made the war worthwhile, and a fierce resistance was one way to preserve honor. The long struggle against superior numbers, the high competence of many Confederate generals, and the skill and courage of the troops all had a part in preserving honor even in defeat.

The choice was made easier by the logic of desperation, the humiliation that would accompany defeat, and the realization of slavery's probable doom no matter what decision the South made. Gradually southerners realized that if the hated Yankees succeeded in nothing else, they had delivered a mortal wound to the peculiar institution. Under such circumstances one could be very practical in advocating the arming of the slaves for, as Mississippi Congressman John T. Lamkin pointed out, one might as well favor black soldiers, with emancipation as their reward, since the slaves would have freedom whether the Confederacy won or not. "And to tell you the plain truth," he wrote his wife, "I dont [sic] care whether they are or not. . . . Slavery is played out." Congressman Warren Akin's wife put the same ideas more strongly: "Every one I talk to is in favor of putting negroes in the army and that *immediately*. . . . I think slavery is now gone and what little there is left of it should be rendered as serviceable as possible."

The psychology of fear, resignation, and projection was clearly operating here; often describing defeat as subjugation to slavery and despotism, Confederates would secure protection by using slaves for soldiers. Mrs. Akin and Congressman Lamkin could more easily think the unthinkable by telling themselves that slavery had reached its end in any event. Hence to use slave soldiers, with the likely promise of emancipation as their reward, was giving up nothing that had not been lost already. Fear also played its part—not only fear of defeat but also fear of large numbers of blacks out of social control. This question of racial adjustment would be solved in a grisly way, perhaps, if blacks went into the army. The thought that if the South put blacks to fighting some would die mollified Congressman Akin's wife. If that were not done, "there will soon be more negroes than whites in the country and they will be the free race. *I want to see them got rid of soon.*" A Virginia newspaper urged its readers to conquer their prejudices so that the war would not destroy the "flower of the country." As for the slaves, "surely they are good enough for Yankee bullets."

In turning their backs on slavery, "giving up the principles upon which we went into the war," southerners also gave up that which most fundamentally distinguished South from North. They were denying the basis of whatever nationalism they had at a time when the Union had attained impressive military successes. This denial and defeat, combined with faltering support from religion, not only resulted in soldier desertion and civilian defeatism but also made many Confederates feel betrayed.

And what of those who agreed to secession only reluctantly, who left the Union for no other reason than to preserve slavery? Would they not feel a particular sense of betrayal when their leadership performed the bait-and-switch tactic that pushed the South toward emancipation? Governor Vance asserted that the proposal to arm and emancipate slaves would "surrender the entire question which has ever separated the North from the South, would stultify ourselves in the eyes of the world, and render our whole revolution nugatory—a mere objectles [sic] waste of human life."

For many Confederates, the implications of slave soldiers and emancipation were much more disturbing than merely questioning why they had gone to war and whether they could, or should, drop out. Independence could be sought for its own sake, an alternative that Paul D. Escott emphasizes, but after defeat, which now seemed close at hand, that goal would be ashes. The southern attitudes enumerated above reinforced each other, added converts to the unconscious acceptance of the bitter pill of defeat, and increased the taste of dust and ashes in the mouths of some of the most determined and valiant Confederates.

On a much more fundamental level, however, the dual questions of slave soldiers and emancipation concerned racial adjustment and thus transcended practicality. Howell Cobb got to the heart of the question:

arming slaves was "the most pernicious idea that has been suggested since the war began," for "if slaves will make good soldiers our whole theory of slavery is wrong." John M. Daniel, wartime editor of the *Richmond Examiner*, remarked to his readers (November 8, 1864) that "we surrender our position whenever we introduce the negro to arms. If a negro is fit to be a soldier, he is not fit to be a slave; and if any large portion of the race is fit for free labor—fit to live and be useful under the competitive system of labor—then the whole race is fit for it." So the devastating logic of people like Cobb and Daniel created more dissonance and not only for those who had harbored misgivings about slavery.

When the Confederate leadership changed southern war goals from slavery to independence in late 1864 and early 1865, it heightened this combination of resentment, guilt, and disillusion. As the ultimate outcome of the Confederate debate on emancipation became clear, remorse and anger struck many reluctant Confederates, for the government's policy created dissonance. Such people could no longer reconcile their country's action (wage war to save slavery) with its object (give up slavery). They would have to change either action or object. Until such a change occurred, the resulting dissonance produced severe discomfort.

And dissonance over war goals aggravated the impact of the costs of the war. Mrs. Chesnut, who confided opinions on so many subjects to her diary, had confessed her unease over the war and the lengthening casualty lists after only a year of fighting. Would success repay all that blood? "After all, suppose we do all we hoped. Suppose we start up grand and free—a proud young republic. Think of all those young lives sacrificed! If three for one be killed, what comfort is that? What good will that do? . . . The best and bravest of one generation swept away! . . . But those poor boys of between 18 and 20 years of age . . . they are washed away, literally, in the tide of blood. There is nothing to show they were ever on earth." By 1863 she had become even more distraught, commenting about the sour remarks of newspaper editors who made the maimed and wounded soldiers "think that all this is for nothing—that they are wounded and die in vain." And Chesnut clearly feared that the dead had sacrificed themselves uselessly because in January 1865 she and her friends grieved over their dead with the bitter thought that "their lives had been given up in vain. . . . What a cohort would rise to view if thoughts took shape. Splendid young life sacrificed—in vain."

Others came to similar conclusions. A North Carolina editor declared as early as July 1863 that he stood for peace because, among other reasons, "there has been enough of blood and carnage, enough of widows and orphans, heart broken mothers and sorrowing fathers." Another editor declared in 1864 that the "Courts of Heaven resound with one great prayer; the supplications of a sorrowing people for the return of *peace*. Weary with blood and slaughter, surfeited with tears and suffering, appalled at the dire calamities which war has inaugurated, the heart of the nation pants for relief."

Those, like Mrs. Chesnut, who had feelings of misgiving or guilt over slavery, must have most acutely felt the anguish of the casualties and could welcome the demise of slavery. Many of the Christian believers asked the inevitable question, why did God let this happen to me? From some Confederates the answer was that defeat was a just punishment—punishment for the sins of slavery, of making war, of pride—take your choice.

The time came, therefore, when the force of events plus the power of guilt overwhelmed the reasoning of those who sought to maintain slavery. They argued that they did not really like slavery; that regardless of the outcome of the war, the institution would end; that if they acted with skill they could still retain white supremacy and the benefits of slave labor without the slave system; and that in any event they were better off without it.

After initial rejection, the bulk of the southern leadership gradually moved toward acceptance of the idea. It became policy in March of 1865, just before the end, by a combination of law and executive order. Southerners approached the question from two directions, one idealistic and the other practical. The idealists were those who always had doubted the institution or who had come to feel some pangs of guilt about slavery; they also included those who saw the hand of God at work as the South lost the war and slavery with it because He did not will that the South should win. Those who may have doubted the institution but who argued for emancipation and the arming of slaves on the grounds of practicality joined the idealists. They considered anything that would assist the war effort acceptable, and if Confederate blacks could have more use free than slave, these southerners saw little reason not to change their minds about the proper role of blacks in southern society. So to the dissonance between the knowledge of God's favor and the success of Union arms and a states'-rights country with such a powerful government, the debate over and decision to arm and emancipate slaves in a war on behalf of slavery added yet another conflict that sapped the will of many Confederates to continue the struggle.

Thus by the end of the war Confederates had begun to raise black regiments, with the implied promise of emancipation. In the face of war, of runaways, of black soldiers in the Union army, and of increasing difficulty in getting slaves to work, southerners could reduce the psychological discomfort caused by dissonant, alternative policies about slavery only by turning to new arguments, thereby adding new cognitive elements. Having taken warnings of war and catastrophe with insufficient seriousness, such people became more penitent and responsive to the fate the future might have in store for them. Thus, as Kenneth Stampp noted, "The readiness, if not always good grace, with which most Southerners accepted the abolition of slavery." "When at last, they lost the profits and conveniences of slavery," says Stampp, "they won the chance to live in peace with themselves and with their age. It was not a bad exchange." Other southerners were relieved, eager, and hopeful because they would no longer have to support slaves they did not need.

For others pragmatism provided the new element. They correctly foresaw that the South would be able to keep white supremacy and most of the benefits of the slave system. In the summer of 1865 a Georgia woman argued that the South could abandon slavery because state laws still would permit whites to control the black population. As an official of the Freedmen's Bureau in Richmond told the Joint Committee on Reconstruction in 1866, Virginians preferred blacks to remain free, and they would not reenslave them if they had the chance: "I think they would prefer to hold him by their laws, &c., in a situation which would be slavery in effect but not in name, so as to have the benefit of his labor without the responsibility of supporting him."

Seeking to confront their difficulties in a practical way, southerners relinquished slavery but not racism. Events proved the correctness of the views of those who said that they could control black labor just as well without slavery. Peonage, contract labor, convict leasing, and lien laws served to perpetuate involuntary servitude well into the twentieth century.

If the South had gone to war because of slavery, white supremacy, the desire to be independent, the wish to preserve honor, and states'-rights constitutionalism, but slavery was abandoned, racial control put in question, and independence lost, then it became all the more necessary to justify in other terms the horror of war, the loss of blood and treasure, and the humiliation of defeat. Only honor and states' rights remained to soothe hurt feelings by serving as war aims that had been attained by Confederate arms, even though southerners actually had compromised those as well in their effort to keep the Confederacy alive. Nevertheless, more southerners became convinced after the war than before it that they had fought the honorable fight to preserve the Constitution of their fathers from the subversive attacks of Black Republicanism and even from some would-be nationalists within the Confederacy. For most, this soon became the new cognitive element that reduced the psychological discomfort caused by knowledge of alternative policies on slavery. They soon forgot the strong central government—a government at odds with the notion of states' rights in its actions if not in its rhetoric—that they had created to fight that war; they also promptly forgot their own decision for emancipation, their high desertion rates, and the suddenness of Confederate collapse.

Chapter Fourteen

States' Rights, White Supremacy, Honor, and Southern Victory

By THE END of the war in the spring of 1865, many Confederates had come to accept a new world-view that was more compatible with the reality of the last few years than their old world-view had been. Having fought a war for slavery, they surrendered it unwillingly to Confederate policy and later willingly (though not graciously) to Union policy, for they were coming to the conclusion that they would be able to control black labor just as well without the peculiar institution as with it. Having fought a war for independence (although some Confederates thought this a secondary consideration), they abandoned that goal too, for they could win independence only by continuing a disastrous war in which God evidently favored their adversary.

Honor, however, remained, for it was an inward feeling of self-worth, supported by integrity, bravery, and social deference, that enemy armies could damage but could not destroy. Yet former Confederates eventually claimed to have secured all three of these goals: states' rights, white supremacy, and honor. How had they been able to do that? Southern goals and southern accomplishments became nicely congruent by a process similar to that which occurred when Confederates substituted independence for slavery.

First, one must recall that southerners possessed and enjoyed states' rights, white supremacy, and honor before the war. These three features of southern society were as closely intertwined after the war as they had been before it. In the institution of slavery white southerners had ensured their supremacy over their black countrymen, and states' rights were supposed to guarantee the maintenance of this supremacy. Any northern

violation of southern rights or attack on slavery tended to place southerners in an inferior position, and hence they felt that their honor was in-
fringed upon. Not to uphold the southern position on slavery was therefore dishonorable. The result was that politicians in the antebellum
South had competed with one another to prove that they were "sound"
on the slavery question but that their opponents were not. This, in turn,
reflected on the opponents' sense of honor, and they replied with the
charge that it was the other fellows who might compromise the peculiar
institution. Thus as southerners attempted to regain their sense of control and autonomy, they sought nothing that they had not already had just
a few years before.

   To assume that because these three elements were present in the antebellum South, therefore they could not be real goals in the war, however,
is to read history backward, whereas southerners had to live it from day
to day. The war did threaten states' rights and white supremacy, if not
honor, and it was perfectly reasonable for Confederates to set their sights
on the maintenance or reestablishment of these threatened characteristics of their culture. If southerners perceived that their social and
political systems had been put in jeopardy, or their honor had been questioned, they would act accordingly. And Lincoln's election did seem to
threaten southern feelings of self-worth in overexcited and sometimes
paranoid, parochial politicians. Furthermore, Lincoln was perceived to
be a threat to slavery—that was what secession and war had been all
about—and he seemed to threaten states' rights as well because the
federal government, if it had a mind to tamper with slavery in the states,
could not do so without trespassing the bounds of states' rights as southerners understood them. The southern achievement of these goals was
therefore a real accomplishment, not simply a return to the status quo
ante.

   Southerners, who had begun the process of resolving their dissonance
during the war, completed it fairly quickly afterward. Immediately they
faced the role of slavery in causing the war. The morality of slavery, so
often asserted in the antebellum and war eras, did not relieve the psychological discomfort of the postwar generations. For many former Confederates, proslavery defenses crumbled so immediately and so totally after
the fighting ended that such an argument would no longer have been
respectable.

   Historians have noted how quickly southerners put aside the role of slavery. Robert F. Durden contends that a major element of the "southern apologia" for the hostilities "was the emphatic denial that the South's primary aim in fighting was the preservation of slavery. Liberty, independence, and especially states' rights were advanced by countless southern spokesmen as the hallowed principles of the lost cause." Clement Eaton noted with agreement the observation of John W. De-Forest, a Union officer, that the southerners he had met in South Carolina ignored slavery as a cause of the conflict, maintaining instead that constitutional issues had brought on the crisis. Kenneth Stampp points out the prevalence of such views. After the surrender southern whites "denied that slavery had anything to do with the Confederate cause, thus decontaminating it and turning it into something they could cherish." James L. Roark contends that this behavior "is evidence of a nearly universal desire to escape the ignominy attached to slavery in the postwar period"; consequently, southerners argued the constitutional point instead.

So many confessed that the South had sacrificed lives for no particular reasons or for reasons no one understood. Therefore, it became necessary to justify that horror and erase that uncertainty; but one could not do so by mere hero worship or battle accounts. Southerners needed something to be *for* that would mend damaged self-respect, not just something to be against. They required this not only for the self-respect of the veterans and their civilian comrades, but to ensure that future generations would interpret the war with proper respect for those who had served. In their speeches to former soldiers, Confederate veterans constantly repeated this theme, so often in fact that it is clear these orators meant and fully believed what they said. "We fought for the Constitution," declared one. "We went to war . . . to save the Constitution as we read it," asserted another. Thus in November 1866, the formerly militant *Charleston Mercury,* run by Robert Barnwell Rhett, Jr., quietly mewed that differing theories of government had caused the war. Rhett, Sr., once a fire-eating secessionist congressman, maintained in 1867 that secession occurred "on account of one cause only—the usurpations of the Northern States. . . . When . . . this whole instrument lost its character, and, from a limited Government, the Government of the United States was clearly lapsing into a limitless despotism, the Southern States seceded."

Long after the war former Confederate Congressman J. L. M. Curry took the argument further back into history. The conflict "originated in the convention which framed the Constitution." Slavery merely presented "the occasion, the incitement, which developed widely divergent, fundamental differences as to the character and functions of the Federal Government." Even the centralizers and modernizers, forgetting the wartime system they had created, made this assertion, as if stating a truth always understood, merely requiring mention to gain universal belief. It seemed axiomatic—independence had not constituted the main issue of the conflict after all, or even slavery, but states' rights.

Jefferson Davis believed this as much as anyone else. Righteously proclaiming states' rights in the postwar period, he forgot the "nationalist" Davis who led a powerful Confederate government and who is so well portrayed in the publications of Emory M. Thomas and Paul D. Escott.

If southerners denied that slavery caused the hostilities, they nevertheless accepted racial adjustment, or white supremacy, as an important precipitating factor. The conflict did not result in the immediate triumph of white supremacy, of course. On the contrary, it seemed to deal a powerful blow to the notion, at least temporarily and on the surface. Although southerners castigated Yankee "Puritans" for attempting to interfere in their affairs, the South did not attempt to restore formal slavery. In the post-Reconstruction period, however, white southerners did impose their ideas of proper racial adjustment by means which, though short of declared rebellion, nevertheless often involved guerrilla violence that enabled them to pass important legislation restoring white supremacy.

Southerners found a second way to use honor and states'-rights doctrine to reduce dissonance by pointing to the positive results of the war and defining them primarily in terms of honor and states' rights. One hardly would think that from the southern viewpoint such a war could have a positive outcome. Bluecoats occupied the South, carpetbaggers and scalawags controlled legislatures, slavery had vanished, and war had killed or crippled an entire generation of manhood. Postdecision dissonance obviously existed. The rejected alternative, not seceding, had tempting features after Appomattox that historians easily can imagine if they are willing to use a counterfactual proposition. Nevertheless, James D. Bullock, writing from his voluntary exile in Liverpool, stoutly maintained that when the "score is made up" it would include nothing about the war to cause shame.

Shame stood in opposition to the honor Confederates had wished to preserve. If they could avoid shame, they would maintain honor. The secession crisis was caused not only by fear of northern interference with slavery. It also involved honor, for to submit to northern aggressions on their private property would violate southerners' honor. If they would maintain honor, they had to oppose the shame of subordination to any man, much less to northern Black Republicans. Thus honor had helped to provoke war. "The inhabitant of the Old South," writes Bertram Wyatt-Brown, "was not inspired to shed his own or another's blood for the right to own slaves. . . . A close reading of Southern rhetoric on the eve of the war should make clear the fact that white Southerners were certain their cause was justified by that prehistoric code [of honor]." But valorous performance in war, even a losing war, was not only honorable in itself but would lend an aspect of honor to the resulting peace. To preserve honor, therefore, Confederates had to avoid the shame of Yankee arrogance, or easy capitulation, or black equality, and they had to fight. Indeed, the seeming totality of defeat had intensified feelings of honor, for even when all else seemed lost, honor remained, and the politics of personal honor, constitutionalism, and racism survived the war and continued well into the postwar era.

Southerners therefore continued to display vigilance in preserving any legitimate rights that seemed to be threatened. An unsuccessful attempt to safeguard rights did not entail as much shame as refusal even to try, and the more determined the conflict that resulted, the more honor that accrued to the defeated victim. Honor would not seem to constitute a sufficient reason to go to war, but in the soft light of the postwar years the jewel of honor and self-respect shone ever brighter. A South Carolina planter reflected this notion in May 1865, when he claimed that "there is no humiliation in our position after such a struggle as we made for freedom from Yankees." The statement proved that in defeat the South could—and did—preserve honor. This removed one of the impediments to peace. No longer did one have to define a peace with honor as a peace with independence.

In 1887, former Confederate General Henry R. Jackson thus summed up the causes of the war. "The people of the South," he said in a public address, "flew to arms not to perpetuate but to imperil their peculiar institution—not to save, but to sacrifice property in defense of honor— nay, to sacrifice life itself rather than tamely submit to insolent wrong. For the right to govern themselves, bequeathed to them by their fathers, they were prepared to immolate all."

If the South could salvage honor from an unsuccessful war, it could also preserve it by recalcitrance in the face of what southerners perceived as a vengeful Reconstruction. If they went along with northern demands in the Reconstruction amendments, for example, southerners would imply acceptance of northern values. To avoid such unmanly conduct it thus became the part of honor to resist.

But by the end of Reconstruction and the compromise following the Hayes-Tilden election of 1876, federal control in matters most important to southerners—race relations and the distribution of political power—had ceased. The Radical Republicans had passed from the scene, and northern Republicans as well as Democrats freely conceded to the southern states their right to dismantle as much of Reconstruction as they pleased, except the Thirteenth Amendment.

Southerners who argued that they had fought the war for states' rights and white supremacy could point to this situation as evidence of victory. And they could argue that this victory had, in a sense, a greater magnitude than the one for which they had fought from 1861 to 1865. Not only did the North now concede southern rights but it had itself accepted the states'-rights philosophy for which the South had battled. The war had not merely brought victory and restored honor to the South but had given enlightenment and benefits to the nation as a whole.

Because southern ideas ultimately prevailed in the Reconstruction experiment, southern pride eventually had satisfaction after the war, if not during it. Not only had they preserved states' rights and white supremacy but honor as well. Such people reduced postdecision dissonance by increasing the attractiveness of the chosen alternative. And because honor remained intact, indeed even augmented in strength, generations after the war could hazard the conjecture that perhaps the lost cause had not been lost after all.

This idea added a new cognitive element, the third way in which former Confederates reduced the dissonance between the knowledge of defeat and the knowledge that their own doctrines had brought on an unsuccessful war. In his discussion of the conflict between the alternatives of postwar collaboration and intransigence, William B. Hesseltine emphasized the "compromise by which the 'results of the war' could be shared by Northerners and Southerners alike." This compromise increased the attractiveness of the chosen alternative. It employed states'-rights theory and the concept of honor to alter the equation by denying that the South had lost the war. True, Lee surrendered to Grant, but as a number of Radicals noted during the latter phases of Reconstruction, often it did not seem that way at all. "The South surrendered at Appomattox," complained Albion W. Tourgée, but "the North has been surrendering ever since." Even on the supposed losing side, a sufficient number of positive results existed to justify a suspicion that victory had not gone exclusively to the larger battalions.

Former Confederate Congressman John Vines Wright was numbered among those who took this position, who increased the attractiveness of the chosen alternative, and therefore claimed some measure of victory for the South. His remarks epitomized the compromise that shared the "results of the war." Wright lamented the conflict and the dangers through which the country had passed and expressed the hope that the experience would serve as a warning for the future. But then he went on to assert that the "North went to war to preserve the Union. The South went to war to preserve the Constitution. Through the madness of the hour both might have been destroyed. In the mercy and wisdom of Almighty God both were preserved." Wright did not lack for companions. Speaking for the clergy, Randolph McKim contended that the Confederates had fought for self-government, which states' rights now protected, and "that the Northern armies saved the Union, while 'the armies of the South saved the rights of the States within the Union.'"

Much of this compromise lives on; white southerners still claim their share of the victory, although white supremacy is no longer respectable, especially since the civil rights movement of the 1960s. And neither does the notion of honor have the strength it once had, though insofar as it does survive it probably has more strength in the South than in the North. But states'-rights constitutionalism still is an important concept today, with adherents not only in the South but throughout the country. The traditional conflict between state and federal authority continues to be a basic theme in American politics.

Only in the South, however, does today's constitutionalism link to the events of 1861–65. "While we did oppose each other, section against section, in a bitter and bloody civil war," observed Jerry L. Russell, the Arkansas editor of the *Civil War Round Table Digest*, "our nation and its form of government was not destroyed . . . but rather strengthened and given a sense of national identity. . . . The American form of government . . . was tested in the furnace of civil war and it withstood that test." Indeed, Russell points out, the test continues because the issues, including states' rights and federal encroachment, still live with us. Russell's perceptiveness was unsubtly underlined by a 1979 article in a suburban Houston newspaper, concerning the local chapters of the United Daughters of the Confederacy. One of the members concluded an interview with the remark that "they [Confederates] weren't fighting to preserve slavery. They were fighting for States' Rights. But I don't suppose we're ever going to get the textbooks changed until they're printed someplace else besides Yankeeland."

It may seem to require amazing mental agility to conclude that the Confederacy had won victory. Yet if one takes as one Confederate goal the self-respect of a people, as another goal the preservation of the notion that Americans anywhere had a constitutional right to deal with their own people and institutions as they desired without outside interference, and, as a third, the desire to exercise that right in respect to their own black population, one has only to look at the century between the first and second Reconstructions to see the correctness of this view. The South had indeed preserved its view of the Constitution, white supremacy, and honor. After the unsuccessful struggle to preserve slavery and achieve independence, southerners had returned to the constitutional issue. If the war was lost over slavery and independence, the peace was waged—and won—for states' rights, white supremacy, and honor. In this way, the South could claim "a moral, if not a military, victory," conspiring with historians "to prove that no one—no white man at least—had really lost the Civil War."

Chapter Fifteen

The Elements
of Confederate Defeat

THE IMMEDIATE popular response to the question of why the Confederacy lost is usually that the North overwhelmed the South with its great numbers and resources. The Union possessed more than twice the population of the Confederacy, and the South endured an even greater disadvantage in military population, for the South included four million slaves, excluded from direct military participation on the Confederate side. But though numbers were certainly important, the inherent advantages of defense, illustrated by the virtual impossibility of destroying an enemy army unless it had an incompetent commander, required a greater disparity before the size and resources of the Union could explain Confederate defeat.

Many Confederates agreed that numbers or resources did not provide the margin, although they disagreed on what did. General Beauregard, for example, claimed that "no people ever warred for independence with more relative advantages than the Confederates; and if, as a military question, they must have failed, then no country must aim at freedom by means of war." "The South," Beauregard asserted, "would be open to discredit as a people if its failure could not be explained otherwise than by mere material conquest." To Beauregard, the Confederates did not owe their defeat to numbers but to faulty strategy and the poor leadership of Jefferson Davis.

Some historians have adopted this view, but many agree with Clement Eaton, who, though seeing flaws in military leadership, found the cause of defeat in a loss of the will to fight. Both sides suffered from this problem, but after July 1863 it was worse for the South. Southerners' "morale rose and fell with victory and defeat, and also with their estimation of the northern will to persevere."

Confederate Senator Williamson S. Oldham of Texas offered his explanation. An experienced politician and lawyer, Oldham in 1861 helped to lead Texas out of the Union over the objections of Sam Houston, the crusty pro-Union governor. Having made his decision for Confederate independence, Oldham served in the Provisional Congress and then in the Confederate Senate throughout that body's existence. Claiming to be a supporter of Jefferson Davis, Oldham nevertheless opposed conscription, suspension of the writ of habeas corpus, and martial law, and he logged a mixed record of support for the government's policy of impressment. Frequently on the losing side of an issue, the intractable senator stuck firmly to his principles—so much so that some critics thought him one of the obstacles to Confederate victory. Indeed, he was the sort of man Owsley and Donald blamed for defeat.

Oldham believed, for example, that the preservation of states' rights was more important than the needs of the military and claimed to have been elected to the Confederate Senate for the purpose of opposing policies that tended toward centralization. Oldham was not, however, numbered among the fainthearted. He proposed a policy of burning the North's cities and its shipping facilities and pretended to know a foolproof way to do it; and, as the Confederacy approached defeat, he was one of the few congressmen to remain in Richmond until the adjournment of the last session of Congress. Then, three weeks before General Lee's surrender at Appomattox Court House, Oldham made his way back to Texas and subsequently into Mexico.

During his exile, first in Mexico and later in Canada, he pondered the question of why the Confederacy had lost, and after his return to Texas he tried to commit his ideas to writing. Oldham disapproved of Jefferson Davis's military strategy, strongly believing that Davis overemphasized the defense of Richmond and Virginia and underemphasized the West. But, Oldham admitted, defective strategy did not bring the ultimate disaster, nor did "the want of men and material resources to carry on the war." He recalled being a member of a joint House-Senate committee that served in January 1865 "to inquire into our present and future means of public defense." Congress considered the committee report in secret session, and apparently never printed it, so no official record of its contents exists. But Oldham claimed that after a thorough investigation, which included interviews with Davis, Lee, and various bureau chiefs, the committee "came to the unanimous conclusion and so reported, 'that we were in possession of resources, sufficient to enable us to carry on the war for an indefinite period of time.'"

The stuff of war was available; the deficiency lay elsewhere. Oldham went on to deny that northern resources overpowered the South. He contended that military strength in November 1864 still stood on a par with that of the Union and believed that many former Confederates used the plea of resources simply because "such an excuse is flattering to one's vanity." He also denied that desertion or an obstructive Congress brought about the failure of the cause—states' rights and internal dissent (as the historian would put it) did not produce defeat. Nor did it result from "want of patriotism, and selfishness of the people." These were symptoms, not causes.

Rather, Oldham perceived other reasons why the South lost the Civil War. Continuing party divisions were important, for "men who had for years attached themselves to their parties and party leaders, who had for years, been taught by the latter to glorify the Union, as the greatest blessing . . . could not in the course of a few days surrender up sentiments, they had entertained all their lives." Furthermore, the "federative power" of the government "was destroyed, and absolute despotic power, was conferred upon the executive and the military." Oldham exaggerated, but such measures as conscription, impressment, and suspension of habeas corpus alienated many Confederates, and instead of strengthening the government, they "weakened and paralyzed it." Thus, despite its control over the material resources of the South, the Confederacy could not "command and control its moral resources." By early 1865, when the Stephens-Campbell-Hunter peace commission reported Lincoln's precondition of Union for peace and pardon, many Confederates had accepted the inevitable. "Already conquered," Oldham remarked of the congressmen with whom he sat, "they were willing to accept the terms of the conquerors." Indeed, it becomes clear after reading Oldham's reminiscences that the erstwhile Confederate senator thought the cause of southern defeat was the flagging of Confederate spirit. The Confederate armies, he thought, were strong and almost equal to those of the Union "in all the elements of military strength *morale alone excepted.*"

Uncertainty about war aims helped to sap Confederate morale. Most southerners who had thought the war was fought to attain security for slave property suffered confusion and even demoralization from the proposal to arm slaves. In denying the original motive for the establishment of a separate country, the Confederacy undermined the fundamental basis of its tentative nationalism and deprived many of its citizens of their motive for continuing the conflict.

Lincoln's Emancipation Proclamation made it difficult for Confederates to feel entirely at ease with their assertion that they were fighting for liberty. It aggravated the misgivings of those who long had harbored quiet doubts about slavery and made many others even more uneasy about their isolation in a world in which the great powers of Europe, now joined by the United States, sought to extirpate slavery. Many southerners felt guilt over the institution or at least unease about their position. Thus, as the struggle drew to a close, the commitment to slavery of many southerners withered in the face of the contradiction it created and under the weight of world moral disapproval, which some Confederates felt acutely.

The change in the Confederacy's explanation for secession and war shows the seriousness of the cognitive dissonance created by the problem of slavery. To consider it merely a contest for the proper interpretation of the Constitution was to deny recent historical fact, but the constitutional question offered a far more comfortable explanation for the sacrifice of so much blood and treasure than the protection of slavery had. But to reject slavery as the cause for secession eliminated the characteristic that most distinguished the North from the South. Common history and language united the sections and so, too, in a lesser and more complex sense, did religion; only slavery truly separated them.

In fact, considering their fragile and insecure nationalism, one could almost ask what induced southerners to make such a powerful and prolonged resistance? Certainly the climate of opinion, which for two decades had reflected a consciousness of divergence between the sections and a hostility to Yankees, had much to do with magnifying grievances and strengthening the feeling of separateness. The churches contributed powerfully to fostering this climate of opinion, but they, too, like slavery and limited government, failed as the conflict wore on.

Owsley's thesis "that the Confederacy collapsed more from internal than from external causes" certainly could find strong support in the embryonic nature of Confederate nationalism. The tangible effects of states' rights, as distinguished from the rhetoric, had little negative effect on the Confederate war effort. Even the total number of exempted men was small in relation to the Confederate armies, and most of them made significant economic contributions, served in local defense forces, or both. The protection of ports and the production of such items as salt had an importance that military authorities and President Davis both recognized, and state local defense forces therefore contributed materially to this effort. Further, state endeavors to supply and equip local defense forces and to meet the needs of their own men in the Confederate service provided a major supplement to the national war effort.

States'-rights attempts to obstruct the Confederate government by resisting conscription or the suspension of habeas corpus, for example, also had a negligible effect. States' rights in writing and oratory provided a rallying cry for opposition that already existed in any case. Just as in England under the early Hanoverians the association of the Prince of Wales with the group out of power showed the opposition's loyalty to the king and dynasty, so an appeal to the universally accepted notion of states' rights provided a legitimacy to the opposition and protected it from accusations of disloyalty during a struggle for national existence. Thus states' rights made a political contribution, one probably necessary in the absence of organized political parties.

In view of the rhetoric of states' rights and the long, disputatious correspondence between Governor Brown and the Richmond government, Frank L. Owsley made a natural mistake in choosing states' rights as the internal cause of Confederate collapse. But in placing the blame on disunity caused by states' rights, he did not show that military causes inadequately explained defeat. Considering the still continuing flow of books and articles about Civil War military operations, he displayed wisdom in avoiding a topic on which he would have had difficulty securing agreement. But in view of the harmony of Clausewitz and Jomini on the relevant strategic variables, it is possible to use them effectively as authorities to provide a fairly firm basis for settling the military questions about the Confederacy. Their essential consensus says that an invader needed more force than the North possessed to conquer such a large country as the South, and one so limited in logistical resources.

Edward N. Luttwak in his 1987 *Strategy: The Logic of War and Peace* shows the durability of this interpretation when he follows Clausewitz in his stress on the importance of "depth of territory" and "tenacity" of the defense in turning a victory into a defeat. In making this judgment

Clausewitz and Jomini assumed a national resistance. This the Confederacy made, so far as its limited national will permitted, as the Union's difficulties protecting its railroads from guerrillas amply attest. Sherman's complaint about invading a country populated by the "meanest bitterest enemies" illustrates the strength of the national opposition that the Union armies initially confronted.

In agreeing that the Confederacy's size and popular resistance would have presented an insuperable obstacle, Clausewitz and Jomini also assumed a competent defense. Two of their chosen means for generals to excel, concentration in space and turning movements, found abundant favor with the Confederates and have a place in Luttwak's approach as examples of what he calls "relational maneuver," which consists of "avoidance of the enemy's strengths, followed by the application of some selective superiority against presumed enemy weakness." This course "offers results disproportionately greater than the resources applied to the effort, and thus a chance of victory for the side materially weaker." Moreover, when the Confederates made surprise concentrations to try to defeat Grant at Shiloh before Buell joined him or to strike Rosecrans's dispersed army at Chickamauga, they made a major innovation by using the electric telegraph, the railroad, and the steamship to carry out concentrations over a completely unprecedented geographical extent. Thus, in its strategy, the agrarian South made exemplary use of the products of the industrial revolution in implementing a strategy modern as well as Napoleonic.

Using as criteria the apparently timeless ideas and comments of Clausewitz and Jomini, the Confederacy clearly provided an excellent army, very capably led. Examples of Confederate bungling, such as Pemberton's losing his army at Vicksburg or Bragg's ineffective campaigning, are counterbalanced by Burnside's fairly reliable mismanagement and the pessimism and slow execution of such generals as McClellan and Buell. Both sides wasted lives in frontal attacks, sometimes because they knew no better and other times because commanders and their subordinates lacked the ability or experience to catch their opponent at a disadvantage.

Since the Confederate army clearly did not have a significantly worse command than the Union forces, Clausewitz's and Jomini's strategic variables of space and supply must control. In view of the experience of the operationally superior French armies in Spain and Russia, one must respect their sophisticated conclusion from appropriate historical experience as well as their authority as experts on the kind of war the Union and Confederacy fought. They might well have added the American Revolution to their example of the virtual impossibility of overcoming a national resistance in a vast space without overwhelming forces, and Jomini did include it in his list of national wars.

T. Harry Williams said Jomini preached cities and territory, rather than enemy armies, as the objective in military operations. If this was the case, and it certainly was not in the instance of the strategic turning movement which Jomini liked so well, it proved a realistic doctrine for both armies. Jomini's fondness for the strategic turning movement does fit with Williams's idea that Jomini favored maneuvering over fighting. As to Williams's idea that Jomini advocated one big effort at a time in a single theater, the precept of the use of interior lines to concentrate on a single line of operations also fits Williams's interpretation. The Confederates practiced this strategy successfully in the Shiloh and Chickamauga campaigns and on a lesser scale in the Seven Days' Battles. The Union did the same after the battles of Lookout Mountain and Missionary Ridge and in a different way by their earlier concentration on the Mississippi. But the Union relied more on concentration in time, advocated by Clausewitz, as well as on Jomini's concentration in space.

Williams and some other historians in this country seem to have misunderstood Jomini enough to overlook his essentially Napoleonic viewpoint and to attribute to him some of the views held by Bülow, the geographical school, and others in an essentially pre-Napoleonic tradition. Williams also noted a differential effect in Jomini's influence on each combatant that is hard to discern in the West Point officers, many of whom served apprenticeships under Winfield Scott and Zachary Taylor in the Mexican War.

So, though there is little evidence of a Jominian influence in either army, some knowledge of Napoleonic campaigns and the influence of the Mexican War led both armies to follow Jomini while they fairly consistently, though unconsciously, responded to Clausewitz's perception of the difficulties of executing decisive campaigns in view of the power of the defense, the lack of overwhelming numerical superiority, and the huge extent of the Confederacy. Clausewitz, who had considerable knowledge of the French campaign in Russia, stressed the obstacle of the size of an invaded country, whereas Jomini, who had served with the

French in Spain, predicted most clearly the trouble Confederate guerrillas caused the Union invaders. These difficulties, foreseen by the authorities and present in abundance in the Civil War, adequately explain the slow progress of Union armies.

In spite of Lee's blunder in attacking the Union center on the third day of the Battle of Gettysburg, and Grant's seriously mistaken assault at Cold Harbor, they and the majority of other generals on both sides adhered more to Clausewitz than to Jomini in their recognition of the power of the defense. Grant best exemplified Jomini's ideal with his victories at Vicksburg and Appomattox, but the failure of other generals to achieve similar successes justified Clausewitz's observation that such maneuvers rarely would succeed. Unconsciously, Hood used the turning movement on the defense in a manner approved by Clausewitz, as did Lee in his Second Manassas, Antietam, and Gettysburg campaigns. This defensive application illustrates the power of Luttwak's relational maneuver to cause "disruption" and also bears a distinct resemblance to the concept of deep battle in the U.S. Army's new doctrine.

Thus we have difficulty following T. Harry Williams in discriminating between Jomini's possible influence on either side or seeing Jomini as a potential inhibitor of action on the part of Union or Confederate generals. That there is so little difference in the prescriptions of Jomini and Clausewitz and that Jomini had more faith in the offensive makes it hard to single out Jomini as hampering offensive action or as an advocate of a pre-Napoleonic form of warfare when no authorities so classify Clausewitz.

So Confederate military competence that capably managed its armies and consciously, and skillfully, used cavalry raids to aid guerrillas in destroying Union supply lines provided the means of validating Clausewitz's and Jomini's judgment about the impossibility of the Union attaining its strategic objective by military means if faced with a determined, unremitting national resistance. If, then, the Confederacy had the means to resist military conquest, one must find the cause of defeat within. If states' rights was not this cause, what alternatives are there to the thesis of insufficient nationalism as the internal cause of defeat?

In spite of the blockade and the steady decline of the railways, Confederate supply did not fail. After each apparently catastrophic shock, such as the closure of communication with the trans-Mississippi or the loss of key railroad lines, the ramshackle Confederate logistic organization, displaying an amazing resilience, continued to make adequate provision for the armies. The accumulation in Richmond during the winter of 1865 of a week's reserve of rations for Lee's army illustrates the South's capability. Lee still had this reserve available in early April, in spite of the earlier closure of Wilmington, the presence of Sherman's army in North Carolina, and Sheridan's devastating raid against supply and communications northwest of Richmond.

So, by remarkable and effective efforts, the South did exploit and create an industrial base that proved adequate, with the aid of imports, to maintain suitably equipped forces in the field. Since the Confederate armies suffered no crippling deficiencies in weapons or supply, their principal handicap would be their numerical inferiority. But to offset this lack, Confederates, fighting the first major war in which both sides armed themselves with rifles, had the advantage of a temporary but very significant surge in the power of the tactical defensive. In addition, the difficulties of supply in a very large and relatively thinly settled region proved a powerful aid to strengthening the strategic defensive.

But production of too much cotton and not enough food crops, like the decline in railway service and the constraints of the blockade, severely affected the home front, already heavily taxed through inflation and diminished in manpower because of the needs of the army and of war production. These costs and hardships, like the casualties in battle and the gloom occasioned by defeats, depressed civilian morale. Many of the deficiencies of Confederate supply affected civilians more than the armies and aggravated hardships inseparable from such a bloody and costly war. And the depressed morale of the home front communicated itself to the soldiers through newspapers and the Confederate postal service, which continued to function throughout the war in spite of numerous obstacles, including a constitutionally mandated requirement that postal expenses not exceed postal income.

The defeats, shortages, reduced standard of living, and change of war goals, as well as the war's length, obviously placed a severe strain on the Confederates' dedication to their cause. The high degree of dependence of Confederate morale on military events meant that setbacks on the battle front usually had a significance far beyond the military importance of the loss of a battle or a fragment of territory. A succession of defeats and territorial losses, though not representing militarily consequential conquests of the South's vast land area, worked steadily to depress morale and confidence in victory. With fewer such military disappointments and less hardship for civilians, or with a shorter war, Confederate nationalism, weak though it was, would have equaled the demands placed upon it and might well have developed real strength after the war; in any case, a greater measure of nationalism during the conflict certainly would have enabled the Confederates to resist longer.

Like the French revolutionaries, Confederates conscripted their citizens and mobilized their economic resources, but, unlike them, southerners directed almost all of their revolutionary zeal outward toward adversaries in their bid for independence. They perceived Yankees as virtually the only opponents of their cause, focused their hopes and expectations on the military struggle, and did not, like their French and American revolutionary forebears, engage in ruthless suppression of internal dissent. Seeing northerners as their enemies, southerners generally failed to perceive dissenters and defeatists as opponents of independence in the way that American Patriots had viewed Tories or French Republicans had reacted against Royalists. The modest military actions against North Carolina and Tennessee Unionists did not compare with the military struggles against internal enemies in the American and French revolutions.

Like other soldiers in other wars, Confederate military leaders constantly attempted to answer questions of morale and spirit in military terms. When military successes eluded them or had no meaning, morale plummeted.

Thus Confederates, though not really overlooking the problem of the home front, did not always define as enemies those who had lost heart or wanted peace, and when they finally did begin to think in such terms, the game had almost ended. "The malcontents, seizing on the restlessness consequent upon long and severe pressure," complained Davis, "have created a feeling hostile to the execution of the rigorous laws which were necessary to raise and feed our armies, then magnifying every reverse and prophesying ruin, they have produced public depression and sown the seeds of disintegration." But Davis and his administration had no policies either to suppress such malcontents or to regain their support beyond refuting criticism, wringing hands, and pointing fingers at those who had not thought and done as the leadership had wanted them to do. For the most part, Confederate leaders made little effort to manipulate public opinion.

In addition, planters felt alienated from a government that seemed to threaten their privileges and property and, in spite of the exemplary relief efforts of Georgia and North Carolina, and the similar, if not so extensive, measures in other states, the yeomen, too, felt disaffection with the Confederacy. Both planter and yeoman paid economically for the immense war effort, but too many yeomen lived too close to the margin of existence not to feel the hardships acutely; the costs of the war deprived them of the means to meet their basic needs, or threatened to do so. At the same time they felt that, with such perquisites as the exemption of the overseers of twenty slaves and the right to purchase substitutes for military service, the rich did not bear their fair share of the burdens. Paul Escott stressed that throughout the struggle the planters gave primacy to their own rather than national interests. He points out that "a selfish and short-sighted ruling class had led its region into secession and then proven unwilling to make sacrifices or to surrender its privileges for independence." These class differences in the demands of the war effort created another drain on the limited supply of Confederate nationalism.

But the resulting decline in commitment to the struggle did not begin to affect the war effort very seriously until after the middle of 1864. Then soldiers began to leave the army in increasing numbers. The fall of Atlanta in early September and Sheridan's victories over Early in the Shenandoah Valley, victories that significantly improved Lincoln's chances of reelection, also signaled the beginning of a marked rise in desertion from the Confederate army. Soldiers left not only from discouragement at these defeats but also from a realization that Union victories increased the likelihood of Lincoln's continuation in office and his policy of prosecuting the war to victory. As the fall elections confirmed this apprehension, the augmented stream of deserters continued unabated. During the fall and early winter of 1864–65 desertion took away 40 percent of the Confederate armies east of the Mississippi. The soldiers were voting for peace with their feet, and the few disaffected conscripts sent to the Confederate army probably hurt morale and effectiveness more than their small numbers could have added to its strength. By the early spring of 1865 the Confederate armies east of the Mississippi had shrunk to barely half their size the previous August.

Adventitiously, Grant's logistic strategy began to play some part in this Confederate decline soon after the Union presidential contest of 1864, when Sherman marched from Atlanta to Savannah, breaking railways, destroying factories, stripping the countryside of slaves, and subsisting an army of sixty thousand men on the country. Sherman perceived the effect of this devastation on southerners when he wrote that his march would show the falsity of Davis's "promise of protection." He believed that there were "thousands of people abroad and in the South who will reason thus: If the North can march an army right through the South, it is proof positive that the North can prevail in this struggle." But Sherman's raid occurred well after the exodus from the army began. His raids through Georgia and later into the Carolinas only reinforced a discouragement that already had begun to manifest itself in a dramatic rise in the desertion rate.

Since Lee's army and the other main armies remained sufficiently supplied until the end of the war, one reasonably can conclude that Grant's military strategy influenced the outcome of the conflict but did not determine it. The Confederacy's forces dwindled and surrendered before Grant's raids could deprive them of supplies. The strategy of raids had, of course, considerable political and psychological significance, reinforcing the effect on southern morale of the defeats of September and October and the return of Lincoln to the Executive Mansion.

In any event, Grant's logistic strategy alone could not have won a war against a people sufficiently determined to maintain their independence. Grant aimed only to break up the Confederacy's main armies by severing the railroads that connected them to their supplies of food, shoes, uniforms, weapons, and ammunition. He provided no means of dealing with these armies should they disperse and thereafter continue offering organized resistance as units ranging in size from a division of several brigades down to independent companies. Facing Confederate forces thus continuing to control most of the South, Union armies would have had to launch campaigns to try to dominate the country and end Confederate political power. At this point the Confederates would have had to decide to yield to occupation or emulate the Spanish guerrilla resistance of a half-century earlier, as they already had done in West Tennessee and elsewhere during the Civil War. But Confederate armies surrendered rather than dispersing into smaller but still formidable groups, and the soldiers went home for the same reason that many had already deserted—they did not want an independent Confederacy badly enough to continue the struggle, and they placed the welfare of their loved ones ahead of the creation of a new nation.

By surrendering before resorting to wholesale use of guerrillas, south-erners had, as John Shy has pointed out, "saved the basic elements—with the exception of slavery itself—of the Southern social, that is to say racial, order. The social order could not possibly have survived the guer-rilla warfare which a continued resistance movement would have re-quired." Yet the wholesale desertion that affected the armies in the fall and winter of 1864–65 showed that, before a full-scale resort to guerrilla warfare could have loomed as the alternative, a critical number of Con-federates had given to the cause all that their commitment warranted.

Clausewitz excoriated such behavior. Although he did not use the word "honor," he demanded that a people fight to preserve it. "No mat-ter how small and weak a state may be in comparison with its enemy," he wrote, "it must not forego these last efforts, or one would conclude that its soul is dead." "There will always be time enough to die," he con-tinued. "Like a drowning man who will clutch instinctively at a straw, it is a natural law of the moral world that a nation that finds itself on the brink of an abyss will try to save itself by any means." Clausewitz felt that a failure to fight to the last shows that the nation "did not deserve to win, and, possibly for that very reason was unable to." But Clausewitz is too harsh. The length of wars and the level of each combatant's endeavor has, as he realized, always varied with the value attached to victory and the cost associated with defeat. Europe has seen wars that lasted inter-mittently for over a hundred years and others much shorter, one in 1866 between evenly matched coalitions lasting only seven weeks.

Whether a struggle had to do with gaining or retaining a province or a whole people's liberty, a decision, whether made by an absolute ruler or a representative assembly, would almost invariabley depend on an implicit interplay between the importance of the goal and the degree of sacrifice required to attain it. So millions of Confederates tacitly weighed these two considerations and more and more came to decide in favor of re-union with the North.

Moreover, Clausewitz's caustic criticism has relevance only if one as-sumes that the Confederacy was a nation—that it was sufficiently sepa-rated from the Union and the glory of their common history to make it a distinct nationality. And Clausewitz did make a similar point in analyzing conflict "between *states of very unequal strength*" when he noted that "in-ability to carry on the struggle can, in practice, be replaced by two other grounds for making peace: the first is the improbability of victory; the second is its unacceptable cost." Powerful Union armed forces and sophisticated and innovative strategy supplied the first ground; the insufficiency of a nationalism based on slavery, states' rights, and honor meant that the cost of continuing the struggle ran too high.

The strength of the armies indicated the decline in commitment to continue fighting until the Union abandoned the struggle. Confederate military strength had remained surprisingly constant, beginning at 326,768 in December 1861, peaking at 473,058 in June 1863, and still counting 358,692 at the end of December 1864. Yet the difference between the numbers of men on the rolls and those actually present with the colors provides an impressive indicator of the broadening gap between military capability and the will to exercise it.

At the end of 1861, Confederate forces had 21 percent of the men on their rosters absent. But by June 1862 the number absent had risen to over 30 percent and fluctuated around 30 percent for the next twelve months. By the end of the fall of 1863 the percentage of Confederate absentees had risen almost to 40 percent. Evidently the dimmed prospects for victory after Gettysburg, Vicksburg, and Chattanooga had raised the desertion rate. But the percentage absent remained constant during the spring and summer. Thus on June 30, 1864, the Confederate armies had about 413,000 men on their rolls but only about 257,000 counted present with their units. Declining morale since the summer of 1863 had helped to increase a tremendous gap between nominal and actual strength. In the fall of 1864 the proportion of absentees increased dramatically, rising from less than 40 percent at the end of June to 53 percent in the return of December 31, 1864. The fall of Atlanta and the reelection of Lincoln had obviously depressed morale. Thus absences, providing a measure of the decrease in the number of Confederates willing to fight, show the growth in the number of southerners who either had already paid as much as they thought independence was worth or who viewed the prospect of victory as hopeless and stopped their losses by ending their contribution to the war effort.

So the Confederacy succumbed to internal rather than external causes. An insufficient nationalism failed to survive the strains imposed by the lengthy hostilities. Necessary measures alienated planters, who, by planting cotton and husbanding their slaves, already had limited the national effort. Privation affected many yeomen, soldiers, and their families as the costs and shortages of the contest reduced their already meager standards of living. These hardships and the perception of inequitable and unwise actions placed an added strain on a nationalism already taxed by the duration and bloodshed of the conflict. Slavery, in a sense the keystone of secession, became a liability as the Union's fight against slavery and the South's own religious beliefs induced more guilt among more southerners. After three years of essentially successful defense against powerful invading forces, these prolonged strains proved more than Confederate nationalism could bear and, frequently encouraged by a sense that defeat must be the Lord's work, Confederates, by thousands of individual decisions, abandoned the struggle for and allegiance to the Confederate States of America.

If one wished to turn the question around and ask why the North won, the South's abandonment of its quest for independence appears as an indirect result of Union military efforts, supplemented by the terms of Lincoln's offer for reunion. The federal logistic military strategy, first as a persisting strategy by land as well as by sea and then with a raiding strategy on land, failed to achieve victory before the Confederates gave up. The traditional view of Grant's 1864 strategy in Virginia has interpreted him as seeking to annihilate the enemy army in battle and achieving it eventually at high cost only by the process of attrition. Yet the casualties of these campaigns were only part of a process of inflicting and suffering losses going on since the beginning of the war. A deliberate adoption of a strategy of attrition acknowledges or exploits the impossibility of decisive military operations, but it is also a normal by-product of almost any military activity. Narrowly construed, attrition describes an effort to destroy hostile military forces by wearing them down in combat; in order for it to work, the user of the strategy must expend a smaller proportion of his forces than his adversary. More broadly understood, attrition may include the employment of a logistic as well as a combat strategy and should not merely mean an effort to exhaust the enemy's material resources before consuming all of one's own, but should also include sapping his motivation for victory before one's own fails. In addition to inflicting material losses, the Civil War's conflict on land and sea acted in the psychological domain as its incidents affected the morale of the combatants and influenced their expectation of both the likelihood and cost of winning. The victory of the United States by such a broadly defined strategy of attrition was not a product of contingent events but an indirect result of all federal military and naval efforts; before the war had drained the Union's will to win or exhausted the Confederacy's material and manpower resources, attrition had raised the cost, past and prospective, of a southern victory beyond its value compared with Lincoln's nonvindictive terms of reconstruction.

If the Confederacy abandoned the struggle with vast areas unoccupied and still able to continue without a widespread resort to guerrilla resistance, how may one estimate its people's nationalism, devotion to independence, and concern for their honor in making more than a merely earnest attempt once they had taken the step of secession? The number of combat casualties offers an index of effort and provides a means of examining the distance between capability and performance. The Confederacy's 100,000, perhaps as many as 120,000, combat deaths certainly argue for a most serious effort to gain independence. But was it all that the Confederacy could have given? Comparisons (offered without intending to suggest any as an appropriate level of exertion for the South) can shed light on the Confederacy's effort.

The battle deaths would amount to no more than 2.2 percent of the Confederacy's 5,500,000 whites, a percentage which clearly differentiates the South from the United States's .4 percent fatalities in the Revolution. On the other hand, such a loss compares with France's loss in World War I of 3.3 percent of its population. At the close of that war France, with a population of 40,000,000 and armed forces in excess of 4,000,000, took the offensive. The strongly nationalistic French, with a highly developed antipathy for the Germans and the assistance of a fresh ally, the United States, surmounted these losses, provided leadership and weapons for the forces opposing Germany, and carried the war to an offensive conclusion; the Confederacy proved unable to sustain a continued defensive as long as the four and one-fourth years of World War I.

In World War II Germany fought longer and suffered even more heavily than France in the previous war, losing through armed forces fatalities about 5 percent of its population. In addition, enemies inflicted substantial civilian casualties in air raids. Nevertheless, Germany fought for five and a half years, continuing an increasingly hopeless resistance after its principal European ally, Italy, left the war. Linguistic and historical distinctness from the enemies with whom it had recently fought another long war and ideological differences, especially with the Russian regime, undoubtedly supported a firm national resistance under the leadership of Germany's powerful autocratic government. Compared to the Confederacy, Germany lost more than double the percentage of combat deaths. But the overrunning of Germany, a comparatively small country, by millions of hostile soldiers cut short the resistance, one that Hitler would doubtless have prolonged had he had the advantage of a land area comparable in size to the South's. Nevertheless, against enemies demanding unconditional surrender, the divergence in combat deaths between Germany and the South may serve as an indicator of the disparity in the intensity of nationalism between the two and the different consequences southerners and Germans saw in defeat, as well as of the far greater authority which the Nazi regime exercised over its people.

Just as the Civil War ended, the landlocked South American republic of Paraguay launched a war that presents interesting parallels with, and at least one sharp contrast to, the Confederacy. The war against the Triple Alliance of Brazil, Uruguay, and Argentina found Paraguay badly outmatched even without important Uruguayan involvement. Brazil's population base alone numbered ten million compared to Paraguay's estimated five hundred thousand; the officially stated strength of the Brazilian national guard nearly equaled the total unenumerated population of Paraguay.

Early in 1865 the armored ships of the Imperial Brazilian Navy smashed the Paraguayan fleet, subsequently imposing a total blockade of the Paraguay River, the country's natural and only useful lifeline to the outside. Paraguayans foolishly swam out into the river to attack Brazilian ships or stole along in canoes camouflaged with water hyacinths. Three thousand Paraguayans held muddy trenches along the river against fifteen thousand invaders and, with a handful of soldiers, maintained a redoubt at Humaita for months against the allied fleet. Interestingly, Paraguay conscripted its few slaves while Brazil offered theirs freedom in exchange for military service.

Contemporaries marveled, as have historians since, at the Paraguayans' tenacity in fighting for five years a steadily losing war against their opponents' larger armies and superior resources. Paraguayans' fanatic resistance depended on the unyielding determination of their autocratic and vainglorious president and their intense, almost tribal, identity. Indian ethnicity and cultural unity lay at the heart of their suicidal fortitude and passionate patriotism, as did a bitter legacy of Brazilian and Argentine encroachments and intimidation.

The military effort raised for this struggle contrasted markedly with that of the Confederacy. Paraguay fielded an army of sixty thousand men on a population base of about five hundred thousand, for a time the largest standing army on the continent. After four years, every male in Paraguay from the ages of eleven to sixty was at the front on the river approaches, and women and children volunteered much, if not most, of the logistical support. Paraguay's 10 to 12 percent of the population under arms compares impressively with the 10 percent typically maintained by industrialized societies in twentieth-century wars and contrasts tellingly with the 3 to 4 percent sustained under the Confederacy. Although Paraguay's government finally resorted to conscription, most soldiers willingly volunteered.

When heavy casualties, disease, and starvation depleted manpower reserves, children from the ages of ten to fourteen volunteered even when the draft age was lowered to twelve. By the end of the war in 1870–71 militia rolls included even the blind and otherwise handicapped.

Casualty counts well illustrate Paraguayan tenacity. Commencing with 500,000 population, Paraguay was reduced to a total of 221,000 a half-decade later. Of these, 106,250 were women, 86,000 were children, and 28,750 were men. In other words, 56 percent of the population failed to survive the disaster.

Obviously, the Paraguayans, who lost the war but retained their independence, displayed an exceptional devotion to their country. Perhaps they would have ended the war sooner, by negotiation if not surrender, had their president not stubbornly refused to consider any concession, even after allied occupation of the capital found him taking refuge in the interior wilderness with the remnants of the palace guard. But Paraguayan tenacity, based on a fundamental commitment to their country and hatred of the invaders, does exhibit how a people can fight when possessed of total conviction. Lacking this determination, the Confederacy yielded after a far less costly resistance against an enemy enjoying resources meager in comparison to the advantage held by the Triple Alliance over Paraguay.

Casualty figures also exhibit that the Union's loss of .7 percent of its population as combat fatalities surely placed a far smaller strain on its morale than did the 2.2 percent suffered by the Confederacy. When one compares the situation of the South with the uninvaded North and its unblockaded economy beset by a less virulent inflation and served by adequately maintained railroads, it is easy to see that the Union's devotion to its cause faced a significantly less severe test than the Confederacy's. When one recalls that Confederate nationalism withstood even the daunting loss of Vicksburg, Port Hudson, and their garrisons in the same month as the defeat at Gettysburg and the retreat from Middle Tennessee, it is difficult not to believe that the United States had a robust enough nationalism to have readily weathered the discouragement of such contingencies as, for example, the consequences of a prolonged Confederate military stay in Kentucky and Maryland in the fall of 1862 or Sherman's having to make an earlier beginning of his Georgia raid without first capturing Atlanta.

On the other hand, the comparisons with France and Paraguay, which were not fighting for their political existence, and Germany, which was, show how much residual and unused strength the Confederacy had available but did not choose to commit to its struggle for independence. Yet these same numbers also exhibit how hard the Confederacy did fight in spite of its lack of the strong nationalism and significant distinctiveness which separated the combatants in these other three wars. And the Confederates fought harder than Americans ever fought, or needed to fight, facing far more formidable opposition than Americans ever confronted, and without allies. And the inadequacy of their motivation to save slavery, their only modest feeling of national distinctiveness, and their fundamentalist Christian faith explain why they did not do more.

Bibliographical Essay

As it originally appeared in 1986, under the title *Why the South Lost the Civil War*, this work had over seven hundred footnotes, the majority of them citing more than one source. The notes spread over fifty-three pages of text and referenced almost four hundred sources. This is not extensive documentation for a study of the Civil War, inasmuch as scholarship in this area has been among the most productive of all fields in American history, with important contributions by contemporaries and by professionals and skilled amateurs in our own time. Indeed, several thousand works had already been published before the war had been over for more than a year or two. Civil War roundtables, crowds at battlefield sites, popular magazines, and even occasional television specials testify to continuing popular as well as academic interest in this rich field. The result is that no one can begin to list the most important works on the Civil War without inevitably missing some of the best, and it is our misfortune to be unable to deal with the arguments of some historians or to examine sufficiently the contentions of many others. This is the inevitable difficulty of being a historian of the Civil War. The difficulty is compounded when publishing what is primarily an abridgment of an earlier work, with a brief essay taking the place of an extensive bibliography.

This version, and the longer work from which it was derived, is largely a synthesis, attempting to examine the contributions of a multitude of historians to the perennial teaser, why the South lost the Civil War, and advancing our answer to that important question. Although we did use some primary sources, we did not depend on them to the same extent as most studies that attempt to plow new ground. For several reasons, therefore, this bibliography is highly selective. For additional references and more intensive discussion of many historians' ideas, the reader should refer to the text and footnotes of *Why the South Lost the Civil War.*

Many of our primary sources went unmentioned, for in our careers we have encountered many helpful ideas that were recorded in our memories without attribution and have become part of our individual thinking. But we should first mention the categories of primary materials we used and some of the most useful primary documents on which we relied heavily. Military records were especially important, most notably U.S. War Department, *The War of the Rebellion: A Compilation of the Official Records of the Union and Confederate Armies*, 70 vols. in 128

(Washington, D.C., 1881–1901). The corresponding series for the navy, U.S. Naval War Records Office, *Official Records of the Union and Confederate Navies in the War of the Rebellion,* 30 vols. (Washington, D.C., 1894–1927), was equally important. These two series were supplemented by other documentary collections, including Dunbar Rowland, ed., *Jefferson Davis, Constitutionalist: His Letters, Papers and Speeches,* 10 vols. (Jackson, Miss., 1923); the *Southern Historical Society Papers,* 52 vols. (Richmond, 1876–1959); and by the memoirs of leading participants, such as Joseph E. Johnston's *Narrative of Military Operations Directed, during the Late War between the States* (1874; rpt. Bloomington, 1959). Several important diaries shed light on military as well as civil events, most notably John B. Jones, *A Rebel War Clerk's Diary at the Confederate States Capital,* 2 vols. (Philadelphia, 1866); Edward Younger, ed., *Inside the Confederate Government: The Diary of Robert Garlick Hill Kean* (New York, 1957); and Frank E. Vandiver, ed., *The Civil War Diary of General Josiah Gorgas* (University, Ala., 1947). These sources not only provided the foundation of the interpretations found in the military portions of the narrative but also provided important insight into civil affairs.

Understanding of Confederate civil affairs is important if one is to comprehend the early strength and enthusiasm on the home front and its final collapse. Primary sources, such as southern newspapers and government documents, provide a great deal of insight and, along with the diaries and letters of ordinary folk, give researchers some notion of the omnipresence of God in the lives of Confederate citizens. Mrs. Chesnut's diary is always quotable, although one must remember that her view was strictly from the top. The best edition is C. Vann Woodward, ed., *Mary Chesnut's Civil War* (New Haven, 1981); like so many other historians, we have probably been seduced by her lucidity, color, and literary qualities into quoting her too often. For similar material, again from the top but with more religious overtones, see Robert Manson Myers, ed., *The Children of Pride: A True Story of Georgia and the Civil War* (New Haven, 1972). Southern newspapers are sufficiently available, if not always with complete runs, to provide the editors' views of Confederate destiny. Such papers as the *Atlanta Southern Confederacy,* the *Lynchburg Republican,* the *Macon* (Georgia) *Telegraph,* the *Raleigh Daily Conservative,* the *North Carolina Standard,* and the several Richmond papers, for example, are essential to an understanding of the vicissitudes of home-front morale. Even a few newspapers can furnish the researcher with important insights into the attitudes of editors and readers in wide areas of the South, thanks in no little measure to the editors' custom of exchanging papers and copying each others' news and commentary.

The most readily available primary sources for operations of the Confederate government focus on Jefferson Davis and the Confederate Congress. See James D. Richardson, ed., *A Compilation of the Messages and Papers of the Confederacy,*

Including Diplomatic Correspondence, 1861–1865, 2 vols. (Nashville, 1905), and Rowland, *Jefferson Davis, Constitutionalist,* for Davis's official correspondence. These sources will soon be supplemented, although not entirely supplanted, by Haskell M. Monroe et al., eds., *The Papers of Jefferson Davis,* currently edited by Lynda Lasswell Crist and Mary Seaton Dix, 5 vols. to date (Baton Rouge, 1971–). For the actions of the Confederate Congress, see U.S. Congress, Senate, *Journal of the Congress of the Confederate States of America, 1861–1865,* 7 vols., Senate Document 234, 58th Cong. 2d sess. (Washington, D.C., 1904–5), which provides a full record of the actions of Congress, and the "Proceedings of the . . . Confederate Congress" (title varies), *Southern Historical Society Papers* 44–52 (June 1923–July 1959). Unfortunately, these proceedings are not comparable to the *Congressional Globe,* their Union counterpart, because they are simply a compilation of daily reports—often incomplete—from the Richmond newspapers. The laws of the Confederacy are found in James M. Matthews, ed., *The Statutes at Large of the Provisional Government of the Confederate States of America* . . . (Richmond, 1864), and in smaller and unfortunately rare compilations of similar title that Matthews published after each session of the First and Second Congresses except the last. The laws of the second session of the Second Congress appear in Charles W. Ramsdell, ed., *Laws and Joint Resolutions of the Last Session of the Confederate Congress* . . . (Durham, 1941). State governments were also important, although the published primary documentation is neither as full nor as readily available as for the Confederate government. Allen D. Candler's edition of *The Confederate Records of the State of Georgia,* 5 vols. (Atlanta, 1909–11) is unfortunately not paralleled by equally extensive publications for other Confederate states. The laws passed by the state legislatures are available, however, and enactments concerning days of fasting or humiliation and prayer, measures for the relief of destitute citizens, and resolutions concerning military affairs serve as an index of the state of home-front determination and public perceptions of events.

Why did the South lose the Civil War? The historians who contributed to David Donald's *Why the North Won the Civil War* (Baton Rouge, 1960) mentioned several possibilities, including Lincoln's superior leadership, effective Union diplomacy, greater Union resources, better federal generalship, and the refusal of the South to compromise its democratic ideals. Other historians have given other reasons. Charles W. Ramsdell, *Behind the Lines in the Southern Confederacy* (1944; rpt. New York, 1969), looked to economic difficulties that reinforced the destructive effects of military defeats to undermine morale. E. Merton Coulter, *The Confederate States of America, 1861–1865* (Baton Rouge, 1950), anticipated some of our own ideas by concluding the Confederates "did not will hard enough and long enough to win" (p. 566). Bell Irvin Wiley suggested that the South was hurt by the unwillingness of some of the Confederate leaders to subordinate their own ideas and egos sufficiently to follow government policy. See Wiley, *The Road to Appomattox* (1956; rpt. New York, 1968). Stanley Lebergott, "Why the South Lost: Commercial Purpose in the Confederacy, 1861–1865," *Journal of American History* 70 (June 1983):58–74, attributes the debacle to bungled economic mobilization and the failure of tax policy and impressment. Such problems were real enough, of course, and yet the Confederacy ended the war with large numbers of troops still on the rolls, who could have fought on had they been sufficiently motivated to do so.

One of the favorite interpretations of Confederate defeat, ever since Frank L. Owsley published *State Rights in the Confederacy* (Chicago, 1925), has been that the Confederacy "Died of State Rights" (p. 1). The deleterious effects of states' rights allegedly occurred when state governors (primarily Joseph E. Brown of Georgia and Zebulon Vance of North Carolina) jealously tried to preserve their prerogatives, provide for the needs of their troops in the field, and aid needy folk back home. As James M. Merrill, *The Rebel Shore: The Story of Union Seapower in the Civil War* (Boston, 1957), points out, however, the governors were under heavy pressure from their constituents. When early Union raids established federal enclaves along exposed coasts, refugees fled inland and pleaded with their governors to defend their homes. In *Parties and Politics in North Carolina, 1836–1865* (Baton Rouge, 1983), Marc W. Kruman examines the North Carolina experience, common elsewhere as well, that white men acted on the assumption that anyone whose liberties were restricted was a slave. To protect themselves from slavery imposed by a strong central government, therefore, North Carolinians voted for states'-rights-oriented politicians who would be sure to preserve local liberties. See also Kruman, "Dissent in the Confederacy: The North Carolina Experience," *Civil War History* 27 (December 1981):293–313. Kruman emphasizes that North Carolina obstructionism, if such it was, was not treason to the Confederacy, but an attempt to achieve peace and freedom within the Confederacy. And since North Carolina contributed more than its share of resources to the Confederate war effort, it becomes clear that either the states'-rights movement was ineffective or that it was a loyal movement. David D. Scarboro, "North Carolina and the Confederacy: The Weakness of States' Rights during the Civil War," *North Carolina Historical Review* 56 (April 1979):133–49, argues (correctly, we think) that the history of state-Confederate relations "show[s] that negotiation played a far larger role than confrontation" (p. 134).

Thus, we find not only that states' rights did not do as much harm to the southern war effort as Owsley and subsequent historians have contended, but that in many respects it actually enabled the South to make more effective use of her limited resources than would otherwise have been the case. Indeed, both Paul D. Escott, *After Secession: Jefferson Davis and the Failure of Confederate Nationalism* (Baton Rouge, 1978), and Thomas B. Alexander and Richard E.

Beringer, *The Anatomy of the Confederate Congress: A Study of the Influence of Member Characteristics on Legislative Voting Behavior, 1861–1865* (Nashville, 1972), agree that states' rights is a red herring. Even while protesting their loyalty to states' rights, Confederates on the national and local levels regularly accepted common-sense wartime restrictions that they would have rebelled against in time of peace (although for some ideologues this acceptance no doubt was subconscious). The amazingly powerful Confederate Constitution did not inhibit wartime centralization to a significant extent. For discussion of the Constitution see Charles Robert Lee, Jr., *The Confederate Constitutions* (Chapel Hill, 1963), and Alexander and Beringer, *Anatomy of the Confederate Congress* (Lee provides parallel texts of the United States and Confederate Constitutions). Curtis Arthur Amlund, *Federalism in the Southern Confederacy* (Washington, D.C., 1966), also emphasizes the power of the central government of the Confederacy, although his work is thinly documented. John Brawner Robbins, a student of Frank Vandiver, goes over the ground thoroughly in "Confederate Nationalism: Politics and Government in the Confederate South, 1861–1865" (Ph.D. dissertation, Rice University, 1964). As Richard D. Brown observed in *Modernization: The Transformation of American Life, 1600–1865* (New York, 1976), the war enforced an institutionalization on North and South, whether they would or not, and both sections were forced by circumstances to move beyond localism toward national uniformity that contradicted the states'-rights ideal.

   This book is based on the assumption that the battlefield was not the decisive factor in the fate of the Confederacy but that a lack of nationalism was the "proximate cause" of defeat of the southern bid for independence. Lacking sufficient sense of nationhood, Confederates also lacked sufficient will to overcome the debilitating effects of battlefield defeat in the last year of the war, to outwait the Union, and to see the thing through. The argument of this case has required us to discuss military affairs extensively. This examination has indicated to our satisfaction that the Confederate army was never really defeated, nor was outright defeat of either army a likely possibility. Unless they were captured, as at Vicksburg, or overwhelmingly outnumbered, both Union and Confederate armies survived to fight—and fight well—another day, even after such bloody maulings as Fredericksburg, Chancellorsville, Shiloh, or Chickamauga. Although numerous battles resulted in perceived defeat, the Confederate army was never destroyed, and it maintained sufficient strength to unsettle the nerves of Union officers and politicians right up until the end. To understand how this could be so, we have had recourse to documentation of military affairs and to contemporary military theory.

   Here we place great reliance on two nineteenth-century theorists, Henri de Jomini and Karl von Clausewitz. The two names are familiar, but it is surprising that for all of their authority, very few historians have read them, at least not well enough to notice that they usually say much the same thing. Upon close examination, Jomini and Clausewitz are more in agreement than disagreement. Both lay down some very common-sense rules for the conduct of war, and though Jomini paid more attention to interior lines, Clausewitz was not ignorant of the concept nor was Jomini as dogmatic in his geometric constructions as many historians, notably the late T. Harry Williams, believed. Our reliance on the authorities does not mean that we believe the Civil War generals were necessarily familiar with their ideas.

In using Jomini and Clausewitz to evaluate Civil War military performance, we have relied on only one of the works of each, their last. We have used the translation of Clausewitz's *On War* by Michael Howard and Peter Paret (Princeton, 1976). For Jomini, we have used G. H. Mendell and W. P. Craighill, trans., *The Art of War* (Philadelphia, 1862). The thinking of both Jomini and Clausewitz is still important in American military doctrine, as exhibited in the U.S. Army's *F-M 100-5, Operations* (Washington, D.C., 1982; new ed. 1986). *F-M 100-5* mentions Clausewitz and deals with such Jominian concepts as the turning movement and interior lines, using Grant's Vicksburg campaign as an instructive example. The legitimacy of the nineteenth-century authorities, especially Clausewitz, for modern military thought is thus generally accepted by military thinkers today. In addition to *F-M 100-5* see Col. Harry G. Summers, Jr., *On Strategy: The Vietnam War in Context* (Carlisle Barracks, 1981). Summers's perceptive commentary on the Vietnam war is laced with references to and quotations from Clausewitz and is promoted as "a politico-military treatise of rare insight offering practical application of the 19th Century definitive work of Carl von Clausewitz on the nature of war" (p. vii). His interpretation of Clausewitz's modern influence is not confined to the United States, for Summers's Army War College study is used by military personnel in Australia, Mexico, and South Korea as well. Two more recent publications, Edward N. Luttwak, *Strategy: The Logic of War and Peace* (Cambridge, Mass., 1987), shows its debt to Clausewitz and demonstrates the place of Civil War strategy within a larger context, and Michael I. Handel, ed., *Clausewitz and Modern Strategy* (London, 1986), offers commentary on Clausewitz's present relevance, derived from an international conference at the U.S. Army War College. For a view of the place of the Civil War in the evolution of warfare and a synthesis of many of the ideas in Clausewitz, Jomini, and elsewhere, see Archer Jones, *The Art of War in the Western World* (Urbana, 1987).

The recent American interpretations of Jomini and his influence began with J. D. Hittle, *Jomini and His Summary of the Art of War* (Harrisburg, Pa., 1947), and David Donald, ed., *Lincoln Reconsidered* (New York, 1956). Working in this Jominian tradition and drawing heavily on his important *Lincoln and His Generals* (New York, 1952), T. Harry Williams wrote his influential essay "The Military Leadership of North and South," in David Donald, ed., *Why the North Won the*

Civil War. Williams believed that most Civil War generals were handicapped by their West Point training in Jominian doctrine, which emphasized limited war for limited objectives. Supposedly Ulysses S. Grant's great virtue was that he was uncontaminated by Jomini and hence made enemy armies, not enemy territory, his objective. Actually, there was very little Jomini, indeed very little of any strategy, in the West Point curriculum before the Civil War.

The disagreement with the theses of a pre-Napoleonic cast to Jomini's ideas and of their extensive influence on Civil War leaders began with Archer Jones, "Jomini and the Strategy of the American Civil War: A Reinterpretation," *Military Affairs* 34 (December 1970):127–31, and Thomas L. Connelly and Archer Jones, *The Politics of Command: Factions and Ideas in Confederate Strategy* (Baton Rouge, 1973). It continued through Hattaway and Jones, *How the North Won* to *Why the South Lost the Civil War,* and finally to this volume.

The most recent interpretation of R. E. Lee is in Russell F. Weigley, "American Strategy from Its Beginning through the First World War," in Peter Paret, ed., *Makers of Modern Strategy from Machiavelli to the Nuclear Age* (Princeton, 1986), 408–43. Weigley sees Lee as a master practitioner of the turning movement, who, rather than using it for essentially defensive purposes, aimed at a "victory of annihilation," a strategic "hope" that General "Grant could not share" (pp. 424, 432). Yet the evidence presented here for Lee's obsession with the offensive does not persuade us to abandon our interpretation of his logistical and strategically defensive objectives.

In his argument that in expending "troops at a rate the Confederacy could not spare" Lee imposed a "mortal toll upon the scarcest of all the Confederacy's scarce resources" (ibid., p. 426), Weigley expressed a view not only in consonance with one advocated by Thomas L. Connelly but more recently, and in broader context, by Grady McWhiney and Perry D. Jamieson in *Attack and Die: Civil War Military Tactics and the Southern Heritage* (University, Ala., 1982). McWhiney and Jamieson believe that a Celtic ethnic heritage encouraged Confederate addiction to bloody tactical offensives and frontal attacks. Certainly frontal attacks were responsible for much unnecessary bloodshed on both sides, but we do not see an ethnic basis for such behavior. This interpretation of the causes of Confederate defeat met strong dissent in Appendix II of *Why the South Lost the Civil War,* which in part relied on Appendix B of *How the North Won.* The Celtic thesis has received vigorous criticism in Rowland Berthoff, "Celtic Mist over the South," *Journal of Southern History* 52 (November 1986):532–50. Contrary to McWhiney and Jamieson, we do not accept the existence of a Celtic way of war. Although their main thesis does not depend on the existence of a special sort of Celtic warfare or on defective Confederate tactics for whatever cause, a more exhaustive examination of the data has not supported their challenging interpretation that the Confederacy lost because of unsustainable casualties.

Nevertheless, the influence of heavy battle casualties on the home front as well as on the men still in the ranks had a major effect on morale and willingness to continue the struggle. For a recent critique of the interpretation and a sophisticated review of the issue, see Albert Castel, "Mars and the Reverend Longstreet: Or, Attacking and Dying in the Civil War," *Civil War History* 33 (June 1987):103–14. Castel believes that frontal attacks occurred so frequently because they were the only "practical alternative" (p. 113).

A historian who agrees with the thesis of a distinctive Confederate tactical ineptitude is James M. McPherson, who, in his very important *Battle Cry of Freedom: The Civil War Era* (New York, 1988), proposes a new basis for the discussion of Confederate defeat. This book, volume 6 in *The Oxford History of the United States*, under the general editorship of C. Vann Woodward, does not see much merit in the notion that Confederates lost their bid for independence because of a weakness of nationalism or a lack of will. He sees some merit in the explanations of internal dissent in the South and the development of superior leadership and managerial talent in the North. He is reluctant to attribute the results of the war to any particular cause due to "contingency—the recognition that at numerous critical points during the war things might have gone altogether differently" (p. 858). Pointing to several occasions when things might have gone differently (the Confederacy's successful western counter-offensives in the summer of 1862, the Confederate repulses at Perryville and Antietam in the fall of 1862, Gettysburg, Vicksburg, and Chattanooga in the summer and fall of 1863, and the bloody stalemate in Virginia in 1864, which threatened to defeat Lincoln in the fall elections), he concludes that the loss of will thesis puts "the cart before the horse. Defeat causes demoralization and loss of will" (p. 858). But clearly the reciprocal is also true—loss of will can—and did—cause defeat.

The army and the navy during the Civil War worked together closely, regularly, and well for the first time in American military history. In addition to the blockade, discussed below, the navy operated on the western waters in direct support of the army and in cooperation with the army in amphibious operations. For a general discussion of naval operations see Merrill, *Rebel Shore;* Rowena Reed, *Combined Operations in the Civil War* (Annapolis, 1978); John D. Milligan, *Gunboats down the Mississippi* (Annapolis, 1965); and Bern Anderson, *By Sea and by River: The Naval History of the Civil War* (New York, 1962). For Confederate naval operations see three works by William N. Still, Jr., *Confederate Shipbuilding* (Columbia, S.C., 1985); *Iron Afloat: The Story of the Confederate Armorclads* (Nashville, 1971); and "The New Ironclads," in William C. Davis, ed., *The Image of War, 1861–1865,* vol. 2, *The Guns of '62* (Garden City, N.Y., 1982).

Some authorities consider the impact of the Union blockade a decisive factor in the result of the Civil War. Coulter, *Confederate States of America,* thought it one of the essential causes of Confederate defeat. Charles P. Roland, *The Confederacy*

(Chicago, 1960), and Anderson, *By Sea and by River*, agree. We come to different conclusions, building on work that goes back to the pioneering research of Frank L. Owsley. In his *King Cotton Diplomacy: Foreign Relations of the Confederate States of America* (1931; 2d ed. Chicago, 1959), Owsley maintained that the blockade was not effective, if measured by the amount of cargo that got through to southern ports. Owsley's conclusions are supported by a series of articles written by Marcus Price, who analyzed shipping through the ports of the Carolinas, the Gulf of Mexico, and Georgia and East Florida. See Price, "Ships That Tested the Blockade of the Carolina Ports, 1861–1865," *American Neptune* 8 (July 1948):196–241; Price, "Ships That Tested the Blockade of the Gulf Ports, 1861–1865," *American Neptune* 11 (October 1951):262–90; and Price, "Ships That Tested the Blockade of the Georgia and East Florida Ports, 1861–1865," *American Neptune* 15 (April 1955):97–132. See also Richard E. Wood, "Port Town at War: Wilmington, North Carolina, 1860–1865" (Ph.D. dissertation, Florida State University, 1976). The number of successful runs of the blockade found by Price and Wood certainly justifies William N. Still's characterization of the blockade as a "Naval Sieve." See Still, "A Naval Sieve: The Union Blockade in the Civil War," *Naval War College Review* 36 (May–June 1983):34–45. Frank E. Vandiver had earlier reached the same conclusion by examining blockade-running through Bermuda, and he concluded in a later study that the Union navy simply could not meet the challenge of the blockade runners. See Vandiver, ed., *Confederate Blockade Running through Bermuda, 1861–1865* (Austin, 1947), and Vandiver, *Their Tattered Flags* (New York, 1970).

Whatever the condition of the armies and navies, the case is often made that the Confederacy lost the Civil War because of inferior resources, referring to both manpower and matériel. Although both were often in short supply, lack of resources is also an insufficient explanation for the outcome of the war. Albert B. Moore, *Conscription and Conflict in the Confederacy* (New York, 1924), gives a full account of the Confederacy's early and effective resort to centralized conscription of manpower. Georgia Lee Tatum, *Disloyalty in the Confederacy* (1934; rpt. New York, 1970); Ella Lonn, *Desertion during the Civil War* (1929; rpt. Gloucester, Mass., 1966); and Wilfred Buck Yearns, *The Confederate Congress* (Athens, Ga., 1960), each illustrates the inequities of the conscription system and the natural resentment against it that was reflected in draft-dodging and desertion. Again the importance of morale is evident, for with greater public determination, men would have been effectively rallied to the colors and, once there, would have stayed. Thomas L. Livermore, *Numbers and Losses in the Civil War in America* (Boston, 1900), has useful estimates of the extent to which the Confederacy realized its manpower mobilization potential.

But what about matériel? Historians generally agree that the great industrial potential realized by the northern economy equipped the Union soldier better than his southern adversary. But the North had a substantial industrial base to build on. What is less known is that the Confederacy successfully met the comparatively simple needs of mid-nineteenth-century war by a remarkable industrial mobilization. Confederates and historians both forgot about this achievement until the mid-twentieth century. See, however, Coulter, *Confederate States of America*, and Roland, *The Confederacy*, who contend that wartime development created interest in industrialization that carried over into the postwar period.

The first studies to delve into Confederate industrialization began to appear in the 1930s and 1940s, when historians first took a close look at the southern economy. Louise B. Hill provided the slogan for these developments. In *State Socialism in the Confederate States of America* (Charlottesville, 1936), she examined the effective measures taken by the Confederate government to impose uniformity on foreign trade. Stringent economic mobilization was not confined to shipping. Railroads were placed under strict control, permitting as much usefulness to the war effort as their rickety and underbuilt condition allowed. See, for example, Robert C. Black III, *The Railroads of the Confederacy* (Chapel Hill, 1952), and Richard D. Goff, *Confederate Supply* (Durham, 1969). Goff treats not only the role of the railroads but all other aspects of the Confederate logistic effort as well. This centralization, which Hill called state socialism and Frank E. Vandiver later called nationalism, had a profound effect on manufacturing. Vandiver first called attention to the effectiveness of Confederate activity in the munitions industry in his edition of *The Civil War Diary of General Josiah Gorgas* (University, Ala., 1947) and in his subsequent biography of the Confederate chief of ordnance, *Ploughshares into Swords: Josiah Gorgas and Confederate Ordnance* (Austin, 1952). Gorgas was justifiably proud that whereas the Confederacy produced almost no munitions at the beginning of the war, it was self-sufficient in this essential item by 1864. Following closely after his mentor, Vandiver, Emory Thomas points up the remarkable Confederate economic development in *The Confederacy as a Revolutionary Experience* (Englewood Cliffs, 1971) and *The Confederate Nation, 1861–1865* (New York, 1979), as Confederates controlled old industries and created new ones to meet their wartime needs. Much of the early matériel was produced at the Tredegar Iron Works in Richmond, the one major iron works that predated the war, and which was so well developed during the war that its capacity often outstripped the availability of raw materials. For this remarkable establishment see Charles B. Dew, *Ironmaker to the Confederacy: Joseph R. Anderson and the Tredegar Iron Works* (New Haven, 1966). Unfortunately, there is only one wide-ranging study of Confederate industrialization. That important work is Raimondo Luraghi's *The Rise and Fall of the Plantation South* (New York, 1978). As an Italian scholar, Luraghi makes observations that the detached foreign scholar can often provide. We do not agree with all of his interpretations, but Luraghi understood that a rapid, even revolutionary industrialization took place under the guns of war. Luraghi sees two devices that levered the Confederacy into industrialization, one being the conscription-exemption laws, which exempted certain skilled workers from the draft. The other was control over transportation. A government with the right to deny the labor to make a finished product, and then the transportation to ship it, has a tight grip on the economy if it wishes to use it.

If the southern nation lost the war in spite of its military strength, the weakness of the Union blockade, and its effective industrialization, perhaps part of the reason may be that it was not really a nation. The Confederacy may have been a country on paper, but it was not a nation in the hearts and minds of its citizens. The term *nationalism* is a slippery one, and it must be made clear that we are not referring to a strong, centralized style of government. Frank E. Vandiver and Emory M. Thomas make a good case for what we might call administrative nationalism because Confederates created a remarkably strong central government that was responsible for much of the Confederacy's success in mobilizing its resources and supporting its army. Vandiver goes so far as to imply and Thomas to state that Jefferson Davis's Confederacy was revolutionary in nature, an interpretation that may very well be correct, although the very idea alarmed Davis. See Vandiver, *Jefferson Davis and the Confederate State* (Oxford, 1964); Vandiver, *Their Tattered Flags;* and the similar ideas expressed in Thomas, *The Confederacy as a Revolutionary Experience* and *The Confederate Nation, 1861–1865.* Paul D. Escott, *After Secession,* has also examined this administrative nationalism, concluding that it was not successful enough to ensure victory because some of Davis's policies alienated important segments of the Confederate population.

We feel that whatever strength administrative nationalism may have had, and indeed Vandiver and Thomas are right in stressing its importance, Confederate defeat may be explained in large degree by understanding that the South lacked a widely shared sense of a distinct nationality and a mystical sense of its own separate nationhood. The major problem was that North and South were not very different; whatever nationality one felt, the other had to feel also. United by language, history, and even constitutional interpretation (Republicans affirmed states' rights in their 1860 platform), these Americans were divided primarily by slavery. As Kenneth Stampp points out in "The Southern Road to Appomattox," in Stampp, ed., *The Imperiled Union: Essays on the Background of the Civil War* (New York, 1980), Confederates were united more by dangers to white supremacy than by a sense of national uniqueness. He sees southern nationalism as "that most flimsy and ephemeral of dreams" (p. 257). In April 1865 southern nationalists, had there been enough of them, could have asserted their nationalism by continuing to resist, just as many other countries have done to combat alien invaders. They might not have won the war, but they would have made things a great deal more difficult for the Yankees than they already had.

Throughout the war, Confederate cavalry and guerrilla raids were quite effective. Each side had felt the sting of guerrillas on occasion; it was not for nothing that Grant and Sherman sought so urgently to capture their adversaries intact. Robert L. Kerby, "Why the Confederacy Lost," *Review of Politics* 35 (July 1973):326–45, believes the decision to fight as a nation-state was the Confederacy's most critical decision. As Stampp notes in "Southern Road to Appomattox," and Carl N. Degler reminds us in *Place over Time: The Continuity of Southern Distinctiveness* (Baton Rouge, 1977), guerrilla war did break out when southerners wanted to ensure local political control and white supremacy, which were threatened by the reformist ideas of Radical Republicans after the war.

To be sure, southern nationalism and Confederate nationalism may be two different things, but that very fact underlines the problem, for the proponents of southern nationalism often forget that large parts of the South did not feel sufficiently distinct from the rest of the Union to enter the Confederacy, and parts of some of the states that did join the new country did so against the better judgment of many of their citizens. Ralph A. Wooster's *The Secession Conventions of the South* (Princeton, 1962), a careful examination of the secession conventions, indicates clearly the strength of Unionism in some parts of the South and the internal divisions that lopsided secession votes sometimes masked. Steven A. Channing disagrees with our skepticism, pointing out in his essay "Slavery and Confederate Nationalism," in Walter J. Fraser, Jr., and Winfred B. Moore, eds., *From the Old South to the New: Essays on the Transitional South* (Westport, Conn., 1981), that the very existence of the Confederacy must prove something. He believes this something was "an ideological core sustaining a latent cultural nationalism" (pp. 221–24). We believe that it was latent indeed. Internal division within the Confederacy was so great during the war that it precludes much of a mystical sense of nationalism. See, for example, the work on the Appalachian chain of discontent by Tatum, *Disloyalty in the Confederacy*, and Phillip Shaw Paludan, *Victims: A True Story of the Civil War* (Knoxville, 1981). It should also be noted that supporters of the idea of Confederate nationalism, or southern nationalism, are talking about the white population only. The whole idea of a distinct southern nationalism, or what James M. McPherson calls "southern exceptionalism," is successfully refuted, we believe, in McPherson, "Antebellum Southern Exceptionalism: A New Look at an Old Question," *Civil War History* 29 (September 1983):230–44; Edward Pessen, "How Different from Each Other Were the Antebellum North and South?" *American Historical Review* 85 (December 1980):1119–49; and Grady McWhiney, *Southerners and Other Americans* (New York, 1973). See also Degler, *Place over Time*, which makes the case that slavery did make the South distinctive, but not so much as to create a special world-view, and John McCardell, *The Idea of a Southern Nation: Southern Nationalists and Southern Nationalism, 1830–1860* (New York, 1981), which seems to confuse nationalism and separatism, though agreeing that northerners and southerners had not become distinct nationals on the eve of the Civil War.

A stronger sense of nationalism probably would also have overcome more of the debilitating effects of war-induced poverty upon large segments of the white population. Frank L. Owsley called attention to this problem in "Defeatism in the Confederacy," *North Carolina Historical Review* 3 (July 1926):446–56, concluding that defeatism in the backcountry was induced by the suffering of the soldiers' families, rather than lack of nationalistic enthusiasm. But if the central government had been supported by a stronger sense of nationalism, it might have been moved to do more to meet the needs of the poor, rather than leave this burden to the states. Escott, *After Secession,* concludes that the common folk were in dire need of government assistance and would not concern themselves about whether it came from Confederate or state governments. He discusses the problem further in "Poverty and Governmental Aid for the Poor in Confederate North Carolina," *North Carolina Historical Review* 61 (October 1984):462–80, and "'The Cry of the Sufferers': The Problem of Welfare in the Confederacy," *Civil War History* 23 (September 1977):228–40. State governments went to unprecedented lengths to meet the needs of soldiers' families, and some of their actions are indicated for North Carolina in Escott's articles cited above and for the rest of the Confederacy in Ramsdell's *Behind the Lines in the Southern Confederacy.* See also Ella Lonn, *Salt as a Factor in the Confederacy* (1933; rpt. University, Ala., 1965); W. Buck Yearns, ed., *The Confederate Governors* (Athens, Ga., 1985); and Peter Wallenstein, "Rich Man's War, Rich Man's Fight: Civil War and the Transformation of Public Finance in Georgia," *Journal of Southern History* 50 (February 1984):15–42.

The reader who would delve deeply into the reasons for Confederate defeat must also take southern religion into account, for not only did it differ from religion in the North, but it was taken seriously by northerners and southerners alike, who saw the hand of God in the events around them. As Samuel S. Hill, Jr., points out in *The South and North in American Religion* (Athens, Ga., 1980), religion was important for southerners, for whom evangelical belief was as much a part of the natural order of society as race. And once the final break between the sections occurred, noted William W. Sweet, *The Story of Religion in America,* 2d ed. (New York, 1950), religion provided one of the glues that held each section together. After the Presbyterian, Methodist, and Baptist churches divided before the war, and as the liturgical churches were divided by the war, the clergy took the part of their respective sections without much hesitancy; indeed, some of them were proud of their roles—see Sydney E. Ahlstrom, *A Religious History of the American People* (New Haven, 1972)—and sought to take an active part in the war. They served not only as chaplains but also as combatants, according to the study by W. Harrison Daniel, "Protestantism and Patriotism in the

Confederacy," *Mississippi Quarterly* 24 (Spring 1971):119–23. For further, more recent discussion of southern religion, see James Oscar Farmer, Jr., *The Metaphysical Confederacy: James Henley Thornwell and the Synthesis of Southern Values* (Macon, Ga., 1986).

Closely connected with religion was the concept of guilt, induced by the knowledge that all have sinned. Although most southerners agreed that slavery was not itself a sin, they knew it could lead to sin. And they knew that sin could lead to punishment, and eventually many became convinced that defeat was a punishment for slavery, or how they had administered slavery. Stampp, in "Southern Road to Appomattox," contends that precisely because of uneasiness over slavery some southerners were easily reconciled to defeat. In one form or another, this guilt thesis was accepted by W. J. Cash, *The Mind of the South* (New York, 1941); Charles Grier Sellers, Jr., "The Travail of Slavery," in Sellers, ed., *The Southerner as American* (Chapel Hill, 1960); Robert Penn Warren, *The Legacy of the Civil War* (1961; rpt. Cambridge, Mass., 1983); Degler, *Place over Time;* and James Oakes, *The Ruling Race: A History of American Slaveholders* (New York, 1982). The feeling of guilt could only have become greater as Confederates moved to their own decision for emancipation, as detailed in Robert F. Durden, *The Gray and the Black: The Confederate Debate on Emancipation* (Baton Rouge, 1972). It is, however, only fair to note that some historians of the Civil War era do not accept the guilt thesis. See, for example, Eugene D. Genovese, *The World the Slaveholders Made: Two Essays in Interpretation* (New York, 1969), and James L. Roark, *Masters without Slaves: Southern Planters in the Civil War and Reconstruction* (New York, 1977).

Problems of religion and guilt could affect both sides, of course, but religion, says Samuel Hill, *The South and North in American Religion,* had followed a somewhat different evolution North and South. The South looked upon itself as purer than the North and believed that it had come closer to millennial perfection. Hill believes that northerners saw a need to perfect society, whereas southerners thought society needed not reformation but stability so that humans could work out their salvation. Both views are millennialism, but with a difference. See James H. Moorhead, *American Apocalypse: Yankee Protestants and the Civil War, 1860–1869* (New Haven, 1978), for the contention that southerners tended to what is now called premillennialism—Christ would come again before the millennium without human action—whereas northerners were postmillennialists, believing that God could be prodded into hastening His coming, which would take place at the end of the millennium. We are not sure that southern Protestant thought was anywhere near so complicated, at least among the rank and file. In any event, most southern theologians probably thought millennialism smacked too much of New England for them to take much stock in it. Nevertheless, a glance at contemporary newspapers indicates the seriousness of southerners' belief that God would be on their side. For the intimate relationship of God and victory and God and slavery in southern thought during the war, see James W. Silver, "Propaganda in the Confederacy," *Journal of Southern History* 11 (November 1945):487–503; Silver, *Confederate Morale and Church Propaganda* (New York, 1957); Bell Irvin Wiley, "The Movement to Humanize the Institution of Slavery during the Confederacy," *Emory University Quarterly* 5 (December 1949):207–20; and Farmer, *Metaphysical Confederacy.*

This study of religion lends a great deal of support to the conclusion that perhaps something besides military defeat was responsible for the outcome of the war. When Ramsdell looked at the economic shambles, he concluded that the biggest problem the Confederacy faced was its finances. But he went on to point out the relation between economic privation and the breakdown of home-front morale. Clement Eaton, *A History of the Southern Confederacy* (1954; rpt. New York, 1965), examined a variety of Confederate problems, including states' rights, the peace movement, and suspension of the writ of habeas corpus, among others, and also pointed to the undermining of public will. Charles P. Roland believes that Confederates had the necessary resources to win and lacked only the extra measure of skill, unity, and will. See Roland, *The Confederacy.* Edward Channing was more forceful, writing in *The War for Southern Independence, 1849–1865* (New York, 1925) that if the South had had the will to fight on, she could have. In *The Collapse of the Confederacy* (1937; rpt. New York, 1968), pp. 167–68, 171, Charles H. Wesley agreed that there was no single cause for Confederate defeat but that "the psychological factor of morale was one of the most influential in the complex scene." Coulter, *Confederate States of America,* even concluded that the South "did not deserve to win" in view of its signal failure in morale and will power (pp. 566–67).

Morale and will are virtually interchangeable terms. What undermines one has the same effect on the other, and it is clear that by April 1865 it was a rare Confederate who had enough of either to continue the fight. How could this be, if God was on the side of right, and Confederates were right? There were several ways southerners could deal with this psychological discomfort—the technical term is cognitive dissonance—to make sense of their crumbling world. Perhaps God was on the side of the Yankees after all, but this was a difficult conclusion to come to. If so, it was for a reason, and what better one than that, like the Israelites of old, southerners had not remained faithful to God? In what way? Many looked to the institution of slavery and began to reevaluate the institution itself or, more often, the way it was run. To others defeat was a punishment for all the bloodshed. To still others, it was a test of God's people, to see how they would bear adversity. By 1864 the alternative decisions not made—Union and peace—had attractive features that disunion and losing the war did not have. Legislatures tried to appease God by passing resolutions of humiliation and prayer, and individuals prayed for understanding. By late 1864 religion had thus undermined will, for to fight on was to fight against God. Morale and will could no longer sustain the war effort.

The theory of cognitive dissonance helps to explain how people reduce the tension between the world as it is and the world as they would have it, between mutually incompatible alternatives, between decisions made and those not made. The Confederate citizen who thought the war was fought to save slave property and to preserve a social order based on slavery had some fancy thinking to do when Jefferson Davis and the Confederate Congress indicated their willingness to enlist slaves as soldiers and give up the peculiar institution so as to win a war for independence. After thousands of men had been slain, such people suddenly discovered that the war goals were not what they thought they had been, and it was too late to turn back, too late to take the alternative road. As Confederates came to see that slavery was doomed, they tried with success to convince themselves that the war had never been for slavery but had been for independence all along. And as independence became less and less likely, they came to believe that they fought for states' rights, white supremacy, and honor—and that, in the long run, they had won all three. We summarize this much from the text because it bears repeating that not only religion but social psychology was at work here, specifically the theory of cognitive dissonance, which is discussed in some detail in Chapter 10.

The theory of cognitive dissonance was systematized by Leon Festinger in *A Theory of Cognitive Dissonance* (Evanston, 1957) and presented in a useful popularized explanation in "Cognitive Dissonance," *Scientific American* 207 (October 1962):93–102. The number of other investigators who have amplified and modified the theory is too great to include here, but historians who are interested in learning more so that they may apply these ideas to their own work should consult the work by Festinger cited above, as well as his *Conflict, Decision, and Dissonance* (Stanford, 1964). See also Philip G. Zimbardo, *The Cognitive Control of Motivation: The Consequences of Choice and Dissonance* (Glenview, 1969); Jack W. Brehm and Arthur R. Cohen, *Explorations in Cognitive Dissonance* (New York, 1962); Abraham K. Korman, *The Psychology of Motivation* (Englewood Cliffs, 1974); and Robert B. Zajonc, "Thinking: Cognitive Organization and Processes," in David L. Sills, ed., *International Encyclopedia of the Social Sciences*, vol. 15 (New York, 1968), pp. 615–22. For discussion of the usefulness of this interpretive method, which has been used by a number of historians in the last fifteen years, see Richard E. Beringer, *Historical Analysis: Contemporary Approaches to Clio's Craft* (1978; rpt. Melbourne, Fla., 1986), chap. 9. For examples of the use of cognitive dissonance by historians of the Civil War era, see Robert M. Cover, *Justice Accused: Anti-Slavery and the Judicial Process* (New Haven, 1975), which explains how the antislavery judges dealt with their dissonance when they were forced to make proslavery decisions, and Escott, *After Secession,* who uses the theory to understand how Confederates changed their war goal from preservation of slavery to independence for its own sake.

One way southerners could reconcile the results of the war with God's will was by finding a scapegoat. After the war Jefferson Davis, various generals, or the weakness of the people were used to explain why the South lost. William Garrett Piston discusses one of the most notable examples of scapegoating in *Lee's Tarnished Lieutenant: James Longstreet and His Place in Southern History* (Athens, Ga., 1987). Southerners came to believe that Longstreet's allegedly tardy attack at Gettysburg caused Lee's defeat and the loss of the Civil War. Thus Longstreet was "guilty," for it was his blunder that accounted "for the failure of a righteous, God-fearing populace in its bid for nationhood" (p. xi). Without this explanation, defeat would be "tantamount to the loss of God's Grace" (p. 112). The Lost Cause legend was created to permit the veteran to conclude that he had been overwhelmed but not really beaten. Honor could thus be saved. One southern poet, and we use the term loosely, put the attitude in verse:

> Man did not conquer her [the Confederacy], but God
> For some wise purpose of his own
> withdrew his arm; she, left alone,
> Sank down resistless 'neath his rod.
> God chastens most who he loves best . . .
> (Piston, *Lee's Tarnished Lieutenant,* p. 114).

The most remarkable use of cognitive dissonance in the Civil War era, however, is in the transformation of defeat into victory. Southerners claimed after the war that they had fought not for slavery but for states' rights. Various aspects of this switch are discussed by Steven A. Channing, *Crisis of Fear: Secession in South Carolina* (New York, 1970); Clement Eaton, *The Waning of the Old South Civilization, 1860–1880's* (1968; rpt. New York, 1969); Stampp, "Southern Road to Appomattox"; and Roark, *Masters without Slaves.* See also Waldo W. Braden, "Repining over an Irrevocable Past: The Ceremonial Orator in a Defeated Society, 1865–1900," and Howard Dorgan, "Rhetoric of the United Confederate Veterans: A Lost Cause Mythology in the Making," both in Braden, ed., *Oratory in the New South* (Baton Rouge, 1979).

For reduction of southern dissonance by defining the positive results of the war in terms of honor as well as states' rights, see especially Bertram Wyatt-Brown, *Southern Honor: Ethics and Behavior in the Old South* (New York, 1982). Wyatt-Brown does not specifically discuss southern concepts of honor after the Civil War, but the tenor of his work and his discussion of prewar attitudes leaves little doubt that many southerners had to fight, even in a losing cause, for the sake of their honor. To fight well and lose was honorable; not to fight at all would be shameful. George C. Rable, "Bourbonism, Reconstruction, and the Persistence of Southern Distinctiveness," *Civil War History* 29 (June 1983):135–53, includes some discussion of the postwar significance of southern honor. See also Thomas L. Connelly and Barbara Bellows, *God and General Longstreet: The Lost Cause and the Southern Mind* (Baton Rouge, 1982). These postwar attitudes are also examined closely and effectively by Charles Reagan Wilson, *Baptized in Blood: The Religion of the Lost Cause, 1865–1920* (Athens, Ga., 1980); students who wish to study the subject more closely should read Gaines M. Foster, *Ghosts of the Confederacy: Defeat, the Lost Cause, and the Emergence of the New South, 1865–1913* (New York, 1987). Foster studies how former Confederates interpreted the loss of the war and the meaning it held for their society, as "veterans and other southerners found relief from the lingering fear that defeat had somehow dishonored them" (p. 6). The Lost Cause movement, Foster successfully argues, preserved southern honor and the social order.

In preserving states' rights, white supremacy, and honor, Confederates truly reconciled the dissonance created by their prewar hopes with the desolation of Appomattox. They, too, as William B. Hesseltine observed in *Confederate Leaders in the New South* (Baton Rouge, 1950), could claim a share of the victory.

Index